Here is what other leaders said about *Living Leadership*

"By living along-side real leaders for extended periods of time, the authors cut through the 'how-to' leadership oversimplification and provide extremely valuable insights for those in leadership roles."

Kai Peters, Chief Executive, Ashridge Business School

"This book strips away the mystique of the heroic and charismatic leader and helps you lead more effectively."

Konstantin Mettenheimer Senior Partner, Freshfields, Bruckhaus Deringer

"[*Living Leadership*] gets to the core of leadership: the gritty reality, not the acceptable face or academic frameworks."

Paul Heiden former CEO, FKI plc & Group Finance Director, Rolls Royce plc

"*Living Leadership* shows how, when you take away the myths and misconceptions, leading can genuinely be made easier."

Hans Straberg, President & Chief Executive Officer, Electrolux

"... it's not just a management book. It's more like being on a psychoanalysts couch. You feel like the authors are getting into your head, empathising with the way you feel and helping you with your thinking."

Quentin Poole, Senior Partner, Wragge & Co LLP

"Captures the human, sensitive and fragile nature of leadership."

Louise Julian, Chair of the Board, EF Education First

"A 'how-to' book that redefines leadership in terms of the realities and choices facing people in organisations today."

Professor Michael Osbaldeston, Director of Cranfield School of Management

"I could see so many similarities between my experiences and those you describe... very few books are as practical and 'real life'"

Stuart Lancaster, Head of Elite Player Development, English Rugby Football Union

"*Living Leadership* is a breath of fresh air – insightful and practical."

Philip Cox, Chief Executive, International Power plc

"Binney, Wilke and Williams have got to the core of leadership: the gritty reality, not the acceptable face or academic frameworks."

Paul Heiden former CEO, FKI plc & Group Finance Director, Rolls Royce plc.

"... an unvarnished account of leadership in action, with all its anxiety, uncertainty, false certainty and crippling expectation. [The authors] dispel the myths of leadership, they eschew recipes and homilies; instead they give us some real insight and wisdom into the constraints and possibilities of 'living leadership'."

Bill Critchley, Organisation Consultant and Leader of the Ashridge Masters in Organisation Consulting

"Since I was taught about *Living leadership* at Ashridge Business School I have been a fan of its main arguments, and the great experience and enormous understanding of human beings it is based on. In the book, *Living leadership*, you are taught that leadership is exactly as tough and hard as real life. A book that is written for everyone working with and delivering through people in business and public sector organisations".

Kim Bohr, Finance & HR Director, Royal Theatre, Opera and Ballet Copenhagen

"*Living Leadership* struck a real cord with me. In the quiet of sleepless nights it's precisely the type of themes explored in this book that have aided my success. Great leadership is not about slick presentation. It's about embracing a continual leadership responsibility as second nature in every interaction. Ultimately it's the ability to connect to people in a 'real time real world' way."

Trevor Bish-Jones former Chief Executive, Woolworths Group plc

Living
Leadership

Living Leadership

a practical guide for ordinary heroes

Second Edition

George Binney • Gerhard Wilke • Colin Williams

Illustrations by Didier Gallon

 **FT** Prentice Hall
FINANCIAL TIMES

An imprint of Pearson Education
Harlow, England ▌London ▌New York ▌Boston ▌San Francisco ▌Toronto ▌
Sydney ▌Singapore ▌Hong Kong ▌Tokyo ▌Seoul ▌Taipei ▌New Delhi ▌Cape Town ▌
Madrid ▌Mexico City ▌Amsterdam ▌Munich ▌Paris ▌Milan

Pearson Education Limited

Edinburgh Gate
Harlow CM20 2JE
tel: +44 (0)1279 623623
fax: +44 (0)1279 431059
website: www.pearsoned.co.uk

First published in 2005
Second edition published in Great Britain in 2009
© Pearson Education Limited 2005, 2009

The rights of Binney Associates Limited, Gerhard Wilke and Colin Williams to be
identified as authors of this work have been asserted by them in accordance with the
Copyright, Designs and Patents Act 1988.

ISBN: 978-0-273-72208-3

British Library Cataloguing in Publication Data
A CIP catalogue record for this book can be obtained from the British Library

Library of Congress Cataloging-in-Publication Data
Binney, George.
    Living leadership ; a practical guide for ordinary heroes / George Binney, Gerhard
Wilke, Colin Williams ; illustrations by Didier Gallon. -- 2nd ed.
        p. cm.
    Includes bibliographical references and index.
    ISBN 978-0-273-72208-3 (pbk. : alk. paper) 1. Leadership. I. Wilke, Gerhard,
1948- II. Williams, Colin. III. Title.
    HD57 .7.B5344 2009
    658.4'092--dc22

                                                                    2008048401

10 9 8 7 6 5 4 3 2 1
09 08 07 06 05

Set by 3 in 9.5pt Melior
Printed and bound by Henry Ling Ltd., at the Dorset Press, Dorchester, Dorset

The publishers' policy is to use paper manufactured from sustainable forests.

Contents

Preface / ix

Introduction to the new edition / xi

part **1** What it is

1 Living leadership / 3

2 The end of superman / 21

3 Get connected / 41

4 Get real / 61

5 Get help / 83

6 Surfing, sinking and swimming / 101

7 Leading in the moment / 111

part **2** How it works

8 Bosses / 133

9 Self / 153

10 People / 171

11 Groups / 185

12 Strategy / 201

13 Change / 221

14 Development / 239

part **3** What comes next?

15 Living with permanent transition? / 257

A summary of living leadership / 269

The research / 273

Acknowledgements / 275

Index / 279

Preface

Living Leadership

This is a book for people at all levels who make organisations work, day by day: a practical guide for ordinary heroes. If you lead a project team or group of workers, a function or business unit, a professional body or company, if you have power and authority over others, or just feel strongly about the direction of your organisation, this book is for you.

This is about getting connected. Leading happens *between* people. It is not the property of the leader or of the followers. Leaders lead when they connect with others in ways that help them to seize opportunities or tackle problems that otherwise they could not address.

Living Leadership is born from the real joy and pain of leading. It is based on extensive international research into the realities of leading in organisations today that found that the business and organisational world is still half in love with the idea of transformational heroes. When the going gets tough, people often look for magical figures that will reduce the issues to easy simplicities and get them off the hook of taking responsibility themselves. This search for heroes is reminiscent of all those Hollywood films where the hero saves the world and ordinary people look on in wonder.

We found the organisational world groping its way towards a more realistic, less idealistic view of leaders. This is one in which people at many levels and places take responsibility. It is one in which leaders connect with others, work with, not against, the people around them and come alive because they bring more of themselves to their leading. It is a more human, do-able way of leading. Each moment contains choices for leaders. Consciously picking them up will get you further than all the heroic fantasies about what leaders ought to do.

Our conviction, following our research, is that people in organisations have the potential to lead much more than they do at present. The way to realise this potential is not by looking out there for the answer, but by returning to things you know, things that life has already taught you.

We want you to stop thinking in terms of deficits. You are good enough as a leader as you are. In this book we will show you how.

Our research

Between 1999 and 2003, with the support of Ashridge, the international business school based in the UK, and Groupe HEC in France, we lived alongside leaders and followers in leading organisations across Europe. We observed them as they worked, we discussed with them, in the moment, the challenges and opportunities that they faced and we made sense, with leaders and followers together, of what was happening. We have checked our findings from these case studies in interviews with business leaders and in workshops and conferences involving more than 700 managers and leaders.

As well as ourselves and Richard Elsner, the core research team included Howard Atkins, Elizabeth Braiden and Kathleen King of Ashridge Consulting, and Gilles Amado and Rachel Amato of HEC.

For further information about the research, look at pages 273–4.

Introduction to the new edition

I t is now four years since *Living Leadership* was first published. The three of us have presented and discussed the stories and ideas in the book with thousands of managers and leaders all around the world: in leading international and local companies, in public service organisations and in a wide range of professional and service firms.

What hit home in these sessions?

The conclusion has been the same: whether we are talking in an organisation with more than 100,000 employees or one with 100, whether we are talking to the private or public sectors, whether we are in Germany, the UK, France, the USA, Brazil, China, Thailand or any other place – the ideas and suggestions of *Living Leadership* resonate with people. They found their reality in the book.

Mary Kennedy, a colleague at Ashridge, puts it this way: "What you say comes as an enormous relief. Instead of trying to live up to some ideal, individuals who want to lead can be who they are. And they see what they can work on: step by step, learning to lead in the moment, be that in a meeting, in a corridor, with their boss or with a client."

People recognise the ordinary nature of successful leading in the moment – how special it is and how difficult it can sometimes be to find the courage and the resources to lead.

We have seen people recall the benefits of taking the risk to "get real" and "get connected". They gain respect and authority. They are more able to delegate and trust and to get the work done through others. They get more space and time to think and work out what is needed. The people around them trust them more and test them less.

People found their experience validated in *Living Leadership*: the constant dilemmas (we call them zones of choice) they face as leaders; the feelings that some days they are sinking, other days they are swimming or surfing; the acute need, sometimes, for self-preservation to be able to function effectively; the challenge of working out what is do-able in an age of endless targets and manic pressures.

Instead of looking outside themselves for some perfect model, they can look within, to their experience of life, to help them to lead and work through others. As one German manager said to us after we had presented *Living Leadership*: "We know all that – and we have forgotten. It is good to be reminded."

What it is

In Part 1 we explore what *Living Leadership* is. Chapter 1 summarises the whole picture. In Chapter 2 we look at letting go of the widespread assumption that leaders should be transforming heroes – a picture that is difficult to shake off because so many managers take it for granted and can't see any alternative.

We then explore the three big themes of *Living Leadership*:

- **chapter 3 – get connected**: how you can connect effectively with others
- **chapter 4 – get real**: how you can practise the art of the possible and not get caught up in fantasies about changing the world
- **chapter 5 – get help**: how you can "be your best" if you value your experience of life and make good use of both your strengths and your apparent weaknesses

In Chapter 6 we look at the importance of recognising that

you will not be at your best all the time and how to learn from moments when you are less effective. Chapter 7 deals with the choices that you make as a leader, from moment to moment, that shape your impact on others and suggests that the more aware you are of these choices, the more effective you can be as a leader.

Living leadership
Find yourself in leading people

The best is the enemy of the good.

Voltaire

iving Leadership describes the leadership that really lives in organisations today. There are a thousand books on leadership theory but little has been done to understand how ordinary mortals lead in real organisations. We offer our view of the reality of leadership, what works and what doesn't – based on more than 20 years of working with leaders and the unique, four-year research project in which we lived alongside leaders and their organisations. The picture we got from being with leaders and followers in the moment was very different from the sanitised, cleaned-up view that you get in most management research when you interview people after the event. When you are with people, as events unfold, you experience the excitement and anxiety, the elation and terror, the self-belief and self-doubt of leading and following.

To hell with great men

Leadership for some people is something they are born with. It is a quality possessed by a few great figures (usually men) that have the ability to see ahead, take courageous stands and inspire others. It is often associated with those who have charisma – an almost magical ability to persuade and inspire others. It is something a few demonstrate "from the school playground" onwards. You either have it or you don't. It's not something you can develop.

We disagree.

The three themes of living leadership

1 **Leading happens between people**

Leadership is not the property of the leader (as many have argued) – nor (as some have suggested) of the followers. It is what happens *between* people in a particular moment or situation. Leadership is a social process – the result of interactions between and within individuals and groups. It is both very personal and a product of groups and the overall business and organisational context.

Leaders are on stage, playing a role for and with others. They embody certain qualities or characteristics for other people. They become public property on to which other people project things – whether the leaders like it or not. Sometimes people make their leader a hero; sometimes a scapegoat. Leaders can't avoid these dynamics but they can work with them and look for opportunities to harness them in the service of their organisations.

They have to focus on the people around them and not just the work to be done. To be effective, leaders have to connect with the people around them. People work for people. The vital ingredient is the quality of the relationships between those designated to lead and those who depend on them.

> to be effective, leaders have to connect with the people around them; people work for people

If leadership happens between people, it is important to look at the dynamics of the situation, organisation or group as well as the individual leader. Leadership books have focused too much on the individual; we need to look at the people around the leader, how leadership works for them. Instead of seeing the leader as *on top* doing things *to* organisations, it suggests we should think about leaders *as part of* the organisation, *in the middle*, having an influence but also being shaped by the organisation and the business context.

2 Leaders are shaped by the context

The leadership that comes to exist between a leader and followers is context specific. The social and political environment, the business situation and the culture of an organisation (its characteristic patterns of thinking and behaving) shape the type of leadership that is given. Yes, the personality and working style of the leader are significant but more important is the context within which people are working.

For many people this is an uncomfortable conclusion. People are so used to thinking – or taking for granted – that individuals can change the world that it can be shocking to be reminded about the limits within which leaders work.

We found that leaders could not transform their business environment, organisational culture and people and group dynamics in the way they hoped. All but one of the leaders studied set out to achieve a complete change – a business turnaround, a fundamental change of culture or the development of a new enterprise. Try as they would to wrench their organisations into submission, their organisations bit back. Without exception, the transformations they sought were not achieved. The results they achieved were more down to earth than the original expectations – though, except in one case, regarded by their companies as successes.

> leaders could not transform their business environment, organisational culture and people and group dynamics in the way they hoped

Successful leadership is a living thing. It cannot be bottled and reduced to a simple formula. What constitutes leadership is subtle and situational. In one moment it can be to direct people, to say clearly, "This is what needs to be done, this is what I want you to do". Or it can be to offer a goal or objective and ask others to decide how to get there. In one moment, it can be to face uncertainty, to say, "I don't know where to go or how to get there but together we'll find out". And in another moment it is not to *do* anything; it is just the way someone *is* that speaks to others.

And because context is so important, what works in one moment, with one group of people, does not work with another. You can test this by seeing how people evoke different responses at different times and in different situations. In one context an individual gets a powerful response from others and is able to lead; at another time he[1] tries to lead but no-one follows.

People recognise this pattern but don't want to talk about it. It's time to talk openly about the realities of leadership, what can be achieved and what can't. The leaders in our study became more effective when they accepted the contexts they were in and focused on how to turn them to their advantage. Instead of wringing their hands at difficult business environments, they looked for footholds for the direction they wished to travel. Instead of denouncing their organisational cultures, they looked for the "magic" in them on which they might build.

> it's time to talk openly about the realities of
> leadership

3 People are most effective when they bring themselves to leading

If leaders are to connect with others and understand the context, they need to bring themselves to the job of leading. Leaders "bring themselves" in that they:

- come across to others as real people, real flesh and blood, and not wearing some sort of mask or pretence;
- draw on all their humanity, their intelligence, their emotions and

---

1 Gender: In this book we use both male and female adjectives and pronouns when talking about leaders in general. There is no significance in the choice of masculine or feminine pronouns for particular chapters. We worked with both male and female leaders. The majority were men but some of the leaders from whom we have learnt most were women. We suspect that *Living Leadership* comes more easily to some women than to many men.

their intuition: they don't stay in their heads and draw just on their rational selves, they make use of all their senses and intelligence;

▍ remember what they know from all their life experiences and make use of them in the world of work.

We observed that when leaders did this, in a particular moment and context, the people around them responded to their lead.

"Bringing yourself" is different from "being yourself". Because leading happens *between* people, any leader is on stage and is performing in the best sense. At the same time people sense quickly if others are wearing a mask or pretending. In any interchange only part of their attention goes to the words you use. People also attend to all the other, often silent, signals that are sent – body language, looks, the feel of the person. It is said that when people see politicians they rarely remember what they said but often they recall how they looked and make their judgements accordingly. The people who work with you are also weighing you up instinctively: "Is this someone I can trust? Can I get a feel for the real person here?"

So leaders play a role – but to be effective it has to be a role they can credibly play, a part to which they can bring themselves. To an extent, it's like an actor considering a role in *Hamlet* or *King Lear*. "Is that a role for me – one in which I will be convincing? Or is it one where I will not be comfortable, not be able to come alive?"

There wasn't a particular type of leader – directive or consultative, outgoing or introverted, visionary or practical – who was more successful than others. We saw many different styles of leadership that were effective. What mattered was that the leaders were playing a role that suited them; one that they could credibly bring themselves to and one that those following saw as authoritative.

There is another part to this "bringing yourself". It is the ability to come alive in the moment, to be fully present, with others. The most effective leading we saw was when leaders had a quality of personal presence, in the moment, which was remarkable. At their best, people who were with them had a sense that they had all the leader's attention. The leaders were focused on the people with them and not distracted by other pressures. They weren't looking over their shoulders at the next person, the bosses in the background or the next task. They were here, now, concentrating on the people around them.

Leaders burdened with unreal expectations

At the same time we were constantly frustrated by how burdened leaders were by the sense of what they *ought to be* as leaders. People in positions of authority often carried a huge weight of expectations about what a leader should be. This was a burden that stopped them bringing themselves to leading. We often saw people in positions of responsibility simply *surviving*, getting through from one day to the next. At these times they were focused desperately on getting the work done. They didn't relate to the people around them. They were in a bubble, largely cut off from others and the world around them. They were bogged down in operational tasks, staggering from one moment to the next under the weight of expectations and lists of things to do.

Sometimes it was almost physically painful to see highly capable individuals, who had the best of intentions about the way they wanted to lead, behave badly as leaders. Sometimes we saw leaders treating their subordinates like children, handing out assignments and publicly assessing their past work. At other moments leaders were detached from the people they depended on for results and failed to communicate essential information. Sometimes they pretended to know things that plainly they did not. It would be easy to write off the managers we worked with as incompetent leaders. They were not this at all. They were successful managers and leaders in world-class organisations, yet at times they fell victim to the impossible pressures placed on leaders today.

It was interesting to see who were put forward as role models for leadership. We often heard the same list: Nelson Mandela, Winston Churchill, John Kennedy, Martin Luther King, Margaret Thatcher. These were extraordinary people for extraordinary times.

But what about the more mundane, day-to-day, yet essential leadership needed in most organisations in ordinary times? As a leader for a business or hospital, a refuse cleaning service or professional firm, do you really need to pretend to be Nelson Mandela?

It's the imperfections that make leaders valuable

We found that leaders are far from perfect. At some level people know this too; yet they still act as if leaders are supermen and women. Leaders are driven by deep-seated, highly personal reasons to achieve something, prove something or fix something about themselves. What is different about leaders is that they are driven to speak and act more on behalf of the "we" than the "me". The leaders we saw were preoccupied with getting recognised and not getting rejected. They used this motivation to become effective leaders of successful organisations. The mosaic of their personalities was not a simple pattern of strengths to be developed and weaknesses to be minimised. There is no competency model that can be applied to build the ideal leader. Leaders are effective when they are able to bring how they really are to the task they have chosen: when they engage fully with others, when they retain the capacity to think clearly under huge pressure, when they recognise self-doubt as a powerful aid, when they accept that "good enough" is often a whole lot better than perfection, when they work with others "as they are" rather than expecting blind loyalty. Leaders command respect because they are real: passionate, hard working and committed, but not perfect.

The stories from our research give a sense of what it really feels like to be in the "eye of the storm". They include the actions, reactions and interactions that made a difference as leaders and others played out their dramas. The stories describe what leaders did, why they did it and the results they expected. Most importantly, we followed each story through to discover what actually happened.

Far from finding a tidy sequential process of creating a vision, then inspiring others through charismatic and persuasive communication, we found intensive, emotional journeys, for both leaders and followers, that were at times unclear, confusing and difficult but often engaging, stimulating, exciting and rewarding. There were highs, lows and all points in between. These were the journeys of leaders "coming alive", giving of their best when it was needed – and finding that they did not need to be superheroes.

Living with uncertainty

The purpose of leadership is also different in our picture. In many of the situations we experienced there was no one person who could see the way forward and guide others. The future was uncertain. The prevailing belief that a leader would come along and show the way to the "promised land" was a myth. Even if the leader was right about the general direction the organisation needed to travel, there was a huge amount to learn about what that direction meant and how the organisation could move in that direction. The applied intelligence of groups and whole organisations was needed if the way forward was to be found.

We recognise that this runs counter to strongly held assumptions that finding the right person – be it chief executive or expert – will make all the difference to the future of organisations. But as James Suroweicki[2] says:

> if you can assemble a diverse group of people who possess varying degrees of insight and knowledge, you're better off entrusting it with major decisions rather than leaving them in the hands of one or two people, no matter how smart those people are ... There is no real evidence that one can become expert in something as broad as "decision making" or "policy" or "strategy". Auto repair, piloting, skiing, perhaps even management: these are skills that yield to application, hard work and native talent. But forecasting an uncertain future and deciding the best course of action in the face of that future are much less likely to do so.

2 James Suroweicki, *The Wisdom of Crowds – Why the Many are Smarter than the Few*, Random House, 2004.

Leadership is not then about knowing the answer and inspiring others to follow. It is the capacity to release the collective intelligence and insight of groups and organisations. It is helping people to find their own answers. There are things that you as a leader need to know if you are to be credible but there are also moments when you need to say "I don't know" if others are to confront difficult issues and learn how to overcome them.

> leadership is not about knowing the answer; it is the capacity to release the collective intelligence and insight of groups and organisations

In our minds, you lead when you help others to tackle an issue or seize an opportunity that would not otherwise be addressed. The focus is on triggering some collective capacity for valuable thought and action. These acts of leadership are not often in the heroic mould of one individual standing resolute against the world. Rather, they catalyse a development for a group or organisation. At the right moment, people follow once the lead has been provided. The act of leadership enables others to shift their thinking, to get moving and to deal with issues that have previously been stuck.

Leading involves taking responsibility, seeing things through over a period, being a beacon to others by presence, word or action. It's not just expressing a view or perspective or making an impact in the moment. It's consistency and courage that act as a guide to others.

Many leaders

Living Leadership implies that *many* people can and need to be leaders, not just the *few*. In our research we were constantly reminded that those with power and position in organisations are not the only ones who need to lead. Very often it was the people who did *not* have formal power over others who were more able to lead in the moment than those who were in positions of authority. It seemed that while the formal leader was burdened, slowed down by the weight of impossible expectations, others were sometimes able to look reality in the face and identify what was needed. Modern organisations need the many to lead at different times and in different ways.

Because leadership is a social process, acts of leadership don't exclusively come from those who have the position of boss. Something that surprised us in our research was how often the groups around a formal leader were more able to lead than the leader.

Authority

We also noticed the reluctance now in many organisations to acknowledge the importance of authority, the need of people to have a safe enough and secure enough sense that there are others on whom they can depend to guide them. Any parent and any child knows the value and importance of authority, someone to rely on, someone to prove something to. Yet in many places managers are reluctant to acknowledge that anyone has authority over others and pretend that their unit or organisation is "flat" and everyone has an equal contribution to make.

We experienced repeatedly that groups and organisations do need leading. The idea of the totally flat organisation is a myth and adds frustration rather than freeing people up. In every organisation we worked in there were key moments when someone had to step forward and lead if the group or organisation was to move forward. We also saw the pressing need for good-enough authority figures.

SVEN'S STORY

Sven was the leader of Information Technology in an international manufacturing company. He was responsible for keeping up with the insatiable demand from businesses around the world for an improved IT service. For nine months he had led the multinational team of IT managers, each of whom had a "dotted line" relationship with him and a "solid line" relationship with the regional business boss. When reflecting privately on a three-day meeting that he had just had with the team, he said he wanted to change the relationship he had with his team: he wanted to develop a "personal contract" with each member of the team. "I have to trust them," he said. "I am not their CEO, I have to find a balance, a managerial process that works with them. I have to hold the pressure for results and give them more room. Am I a template manager, someone who feeds in lots of processes and templates for others to use in completing their tasks? Yes, I have driven that approach too much." After exploring the costs of excessive use of templates, he suddenly blurted out, "So, what I need to do is relate to them more as people, is that it?"

Implications of living leadership

If this view is correct, if leaders are most effective when they bring themselves to leading, if leading happens between people and is shaped by the context, what are the implications for you? If you want to lead, what should you do or think about? When you are a follower, what helps?

Get connected

The first priority for leaders and those around them is to get connected – for leaders to relate well enough to the people around them as well as to the task to be done. This requires leaders and others to "get personal" and to show something of themselves. It may mean getting to know people on a social level – but often we saw that the connection was made just in a work setting.

By "getting connected" we mean:

■ enough openness and trust to confront difficult issues openly;

■ enough respect to make people want to work with others and make the extra effort for them;

■ enough shared values and perspectives to enable effective joint working;

▌ enough conflict to widen and deepen the exchanges and make real trust possible.

Such characteristics are easy to describe but difficult to achieve. One of the experiences we had repeatedly in the research was leaders espousing values like openness, trust and respect and then, despite apparently having the best of intentions, practising something very different. The practical question is therefore: "What gets in the way, in reality?" "What are the obstacles that stop you connecting well enough to the people around you?"

In our research it was obvious to some leaders that they had to connect at a personal level – and a mystery to others. Some leaders at some times focused only on the work to be done together and tried to ignore the need to build good-enough, working relationships. The price they paid at these moments was that they got, at best, compliance from their people and, at worst, sullen opposition. At other times, when they connected with the people around them, they discovered energetic and insightful followers.

Get real

The challenge for the leader is to work with "what is":

▌ the relationships in the room;

▌ the connections to others;

▌ the culture of the organisation;

▌ the business and social environment.

Living Leadership connects up the work, the people and the interactions in the group in a way that provides enough safety, over time, to tackle the real difficulties and opportunities.

Living Leadership focuses on making the best use of what *is* and not attempting to transform everything. The effort to bring about revolution within individuals, groups and organisations is both mad and dangerous. Mad because sane adults, groups and organisations don't change utterly. Dangerous because we have enough examples from history – from Lenin to Hitler to Mao – to know that revolutions often start by drawing on people's idealism but end in abuse and dictatorship. Leadership should be about fulfilling the purposes of organisations and not pretending to transform them every time leaders change.

There is no formula people can follow that will tell them how to lead in a particular situation. What constitutes effective leadership, now, here, today, needs to be discovered in the moment. It's no good looking outside the organisation for *the* answer. It does not exist. The picture we offer of leaders is not another business school model. There is no one model of leaders. It's absurd to say there is one set of rules for a successful marriage or relationship. So it is laughable to say there is only one way of being a successful leader.

A "living leader" exists with others: he is in tune, playing in the same key, within the same overall structure. He is giving and taking energy from others, helping and being helped simultaneously. He has an understanding of harmony and dissonance and yet is not constrained by a score or script.

He is ordinary and extra-ordinary. Sometimes he "plays a solo" that is inspiring, uplifting, hugely rewarding and personally

Coming alive as a leader

exhausting – and it makes or breaks the overall performance. Most of the time he is "pumping chords" quietly in the background to keep the rhythm steady. Like the jazz musician, he has worked hard for years to acquire a range of basic skills, practising and polishing them regularly, yet nothing exists to tell him exactly what to do at a given moment. That requires intuition, adaptability, an understanding of the context, a range of possible options to draw from, a feeling for what others need from him, a generosity of spirit to give and the courage to put himself "on the line".

Get help

The third requirement for effective leading is being able to ask for help when you need it – and knowing when to offer help to others. This requires leaders to use themselves well, drawing on their emotions and feelings, intuition and intelligence.

Can people learn how to be a better leader? You bet they can! However, leaders don't become more effective by trying to learn some formula. If, as we found, there is no one model or tool kit that says how to be a successful leader, then the education needed is in self-awareness. The more aware leaders are of who they are, how others see them, what choices they are making and the consequences of those choices, the more effectively they can use themselves and have the impact they want to have.

Our experience with the research reinforces our view that the place to focus development is on leaders appreciating who they are, not trying to be somebody they are not. We found that leadership competencies can be a useful tool but can also be damaging as a means for assessing potential leaders and their learning needs. Comparing individuals against an idealised picture of what leaders should be leads to "deficit thinking" in which people become preoccupied with filling "gaps" in their competencies and end up trying to be somebody they are not. In fact it is the flaws in people that make them interesting and give them their drive. The practical and encouraging question is not how to "correct" flaws but how to make best use of the special qualities each individual has and how to complement what they haven't got with the special abilities of others.

When leaders were most effective they were able to make use of the full extent of their own resources and skills. They gave of their best and enabled others to give of their best. They didn't just survive. They remembered what they knew from all their life experiences and made use of it in the world of work. They drew on their intuition and their feelings. They stopped being one-dimensional change agents and made use of their humanity. They stopped trying to live up to an impossible ideal and were free to adapt themselves to the needs of the moment. They gave up trying to shape the world as they would like and faced life as it is.

Like Philip Pullman in his award-winning *His Dark Materials*[3] trilogy, we say that the effort to cut yourself and others in half, and describe one side as "evil" and the other as "good" – one part as strength, one part as weakness – is a denial of humanity. It is an illusion that is profoundly damaging. How much better if people can value themselves and their organisations as a whole, to see themselves and others not as black and white but infinite colours and both good and bad. How much better to see some of the contradictions and links and not try and change them – to see how demons can be strengths and assets can be liabilities, depending on the context.

Character not charisma

Many people have asked us: "Do I have to be charismatic to be a leader?" For us the answer is "No". Leadership does not require charisma. People can be triggered to see issues and possibilities differently without leaders being charismatic. Our view is that charisma is a social process, as is leading. Charisma exists *between* people in particular moments and circumstances and is not a quality of one individual.

Charisma can be a wonderful thing. We experienced it sometimes in our research and we were bowled over by it. But we are also

---

3 Philip Pullman, *His Dark Materials* trilogy, Scholastic Press, 2001.

suspicious of it. We wonder why people want to abandon responsibility and be led by a masterful, charismatic leader. We ask whether the charismatic person is meeting their own needs at the expense of those of others. Jim Collins, author of the book *Good to Great*, puts forward the interesting proposition that, "A charismatic CEO can win every argument regardless of the facts. A non-charismatic CEO has to win on the merits of the argument."[4]

Character, on the other hand, we found, was an essential ingredient of leadership. It was people who had a moral strength – with views, opinions, feelings, beliefs that did not change from moment to moment but gave others a sense that "you know who you are dealing with". When we saw people being effective leaders, they were not necessarily colourful or outgoing. But they were people of substance.

> character was an essential ingredient of leadership; when we saw people being effective leaders, they were not necessarily colourful or outgoing but they were people of substance

The ethics of leading

There is, of course, an ethical dimension to leadership. The picture we offer here is of human leadership, one that is respectful of other people and oneself. There could be other types of leadership that deliver results, at least in the short term, but that abuse people or treat them dishonestly and are unsustainable.

We take issue with transformational leadership not least because it is associated with people being treated as cogs in a machine, resources to be recruited and thrown away as if they are pieces of machinery. That does not seem to us an acceptable way of leading people. Part of leadership is taking tough, uncomfortable decisions. However, tough decisions and actions can still be handled in a way that is respectful of individuals, groups and institutions.

4 Jim Collins, *Good to Great*, Random House Business Books, 2001.

What is needed is a realistic, down-to-earth rethinking of what leaders can and should do: a willingness to say out loud what people already know at some level. Leaders in organisations need to feel "empowered" at least as much as followers. Leaders need to be allowed to do what is best, in the moment, in relationship with others. They need to come alive as thinking, feeling human beings. It really is as simple – and as complex – as that. And it works! When, in our research study, we saw people bringing themselves to their leading and connecting with others, they provided the leadership that was needed. Bringing yourself – it's the best you can do and it's good enough.

LESSONS FROM OUR RESEARCH

* Leading is a social process; it happens between people.
* The success or failure of leaders is dependent on the ability to work with the context.
* It also depends on the ability of individuals to bring themselves, warts and all.
* Using your life experience is more productive than seeking to perfect your leadership competencies.
* You don't have to be a superhero to be a leader.
* What works is to get connected, to get real, to acknowledge your limits and value who you really are.
* It takes time.

Before we explore in more depth what *Living Leadership* is and how it works, however, we need to tackle the idealised picture of leadership that many managers have in their minds. In our research we saw many leaders and followers trapped in the idea that leaders should be transforming heroes. It is so pervasive in the business and organisational world that often people don't see the model. They take for granted that is how leaders *should be* – even if it is not how they are in reality. The picture of heroic leaders can be inspiring. It plays to the age-old need for heroes. Yet, in the end, it has been deeply damaging. In Chapter 2 we explore how and why.

The end of superman
Don't be a hero

Heroic leaders, once a godsend, are now a public menace. We need to think about organisational leadership in a new way — a way that fits the times in which we live.

Dee W. Hock, founder of Visa International

We have a bold message in this book. In the last 20 years the business and organisational world has overdosed on the idea of leaders as transformational heroes. The age-old desire for heroes has been overlain with a largely American business model. Leadership has been identified with transformation and transformation with leadership. In a time when people generally are sceptical of heroic figures, business keeps looking for great individuals to bring about heroic change.

We found in our research that the model doesn't work, has many damaging consequences and is now crumbling. It's time to kick the habit and get back to reality – time for a more realistic and more flexible picture of leadership to emerge.

> the [transformational] model doesn't work, has many damaging consequences and is now crumbling

The would-be transformational leader trying to keep up appearances

There has been much talk in recent years of "empowerment". Yet what we have experienced more often is organisations skilled at *disempowering* their potential leaders. In many places there is a lack of leadership. People in positions of authority and power – and others – fail to take opportunities to lead. They don't speak up when they feel there is something important to say; they don't challenge when things are going wrong; they don't follow through on good ideas. To understand why there is this leadership shortfall, we need to look in more detail at the picture of leadership that dominates the organisational and business world.

Looking for superman

It's a strange thing. Most of the heroes have fallen. Jack Welch, Percy Barnevik, Kenneth Lay, Martha Stewart, Dick Grasso, George Simpson and many others have bitten the dust. And yet, people in the business and organisational world keep looking for heroic figures. The idea of heroic transformational leaders persists. Over the last 20 years book after book – by writers as authoritative and diverse as John Kotter, Warren Bennis and Rosabeth Moss Kanter – has said that leadership is transformation and transformation is leadership.

The idea of "transformational heroes" is simple to state. It was neatly summed up for us by the number two in an organisation (who was criticising his boss for "not understanding what leadership is"). "A leader", he said, "must have a clear vision of what he wants the organisation to be in the future. He must communicate the vision powerfully and inspire others to adopt it. And he must demonstrate a steely resolve to align decisions and actions so that they support the vision. He should measure performance to ensure that the organisation is moving in the right direction and that corrective action is taken if actions are not aligned." And we can add that in the modern version of transformational heroes, the leader is also tasked with "empowering" people to find their own ways of contributing to the vision.

TRANSFORMATIONAL LEADERSHIP

- ✴ Visionary
- ✴ Inspiring – "an outstanding communicator"
- ✴ Makes things happen – "a steely resolve"
- ✴ Heroic
- ✴ Empowering

Exhibit 1 Transformational leadership – an ideal, often taken for granted

As former Harvard Business School professor John Kotter puts it:[1]

> Leadership is about coping with change. Part of the reason it has become so important in recent years is that the business world

---

[1] Reprinted by permission of *Harvard Business Review*. From "What Leaders Really Do" by John P. Kotter, December 2001. © 2001 by Harvard Business School Publishing Corporation; all rights reserved.

has become more competitive and more volatile. Faster technological change, greater international competition, the deregulation of markets ... have contributed to the shift. The net result is that doing what was done yesterday, or doing it 5% better, is no longer a formula for success. Major changes are more and more necessary to survive and compete in this new environment. More change always demands more leadership.

He goes on to say that leading involves:

Setting a direction – developing a picture of the future (often the distant future) along with strategies for producing the changes needed to achieve that vision.

Aligning people ... this means communicating the new direction to those who can create coalitions that understand the vision and are committed to its achievement.

Motivating and inspiring – keeping moving in the right direction, despite major obstacles to change, by appealing to basic but often untapped human needs, values and emotions.

The red thread running through this picture of leadership is that leaders are *doing things to* their organisations. They stand outside their organisations, they know the way forward and they struggle heroically to make their organisations understand and implement the way forward that they have decided on. Their job, over a period, is to bring about fundamental change.

Leaders are seen like rodeo riders seeking to impose their will on their organisations. The more resistance there is, the more leaders

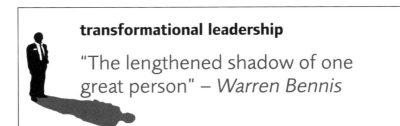

transformational leadership

"The lengthened shadow of one great person" – *Warren Bennis*

Exhibit 2 Transformational leadership

need to push back and bring them under control. They have to make their organisations understand where their true interests lie.

The spotlight in this picture of leadership is on the heroic individual – his qualities (it usually is a man), his experience and understanding, his determination to drive through change. The clear, if implicit, message is that the strength and ability of the leader are the decisive factors. If you want something strongly enough and you understand the business, you can change the world. Are you up to it?

Business leaders are regularly heard committing to turn their companies round or to change their cultures and ways of working or to transform them into enterprises that will deliver reliable increases in shareholder value year after year. Others promise to reshape their companies and move to faster growing or more profitable sectors. Politicians and managers promise to transform public services. The pressures on them to promise to change the world are intense.

> Leaders believe they must behave in some larger-than-life way. With the expectation that they must see things the rest of us do not, they make riskier and riskier decisions, desperate to prove they deserve the role.[2]

People have had a need for heroes since time immemorial. Identifying with famous figures can make followers feel stronger, more powerful. It can simplify complex problems and make them apparently easier to tackle. It can also mean the abdication of responsibility, sitting back and passing the buck to the leader.

The origins of the idea of transforming heroes lie in the revolutionary ideas and practice of the nineteenth and twentieth centuries – Nietzsche and Hitler, Lenin and Mao. Now it is a view with a strong American accent (all the business writers cited above are Americans). It reflects the American "can-do" spirit – the sense that we can change the world if we will it hard enough – and the

2 Vicki Ten Haken (visiting professor of management at Hope College in Holland, Michigan), "Everyday Leaders", *International Economics & Business Research Journal* May 2003.

American view that change is led by individual heroes (from George Washington to Jack Welch and Alan Greenspan).

The consequences of this thinking are enormous. As Merrick Rosenberg puts it:[3]

> Heroic Leaders and their followers get trapped in a never-ending cycle of heroism and passivity. The hero leader sees a crisis and jumps in to save the day. The followers see that their manager is going to handle all of the "big crises" and thus, back off when they occur. The manager sees that the staff is neither willing, nor capable to handle to big issues, which serves to reinforce the need for his or her heroism. And the cycle begins again, with each occurrence serving to solidify the pattern of heroism and passivity.

The transforming hero has become the dominant picture of leadership

We found in our research that the heroic idea of leadership was pervasive – for leaders and followers. Everywhere we went we met it. It exists as an idea, often as an accusation, "Here's what I – or my leader – ought to be." The transformational hero idea sits on the shoulders of managers as a sense of what they *ought* to be doing as leaders – even if they cannot quite live up to the ideal. Other ideas of leadership – the leader as servant, as steward, as figurehead – have been crowded out. People believe that if leaders are not there to transform their companies or organisations, they are not real leaders.

All but one of the leaders in our research were called upon to bring about transformations – the turnaround of a failing business, a radical change in organisational culture or the creation of a new enterprise. The only one who was not – because he was waiting to take over from another leader – was soon parachuted into another division of his company and asked to transform the costs structure and service level of that business.

---

3 Merrick Rosenberg (president, Team Builders Plus), *One Team Newsletter*, March 2005.

Leaders seemed to have the idea that not only were they there to bring about transformation but that they needed to be inspiring individuals and outstanding communicators to achieve the required change. Communication has become a priority for many leaders and many business writers. The assumption is that the leader knows where the organisation should go – and how to get there – but sometimes does not do enough to communicate that direction to others.

We often heard managers say that organisations from time to time need a "tough guy" – someone who is insensitive to people, ruthless and determined – to ensure that they confront the changes that are needed if they are to succeed. We were struck in our research by how powerful this folk image is, how often managers talk about the risk of organisations becoming complacent unless challenged, occasionally, by this "tough guy". When costs need to be cut, bureaucracy challenged, organisations or activities sold or closed – who will do it unless the "tough guy" wields the knife?

Transformational leadership is a true paradigm – an idea so well embedded that in many places it is taken for granted. In the third, validation phase of our research, we often met managers who could see no other option. For them leaders are heroes or they are nothing. They exist to bring about fundamental change. They just don't see any other option.

Like any well-established paradigm, the idea of transforming heroes is difficult to challenge. For thousands of years it was obvious to anyone who cared to think about it that the Earth was the centre of the universe and that the Sun and the planets revolved around it. Then along came an obscure Polish monk called Copernicus to argue that we live in a solar system. It took 150 years, even for educated people, to accept his view. Yes, when people looked, they found that, viewed from Earth, the planets seemed to move backwards and forwards. But they devised ingenious orbits within orbits to explain that the planets did move around the Earth and not the Sun. When a paradigm exists, people don't see the evidence and can't make sense of arguments that contradict their picture.

> we found in our research that the transformational leader is an emperor without clothes

Yet we found in our research that transformational leadership is a myth – an idea that exists in the minds of people but that bears little relationship to the leadership that is provided, day-to-day, in real organisations. People know at some level that the transformational hero is an unattainable ideal. Think about it. How many transforming heroes do you know in your organisation? In our research we saw many people attempting, none succeeding, in being a transforming hero. The emperor has no clothes.

From hero to zero

> "Kings are not born – they are made by artificial hallucination."
>
> *George Bernard Shaw*

The recent history of business and organisations is littered with examples of leaders who sought to bring about transformations – only to find their dreams crumble to dust. We remember colleagues only a few years ago who identified Enron as a new type of business model and Kenneth Lay, Jeff Skilling and the other leaders there as visionaries who were pioneering the "new economy". Now Enron seems like a very old type of business model, the latest in a long line of business scandals in which managers encourage investors to part with their funds by persuading them that they have found a new way of making money.

Not long ago Jack Welch, the chief executive of General Electric, was held up as a business icon in the USA and Percy Barnevik, the chief executive of ABB, was a hero in Europe. Both were credited with transforming their companies and turning dull engineering companies into reliable money-making machines. Now the achievements are seen more critically. The regular increases in shareholder value were not so assured after all.

One of us worked as a young manager for the British General Electric Company, then run by Sir Arnold Weinstock, a brilliant but not at all charismatic leader. He remembers at the time longing for Weinstock to bring about change in the relatively dull electrical engineering and defence companies that he led. It seemed to us obvious that he should invest more and exploit the potential of the extraordinary technologies the company possessed. Weinstock refused and went on managing cautiously, extracting profit and building up a legendary cash pile. Twenty years later, Weinstock at last retired and was replaced by a would-be transforming hero, George Simpson. Simpson transformed the company. He sold all the defence and heavy electrical engineering businesses, bought a stack of telecoms companies in the USA and declared that in future the company – now to be called Marconi – would be a high-growth technology business. In two years the transformation was complete – only it was not the transformation that Simpson had in mind but a journey to near-bankruptcy. Far from being a high growth area, the telecoms market crashed, companies in the USA turned out to be much less valuable than expected and the famous cash pile evaporated. Shareholder value of £35 billion was turned into half a billion and innumerable individual lives turned upside down.

Exhibit 3 Many Business heroes have fallen

Where is the evidence that changing the chief executive is the way to revive a company? There isn't any.

> Margarethe Wiersema, Professor of Strategy at the University of California, studied the 500 largest companies during 1997 and 1998 and discovered that 83 had changed their chief executive during that time. She found that 71 percent had left involuntarily, either because they were fired or took "early retirement", which is often a euphemism for the same thing. This was more than double the rate of the 1980s.
>
> How did the companies fare with their new chief executives? Not very well. Professor Wiersema's research, published in the *Harvard Business Review* in December 2002, found that companies that dismissed their chief executives showed no significant improvement in their operating earnings or their relative share price performance in the subsequent two years. "I couldn't find a single measure suggesting that CEO dismissals have a positive effect on corporate performance," she wrote.
>
> As Professor Wiersema observed, "Poorly performing companies don't get that way because of any single decision or for that matter any single leader. Patterns of historical decisions, strategic neglect and misallocation of resources all contribute to the deterioration of performance; some contributing factors may even lie outside the company's control.
>
> Where company fortunes do revive, it is seldom because of one individual. No chief executive, however talented, acts alone. It requires large numbers of people, from middle managers to front line staff, who are committed, able and know the business well. The person at the top can set the tone and make the right appointments. Even then some of those famed turnarounds turn out to be illusory."[4]

Luc Vandevelde was first widely credited with reviving British retailer Marks & Spencer. Later he was criticised for not doing enough and the company was struggling again.

Stuart Rose took over as CEO from Luc Vandevelde and led a rigorous, challenging assessment of the organisation and strategy.

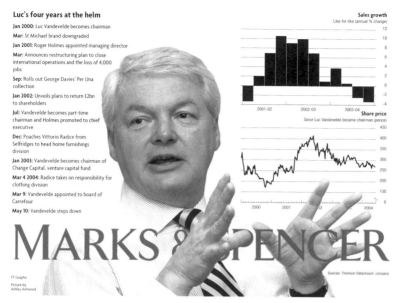

Luc's four years at the helm

Jan 2000: Luc Vandevelde becomes chairman

Mar: St Michael brand downgraded

Jan 2001: Roger Holmes appointed managing director

Mar: Announces restructuring plan to close international operations and the loss of 4,000 jobs

Sep: Rolls out George Davies' Per Una collection

Jan 2002: Unveils plans to return £2bn to shareholders

Jul: Vandevelde becomes part-time chairman and Holmes promoted to chief executive

Dec: Poaches Vittorio Radice from Selfridges to head home furnishings division

Jan 2003: Vandevelde becomes chairman of Change Capital, venture capital fund

Mar 4 2004: Radice takes on responsibility for clothing division

Mar 9: Vandevelde appointed to board of Carrefour

May 10: Vandevelde steps down

Sales growth
Like-for-like (annual % change)

Share price
Since Luc Vandevelde became chairman (pence)

FT Graphic

Picture by Ashley Ashwood

Sources: Thomson Datastream; company

MARKS & SPENCER

Exhibit 4 What goes up – often also comes down

He was initially seen as an "insider, a safe pair of hands" but perhaps not charismatic enough. He oversaw a turnaround in performance that put M&S back in its previous position as one of Britain's leading retailers, fighting off an aggressive acquisition challenge along the way. At the time of writing (autumn 2008) his star is, in turn, waning …

In late 2007, Wyeth's announcement that chief operating officer Bernard Poussot would be taking over as CEO was abrupt and unceremonious. But the unexpected departure of Bob Essner, who was nearing 60, signalled the end of an era at the country's fifth-largest pharmaceutical company:[5]

> In his roughly six years on the job, Essner reinvented Wyeth – selling off non-pharmaceutical businesses and changing the company's name from American Home Products – all in the wake of a massive product liability lawsuit. More importantly, Essner invigorated the company's research labs. He also boosted revenue 30 percent, to $20.4 billion.

5 *Fortune,* 1 October 2007.

So why the sudden exit? Early reports speculated that Essner fell victim to investor discontent after the FDA failed to approve three Wyeth medicines this year.

But the reasons for Essner's departure, announced last week, are more complicated. Regulatory setbacks are hard to take, but anyone who invests in Big Pharma these days expects rejections and delays. Ever since Merck (Charts, Fortune 500) recalled its Vioxx painkiller medication in 2004, the FDA has been stingy about rubber stamping new drugs. CEOs aren't to blame for that – and investors know it.

This doesn't mean that Essner didn't make mistakes. Indeed, he appears to have landed in the hotseat for a common CEO sin: excessive hype.

Straightforward, stout and sporting a gray beard, Essner exudes a grandfatherly sense of calm. But, while he is hardly a Steve Jobs-like hypemeister, he's been trumpeting Wyeth's pipeline over the last three or so years, including the three drugs recently held up by the FDA: Pritiq, an antidepressant; the antipsychotic bifeprunox; and Vivant, an osteoporosis treatment.

Wyeth's pipeline appeared plentiful. Essner, with the help of chief scientist Robert Ruffolo, had revamped the company's labs, and Wyeth's scientists were investigating more compounds than many of its peers.

Investors took the bait, driving Wyeth's stock up 55 percent from October 2004 to June, when it hit an all-time high of $58 a share. Investors were hopeful that the upcoming drugs would help Wyeth to offset the loss of patent protection for two of its top-selling drugs – the antidepressant known as Effexor XR and Protonix, an antacid medicine.

Both medications, which accounted for more than a quarter of Wyeth's $20.3 billion in 2006 revenues, could face generic competition as soon as 2010.

With Wyeth's recent FDA rejections, investors woke up to the fact that the company's pipeline won't be able to make up for the coming patent losses.

Even if the drugs had been approved, some analysts question

whether they would ever have reached the blockbuster status that Essner promised. He had estimated, for instance, that bifeprunox could garner as much as $2 billion at its peak. Some analysts predicted sales of the schizophrenia drug would be roughly a quarter of that. Says Deutsche Bank analyst Barbara Ryan: "The company was extraordinarily bullish about the pipeline. Our view of those products was poor, even without the regulatory issues, the products were not all that compelling."

The curse of the superstar CEO

Rakesh Khurana[6] describes the cult of recruiting charismatic chief executives – often in a crisis and usually from outside a company: "The charismatic leader was supposed to have the power to perform miracles – to bring a dying company back to life, for instance, or to vanquish, much larger, more powerful foes." To achieve these miracles, "they deliberately destabilise their organisations". Some, like Jack Welch at GE or Jacques Nasser at Ford, become known for their willingness to "lay waste" to parts of their organisations. As Khurana points out, destabilisation carries dangers:

- Who and what comes after the charismatic leader?: "... passing the torch from one leader to another is fraught with difficulty".
- The charismatic leader risks damaging an organisation by the wanton uprooting of the traditions and skills that made it successful.
- Sometimes – as at Enron – "the demands of the leader induced blind obedience in his followers".

> the leaders in our research had to let go of an initial dream and come to terms with a more ordinary – yet still satisfactory – achievement

In our research too – on a much less dramatic scale – the would-be transforming heroes did not achieve the transformations they sought. All the leaders in our research had to let go of an initial dream and come to terms with a more ordinary – yet still satisfactory – achievement. With one exception, they were all seen by their organisations as successful leaders; yet none achieved the transformation they originally sought. Examples included:

▊ One who tried in a few months to turn around a business that had been declining for at least 10 years. After one year the business was still not making adequate returns and was sold to a competitor.

▊ Another dreamed of creating a new hybrid organisation, halfway between the utility company parent and an Internet start-up. The strong culture of the parent and the end of the dotcom boom meant that the original objective was not achieved. Some Internet businesses did develop but they were brought firmly under the wing of divisions of the parent company.

▊ Another leader who was setting up a new mental health trust dreamed of creating a patient-centred organisation. He was seen after two years as a highly successful leader. However he had little impact on the underlying relationships between patients, doctors and other health professionals.

▊ The head of Information Technology dreamed of helping to make his European-based multinational more results and business oriented (and less focused on technical excellence and internal harmony). He helped to improve the IT service to businesses. The wider cultural transformation was put on hold when markets turned down and senior managers changed.

None of these leaders was a particularly charismatic individual. They were ordinary, competent managers whom their organisations saw as successful. Most were promoted within two years – and some have been promoted twice since we worked with them.

Transformations don't happen to order

But don't organisations sometimes need transformations? Sure they do. And isn't it part of the job of leaders to lead change? Yes, indeed. Our point is that transformations do not happen to order. What we saw in our research was a reminder that transformations in organisations do not occur because one person, or even a number of leaders, will the change. They happen as a result of the complex interaction of business circumstances, political and social forces, technical change, organisational culture, the dynamics of groups and the choices of both leaders and followers.

People can decide – as they often do – to personify change, to identify it with a particular leader. We saw often how people simplify and dramatise change – and seek to make sense of it – by associating it with individuals. But this is different from saying that the leader caused the transformation. A Jack Welch is the symbol of change – and later of a disappointment – more than the cause of it.

And don't leaders have a huge impact on their organisations? Yes they do. But there are two qualifications. First, it takes time. We found in the research that it takes between 18 and 24 months for the transition connected with a new leader to work through and the new leader to become fully effective. Until that time the new leaders were too anxious and the people around them too unsettled for the leader to have full authority. It takes many more years for powerful leaders to leave their imprint on organisations.

Second, the impact of leaders is not necessarily the one they expect or want. Effective leaders are constantly learning about the impact of their statements, actions and behaviours because they know from experience that the impact they have is often not what they intend. You say one thing but people hear another. You focus on one issue but people are more interested in something else. You take a position that you think is important but no-one notices, while another message you send out inadvertently strikes a chord for many. The most important signal a leader may send out may be a chance conversation or remark or action that at the time he hardly notices.

> The British subsidiary of one well-known US multinational traditionally had American bosses who came over for tours of duty of about two years. One member of the local management team told us that the British managers in the company had a proven way of assessing newly arrived bosses. "If, on his first day, the new boss can find his way to my office and asks about my work, he will be OK. If, on the other hand, he calls us in to see him in his office, we reckon he won't be much good."

The gap between intention and impact does not exist because leaders are stupid or incompetent. It's how human interactions work. Everything you do as a leader has to pass through other people's filters and be interpreted by them. There's no use complaining about this. The best you can do as a leader is have some good feedback mechanisms to see what the impact is.

Trapped in the future?

The emphasis on future visions, associated with the transforming hero idea, reminds us of a story from the 1930s:

> The German, Wolfgang Leonhard, grew up in Moscow in the Stalinist 1930s. He describes his confusion when he and his mother sought to replace their outdated 1924 map of Moscow. They found that the new map contained all the improvements destined to be completed by 1945, "We used to take both town plans with us on our walks from then on – one showing what Moscow had looked like ten years before and the other showing what it would look like ten years hence". As Brooks says, "What had vanished or, more exactly, become compressed between two dream worlds was the present".[7]

Some leaders seem to believe that they are already living in their imagined future world.

The damage done by the transforming hero idea

1 Unreal expectations

We were struck during our research by the senior figures – headhunters, company chairmen and Human Resources directors – who told us that the current expectations of leaders are unsustainable. They said that too much is expected of leaders, in too short a time. Some headhunters suggested that the pool of credible candidates for chief executive roles is shrinking rapidly.

---

7 Brooks, J., *Thank you, Comrade Stalin!: Soviet Public Culture from Revolution to Cold War*, Princetown University Press, 2001.

The chairman of a major international search company reckons that the current situation is unsustainable. "In the last 10 years expectations of leaders, and the risks, have risen, while average tenures have fallen. Increasingly the good people, after one stint in the pressure cooker role of chief executive, don't want any more of it and opt for less strenuous roles as chairmen or non-executive directors."

The transformational view of leadership is becoming unsustainable. Fewer and fewer individuals are willing to accept being thrust into the glare of the top job: "More than half (54%) of the senior executives surveyed say they would turn down the CEO position, according to a Burson-Marsteller and Wirthlin Worldwide study [in 2002]. The refusal rate doubled (26%) from one year ago." The expectations are unrealistic and the pressures unreasonable.

> "Today's CEOs have little time to prove themselves, according to a new national study by Burson-Marsteller. *Building CEO Capital*™ reveals that today's CEO has only five earnings quarters on average to prove him or herself".[8]

2 Followers lean back

The heroic leader idea encourages followers to be passive onlookers. The natural reaction, if the leader has all the limelight, the applause and the rewards, is to lean back and think: "OK you're the hero, you do it. Let's see how you get on ... Only don't expect too much of us. We're just the audience, ready to take instruction when you're ready."

3 Destroying the connection between leader and followers

If the leader is the hero, who knows the answer, and is making others see things his way, then there is no chance of the mutual respect, trust and engagement that we described in Chapter 1 as

---

8 Burson-Marsteller, *Building CEO Capital*™, 2001.

The transformational leader feeling the heat

essential to "getting connected". If you treat others as the audience for your performance, then they will applaud from time to time – or throw rotten eggs – but they are unlikely to get up on stage and help you.

> The problem with the notion of heroic leadership, of course, is not just that it's preposterous on the face of it. It is also corrosive to the connection that needs to exist between a real leader and the people who make the company work. Real leadership is connected, involved and engaged. It's often more quiet than heroic. Real leadership is about building an organisation slowly, carefully and collectively.[9]

4 Leaders feel they can't live up to the ideal

The identification of leadership with lone individuals standing apart and wrestling their organisations into shape paradoxically disempowers leaders and stops them giving of their best. The leaders themselves feel they cannot live up to the hero ideal. They are uneasy. In their gloomier (or more rational) moments, they know they are unlikely to be – or find – a transforming figure. Yet the ideal sits on their shoulders – reminding them of what they

---

[9] Henry Mintzberg, "Memo to CEOs", *Fast Company*, June 2002.

feel they *ought* to be doing as leaders. Leaders and followers are seduced by the idea. "What would it be like if only we had a hero who could transform this organisation? How wonderful would that be?"

LESSONS FROM OUR RESEARCH

* The transforming hero picture of leadership is everywhere in the organisational world.

* In many places it is taken for granted that leadership involves visioning, knowing, directing, aligning and measuring.

* It's a myth – leaders could not live up to it.

* The pretence is becoming unsustainable.

* It's deeply damaging. It preaches empowerment but in reality overburdens leaders and paralyses leaders and followers.

* People are looking for a new picture of leadership.

But how does a more human, more realistic and less charismatic way of leading work? In Chapter 3 we explore how real people in the real world get connected.

Get connected
You depend on others

Coming home from a concert one evening one of us met a musician friend who asked, "Where have you been?" He answered, "I have been to a concert of a famous orchestra". Whereupon she enquired, "Did they play together or merely at the same time?"

In this chapter we look at the first leg of *Living Leadership*: how effective leaders connect well enough to the people around them. As we said, *Living Leadership* exists *between* people. It is not the property of individual leaders nor do followers create it. It is the product of the subtle interplay of the individual and others in a particular context and moment. The quality of working relationships is all-important.

Relationships come first. They are the basis for everything – strategy, vision, operations and all the rest. Relationships are not the nice-to-have, extra room that, one day, you might add to your house, but the foundation for everything that leaders want to do.

In our research we met many leaders who focused on task, task, task – at the risk of never making enough links at a personal level with the people around them. There was so much to do, so much to think about and keep in focus that the human part often seemed to get lost. On top of all the other pressures, working at improving relationships seemed like too much to handle. It felt like a diversion from getting the work done when in fact it's the opposite – the precondition for reaching the targets.

Latent energy is released when leaders connect with others

We saw in our research that it was the quality of relationships that leader and group establish which delivered results. People work for people – not for visions or strategies or targets – and give of their best when they feel connected to the leader and the leader feels connected to them.

Relationships that work – at work

But what do we mean exactly by quality of relationships? Everyone who has worked in an organisation for any time knows at some level. It is a subtle, delicate phenomenon. Do you do things for your boss because he has power over you, can influence how much you get paid – and could sack you if you didn't do what he wanted? Or do you do things for your boss because you respect and trust him (enough)? Do you follow his lead because he has credibility and authority in your eyes? If you are the leader, do you value and respect those who work for you? Do you have confidence (enough) in them to deliver and to support you?

We are not talking about friendship or love here, though, of course, those relationships can happen at work. We are talking about reaching a point where:

▌ a leader accepts the subordinates (enough) as they are (even if they are not the people he might want to have working with him in a perfect world);

▌ people accept their boss as good enough (even if he or she is not, sometimes, the leader they might ideally want to have).

It's the organisational version of "I'm OK, you're OK".

It's also vital to have an absence of distrust – which is not quite the same thing as enough trust. Leaders and followers have to feel that the other side is not going to attack them personally or try to undermine them or get them sacked.

Examples from our research when leaders in our cases connected (enough) with the people around them were:

▌ Diane, when she arrived in her company as the new boss, engaged with people up and down her own company by asking good questions and being interested in how they worked and what ideas they had to improve. She later won a lot of street credibility by opening up a difficult conversation about the financial targets with her bosses and negotiating a one half reduction in the first year objectives in return for a commitment to integrate her operation more into the international company.

▌ John connected with his people when he looked openly at how his executive group worked together. John didn't like the picture that emerged – of "hub and spokes" working, with John keeping control of the key issues and never fully delegating – but he did allow it to be talked about openly. In the circumstances the unit faced, John decided not to change the way of working. Nevertheless, the understanding between managers and the willingness to work for John and each other increased.

▌ Peter, the newly appointed Swedish head of IT reporting to Sven, helped the whole IT group connect when at his first meeting he took the risk of challenging the way Sven handed out assignments. As the newcomer, Peter voiced an issue that others had not been prepared to raise but which had reduced the effectiveness of the group.

▋ Mary, the head of nursing, at an early meeting with her team, talked about the opportunity for nurses to improve their status and be more influential in the hospital. Judging by people's reactions after the meeting, she struck a chord with her fellow nurses and increased the sense of shared identity and commitment.

Times when leaders did not connect with the people around them included:

▋ Sven mentioned that business had turned down and budgets would be cut but failed to deal publicly with the implications for his IT group.

▋ Pierre was absent when the supply chain team for which he was responsible was receiving an award. He was outside the award ceremony on his phone talking to his boss's boss.

▋ Mary arrived for a meeting of her group to find that someone had rearranged the furniture. Instead of the usual large table with chairs around it, the chairs were set out in a circle without any tables. Without hesitating and without discussion, Mary said: "We can't have this. We'll put the chairs and tables back."

▋ James, the new head of a health trust, made speeches about "reconfiguring" health services and "putting patients first" but failed to mention a financial deficit that was likely to lead soon to service cuts.

▋ Max tabled some important issues at a management team meeting but, when the discussion became difficult and no clear conclusion was in sight, he grabbed back the issue himself, saying: "I'll look into this and let you know what I have decided".

We imagine you will have many of your own examples of when leaders did or did not connect with others. For us it is important to note that we are not talking here about playing golf together or a drink in the bar – though those activities may contribute to developing relationships. In our research we saw that the key connections were made as individuals experienced each other at work.

How do you know if there is enough connection?

Tell-tale signals of good enough relationships were moments when people:

▌ were confident enough to ask for help;

▌ "said it like it is" – spoke the truth as they saw it;

▌ disagreed without personal attacks and tolerated conflict;

▌ appreciated publicly and genuinely the contribution of others;

▌ felt heard by their boss;

▌ listened carefully to others;

▌ inquired into how others see things.

Signs of inadequate connection were:

▌ "I don't really know who David (my leader) is ...";

▌ "PowerPoint festivals" – long meetings devoted to hearing formal presentations and avoiding spontaneous conversation of what's really on people's minds;

▌ people sounding off in private about their frustrations;

▌ managers ignoring or rejecting the views of the awkward member of the group who expressed a truth that others didn't want to hear;

▌ people appearing to go along with policies or initiatives that they thought made no sense;

▌ the rejection of another's potential contribution: "He has nothing to offer me";

▌ flights of fancy – developing plans that didn't take account of awkward current realities.

From "templates" to "people person"

Sven was the head of IT in a manufacturing multinational. His background was in finance. Though knowledgeable about IT, he could not match the expertise of his IT team. He had a difficult task. With his boss he was seeking to change the culture of the company through providing integrated IT systems for the corporation as a whole. He had a dual mandate: develop a good enough day-to-day service to the business units and help make the company less complacent, more profit oriented.

Early in Sven's time as IT leader, business in the USA turned down sharply. Budgets were cut and what had appeared a difficult task now seemed to many to be impossible. Sven was surrounded by uncertainty. He did not know what his bosses on the main board of the company would now regard as an adequate result for IT. He didn't know how the business situation would develop and whether the downturn would spread to Europe and Asia/Pacific. He couldn't be sure how the international IT team would respond, who would support him and who would not, who would be effective in this new environment and who would not.

It was in this context that the international team came together for a three-day meeting in Sweden. For most of the time team members sat behind their laptops listening to each other give PowerPoint presentations on latest projects and developments. The energised and powerful conversations took place in the corridors and over coffee breaks, not in the formal sessions. There was no public discussion about the effect of the budget cutbacks even though, in private, most team members said that these made their targets impossible to achieve. As a former consultant, Sven offered a series of templates to team members: "Here's the information we need on that topic, here's the steps you should go through to tackle that issue." He talked about team dynamics but only to exhort participants to trust each other. He did not deal with the topics and feelings that were evident in the margins of the meeting but not put on the table. Participants listened politely to Sven's templates and found some useful suggestions but did not feel any leadership in the room. Out of his hearing, people joked about Sven being a "template manager".

The dynamic of the meeting only changed when one American manager began to challenge Sven overtly for leadership of the group. He questioned the agenda Sven had set and Sven's competence to do the work. Instead of a Swedish consultative model of leadership, the American suggested that a "shoot out" was needed in the group to decide who was really boss and which style of management should prevail.

The challenge galvanised Sven. Instead of talking in abstractions like trust and describing templates, he signalled that he had heard the challenge and that he would confront it one-on-one after the meeting. This he did, travelling round the world to meet all the team members. A reorganisation of the team followed. The American challenger was given a new role focusing on strategy – which was his area of strength and which appeared to satisfy him. A new structure and strategy were developed.

The view that team members had of Sven changed. Instead of standing on the sidelines, team members began to feel that here was a leader who might be worth following. Sven had taken a risk and confronted the challenge from the American. He refused to give the American the job he had sought and promoted others over the challenger's head. After taking careful soundings and listening to team members' views, he had mobilised a working majority in the group.

For the first time as IT leader, Sven "got real" and connected with the team. Instead of worthy slogans, team members felt they were beginning to learn how to work together. Instead of dealing with someone who offered them management consultancy templates they felt they had discovered something about Sven as a person, what his limits were, when he got angry and what his real priorities were.

Another breakthrough came about 12 months later. The main board director, who was Sven's boss, visited the group as it met for one of its quarterly gatherings, which this time was held in Italy. The boss was a big man with a big personality who filled the room when he came in. He joined the group for the afternoon of the first day and announced that the strategy of the group was wrong. He told the group that in future they would go in a different direction. He put up one slide which, he said, captured the essence of the new plan. He now expected the group to work out how they would implement the new plan.

The impact of the boss was overwhelming. In the moment it seemed that everyone was persuaded. The strategy of the group did need to change. Resources were less, obstacles greater than originally planned. There was sense of relief that a critical issue had been named and tackled.

The problem was the next day. The boss had gone and there was a "morning after" feeling. How dare the boss tear up their plan and unilaterally impose another? How could he humiliate Sven like this in front of his group? How realistic was the new plan?

Sven was able to give voice to his own frustrations and those of the team. Suddenly the work of defining objectives and plans became a real shared work. In opposition to the charismatic boss, the group came together and began to take shared responsibility for shaping the future. There was energy in the room, a determination to show the boss that they would not tolerate being treated like children. Within the broad objectives he had given them, the group would decide what to do and how.

The change was crystallised near the end of the meeting by Peter, the newly appointed Swedish head of the IT centre in Europe. He had looked for some time as if he was about to say something. At last he spoke. "Kirkegaard", he said, "stated that being a change agent is the loneliest job in the world. Those who will benefit from change are invisible while those who oppose it are aggressive." He continued, looking at Sven: "I find it surprising you hand out 'to do' lists. We are experienced managers. Why don't you ask us first what's on our 'to do' lists? We have a lot of energy for change and we are anxious to go on. Please change the way you interact with us."

After the meeting the group was more productive than before. Problems and issues were more easily shared. This was no wonderland of extraordinary performance. But it was a group that was honestly working its way through a difficult landscape and helping each other to do a good enough job.

Sven focused initially on attaching to his boss and to the corporate management group. He seemed to identify with them and see himself as their representative when dealing with the IT group. He discovered over 18 months that he was very much "in the middle". To be effective, he had to join the IT group. He was between the corporate management group and the IT team, between the IT group and the different business divisions, between his boss and the other senior directors. He became really effective as he recognised the complexity of these relationships and, instead of relying on a single relationship to the most powerful boss, he took responsibility for managing the whole network.

Patterns of disconnection

It may seem obvious that leadership includes *getting connected*. In today's organisational world, however, it is not self-evident. Many organisations have lost sight of the simple truth that you have to connect with people before you can lead them.

The pressure for short-term results, the sense of overload – too much to do and expectations that are confused or impossible to achieve – constant changes in people and organisation and the picture of leaders as transforming heroes have led to two damaging and self-reinforcing patterns in groups. The first is the leader staying distant from his people and looking for security in attaching upwards to those who seem to have power. The second is followers leaning back and refusing to take responsibility for shaping events. Followers are let off the hook at the same time as leaders are impaled on it.

1 Preoccupation with managing upwards

We were struck by the sense, in a majority of the cases in our research, that the leaders focused for long periods on managing upwards and were much less engaged with their own teams or the rest of their organisations. They seemed not to want to get too involved with the people in their groups. They did not want to get to know them as people but only as objects to whom they could assign work. There was often a lack of awareness or caring for people in the immediate team. In discussion, the leaders seemed to identify with, and attach themselves emotionally to those above them, but very little to those below. They seemed to fear that if they became intimate with their people, they would lose their clarity of view and objectivity and find it impossible to take the tough decisions that might be needed.

In an era of constant reorganisations and abrupt changes in structure and people, it's not surprising that people see safety in getting close to those above them who seem to have power. For some individuals it was a successful strategy. However, it had serious costs – in terms of lost effectiveness with the people on whom leaders depended for results – and sometimes it didn't work at all. The bosses to whom the leaders tried to get close proved unreliable. Sometimes they did not return the loyalty of the leaders and sometimes the bosses lost their own positions of power.

In one case, there was a full reorganisation of a team by a leader who, in one-on-one conversations, came over as personable, sensitive and caring. He put a great deal of care and effort over five months into planning, preparing and executing a reorganisation of his team, with new definitions of the overall task, new structures, new people and new roles. Yet, we were surprised to find that, in the course of implementing his ideas, he did not make time to talk to some people in the team about their futures. These were people that the leader valued and wanted to keep. Yet they were left in a semi-vacuum, with new job titles, but uncertain how the leader (or other bosses) regarded them or how they could contribute best to the new organisation.

It seemed to us that the leader saw his primary relationship as being with the corporate leadership team, of which he was part, and not with the group he was managing. He was so preoccupied with the need to push through a difficult international reorganisation that he was "out of energy" when it came to talking to individual members of his group about their personal futures. It wasn't that he didn't care. It was that his concern to handle all the pressures from those above him left him no space.

2 Followers who lean back and say: "It'll pass"

If the leaders stayed apart from people, the groups with whom they worked often mirrored the distancing by acting out the attitude, "It [the new boss, the new structure, the new strategy] will pass. Let's keep our heads down and wait and see." This is the response of the proverbial Russian peasant: being used to repeated changes of regime and direction but refusing to take any of them too seriously and meanwhile getting on with the business of making a living. We sometimes saw followers who were delighted to sit back and leave responsibility with the leader. Implicitly they were saying to their leader: "You're the hero, you're paid all this money, you get all this attention . . . you do it." The followers saw their job as getting by, surviving the meetings and avoiding taking on extra responsibility while, all the time, being compliant.

> Subordinates greeted one new leader by telling him that the average tenure of his four predecessors had been one year. They asked him, "Why should we believe that you will stay any longer?"

Over a period – 18 to 24 months – most of the leaders in our research overcame these pressures and connected enough with their teams. They discovered that managing upwards was essential but not enough. The bosses to whom they tried to attach were themselves only "passing through". The leaders learnt that their performance, of course, depended on their teams and that their teams did not perform unless there was enough trust and respect between them and their managers.

The one exception was Pierre, the head of supply chain for a multinational. In very difficult circumstances – subordinates spread around the globe, a highly political environment, a boss in manufacturing who had a vested interest in him failing – Pierre never did connect sufficiently with his team. After 18 months the company "reorganised him out of a job".

What does it take to connect, well enough?

So what does it take to develop good enough working relationships between you and your people?

We saw in our research that it's not a question of speeches about trust and respect – nor workshops on team building. What mattered most was how leaders handled themselves as they did their work, what they kept in mind as they sought to achieve their business objectives.

Give up the idea that you are "on top"

If you are to connect with people, you need to see yourself, sometimes, as "in the middle", rather than "on top".

Tom Gilmore has written perceptively about the way in which leaders' experiences are those of being "in the middle" rather more than "at the top" of organisations:

> In the American culture we think of leaders standing apart. The word "leader" stimulates powerful associations: the loneliness of the leader, the awesome responsibilities of the leader, JFK in the window at the White House the night of the Cuban missile crisis, Lee Iacocca single-handedly turning Chrysler around, Jack Welch revitalising GE. Increasingly, these images of the leader alone, the leader at the top, are at variance with the experience of leaders who feel in the middle, hemmed in, beset, besieged, crowded with people and forces impinging on their prerogatives or space to lead.[1]

Most of the case study leaders set out to be "tops". They wanted to be at the top of their units or organisations. They attached themselves to the bosses above them. They were rather disconnected from the teams around them. And yet they often found themselves, uncomfortably, "in the middle" – working hard to interpret the expectations and goals of bosses and make them realisable by their teams. They felt buffeted by pressures from above, below and around.

1 T. Gilmore, "Leaders as Middles", unpublished paper, Center for Applied Research, Philadelphia, June 1997.

It pays to come down and see the options at ground level

The leaders were also on the edge of their groups, sometimes in and sometimes out. On occasions, they even felt they were at the "bottom", with little or no control over events. The whole picture turned out to be much more complex and shifting than being "at the top" of their organisations.

We saw key moments when leaders built their credibility and connected with others by joining others in seeking to tackle a shared problem. Usually these moments came along unplanned. The choice you have is how you respond. Do you grab the opportunity to work together on problems that none of you yet know the answer to? Or do you hold back for fear of being exposed?

The moments when we saw leaders engage with their groups in tackling a problem were pivotal. The leader was seen as big enough to recognise his need of others – as being confident and authoritative enough to say "I don't know". Team members felt valued because they were invited in to help to tackle the issue. They learnt that it was safe for them to take things on – even though they weren't sure what the solution was. For the group as a whole it was also critical: a signal of trust in the people in the room; a sign that it was safe for the group to connect with the leader.

As Ron Heifetz puts it,[2] sometimes as a leader you need to be on the balcony and sometimes you have to be with your people down on the dance floor.

Dare to admit vulnerability and say "I don't know"

Showing some vulnerability is a key element in leading. Repeatedly we saw that it was essential to making an emotional link with followers. Weakness and fallibility can resonate with others in a way that strength does not. As one manager said to us, "When you work with a leader who seems to be perfect, there is nothing to relate to".

The story of Sven, the head of IT, illustrates the shift we saw when followers felt they began to know their leader as a person and attach to him and to his strengths and weaknesses. Often it was some personal disclosure that brought people together. As people know from their experience of life, it is often the expression of some weakness or vulnerability – particularly one that others identify with – that makes leaders people to follow. So it was that when Sven admitted to his relative (compared to his group) lack of understanding of IT and his annoyance with his boss in seeking to impose a new strategy – that was when he connected to the group.

It's not easy. Too much vulnerability and a leader is no use to others, no vulnerability and followers will not engage with them. What is important for both leaders and followers is to acknowledge that vulnerability is part of the picture.

A leader was sitting down with a friend to prepare her application for a very senior job, one that she was determined to try to win. With her

2 Ron Heifetz and Marty Linsky, *Leadership on the Line*, Harvard Business School Press, 2002.

friend's help, she was trying to spell out as clearly as she could the qualities that she offered – what was special about her that would be attractive to the selection group. Her friend, a scientist, felt one point strongly but had difficulty saying it out loud. At last he blurted out: "What's special about you is that you don't pretend to know all the answers. You're happy to say you don't know and to ask others. That's why people warm to you."

> when you work with a leader who seems to be perfect, there is nothing to relate to

Learn from "resistance"

We also saw in the research that "resistance" often has a value and a message for the leader and the group. The "change management" literature is full of injunctions about how to "overcome resistance to change". This approach reinforces the splitting process that goes on in organisations: "us" – good, "them" – bad. If leaders are to connect with others they need to avoid this simplistic splitting process. They need to think, "What lies behind the position these people are taking? The 'resistors' may be driving me nuts but what is the point or message I need to pick up from them? How might they be carrying something for the group as a whole which I need to hear?"

In one company a new boss divided the management team into "us" – the professional, modern managers, brought in from outside – and "them" – the managers who had been in the business for many years and who were, in his mind, in part, responsible for the current, weak position of the company. In management team meetings, the boss – without meaning to – signalled clearly who he respected and who he did not. His voice, his body language, his manner said clearly who was "in" and who was "out".

As the leader became increasingly frustrated by the failure of the business to turn round, he more and more saw "them" as resistors, sabotaging his change process. One by one, over more than a year, he asked several of the recalcitrant managers to leave the company and he replaced them by managers from outside whom he felt would be completely loyal to him and his change agenda. In fact the business results still did not improve. Ultimately the parent company sold the business to a competitor.

The missed opportunity, it seemed to us, was to engage with the "resistors" and try and hear what was underlying their concerns. Some of their resistance was purely emotional – resentment at earlier bosses and changes. Some of what they had to say, however, was of direct value to the business. The managers were trying to say that this business was not like other ones the managing director had managed. Customers cared about different things. In order to provide superb customer service, the company needed to use the experience of the "resistors" to understand what worked for customers and what did not.

VERONIQUE'S STORY

Talk to people – and listen

Veronique is the manager responsible for a large call centre for a European-based, global bank. She leads 400 people drawn from more than 20 nationalities. The nature of the business is immediate, pressurised and stressful. Customers are demanding and impatient – satisfaction is measured in seconds, not days or weeks.

The workforce consists mainly of young, well-educated people who have moved to an English-speaking country to improve their language skills. For this reason the average length of employment is two to three years. Having dual nationality herself – her parents are English and Italian – Veronique is sensitive to the pitfalls in leading such a multicultural group.

Some of her people are fiery and passionate: quick to blame and equally quick to forgive. Others are more level-headed and dispassionate. Some are respectful of authority, others much less so. One of the traps she identified early in the life of the centre was the potential for miscommunication. To this end she instigated a policy (for herself personally and all her managers) of over-communication. They consciously avoid wherever possible the crisp, impersonal e-mail, knowing that it will be interpreted in many different ways – potentially leading to confusion and unrest. Wherever possible, communication takes place face-to-face, with plenty of time allowed for feedback and discussion.

This approach, which may seem time consuming, actually saves huge amounts of lost time as potential problems are cleared up before they develop. An example of this was the day that the USA and Britain invaded Iraq. This was a contentious issue that provoked debate around the world. In the multicultural hothouse of the call centre it could have led to major problems. Veronique was informed during the course of the morning that the Greek employees were circulating a petition demanding that everyone stop work for five minutes to show their disagreement with this "illegal" invasion. She invited the Greeks to discuss their concerns directly with her. Because she had a reputation for being fair and open-minded, they agreed. She was able to discover, simply through listening to them, that their action was motivated by very personal concerns for the safety of relatives rather than a political gesture. She was then able to diffuse a potentially explosive situation.

Veronique's willingness to listen, to be available and to genuinely try to understand other people's point of view rather than dismissing it as wrong are key factors in her success. She has maintained her distance when needed at the same time as building intimacy skilfully, recognising the needs of different cultures. She also brought her life experience to her work in a way that enriched her ability to lead.

Focus on the group around you – it's good enough!

The good news for leaders is that they don't have to connect with every group or person in the organisation. We remember the look of relief on one leader's face when he decided that if he focused on connecting with his executive group that would be enough. He didn't have to worry about reaching every person on the shop floor. He could trust that if he got it right with his executive group, the right messages and feelings would spread "by osmosis" throughout the organisation.

In recent research[3] our colleague, Phil Hodgson, has confirmed the importance of the top team, the group immediately around the leader, as the amplifier – or dampener – of the leader's energy. If the group around the leader is "on song" with the leader, then together the impact on the organisation over time is powerful. If a leader and his executive group are discordant, then that also has a powerful impact.

The pot of gold in connecting with the group

The *getting connected* is not just between the leader and individuals. A distinguishing characteristic of *Living Leadership* is that the connection is between the leader and the group *as a whole*. We saw repeatedly in the case studies the critical moments when the leader shifted from fear of a group to engaging with them and the group as a whole began to take responsibility for shaping the future.

The gain is not a magical transformation. It is going from the stratosphere of idealised expectations down to the ground level of pragmatic ways forward. We saw groups beginning to take their fates in their own hands. People were freed up to deliver. The groups were connected up and people overcame their sense of isolation. They felt supported, less frightened and defensive. They were more able to take risks intuitively and explicitly. The resources of the leader and of the team were freed up.

People often talk about the loneliness of leaders. We found that they don't have to be so lonely! They can draw on their immediate teams to talk, to be supported, to be nurtured. There is enormous relief if and when the leader says to herself: "I don't have to do this on my own." There is exhilaration in the group if and when it finds it is sharing responsibility for the future.

Work it out together

Most of the situations we see leaders and organisations battling with are where they are entering uncharted territory – a new

3 Phil Hodgson et al., *Top Leader Journey* research programme, Ashridge, 2004.

business environment, a new organisational culture, a new group of people. In small but critical ways the context they are working with is different to what has gone before. No-one has ever visited this place before or been quite on this route. There may be parallels with previous developments and there may be many useful lessons to be learnt. However, the future is uncertain and the journey from here to there cannot be known in advance.

The transformational hero view suggests that in these situations leaders look ahead, have the answer and then inspire others to follow them. *Living Leadership*, by contrast, takes the less idealistic, more realistic view that no one person has the answer.

The job of the leader, then, is not to pretend to know the answer but instead to release the collective insight, intelligence and wisdom of the many that will be needed if the new way through is to be found. *Getting connected* is the prerequisite of tapping into this understanding.

As a leader, you have a choice. You have to deal with the group around you anyway. You depend on them for results. The choice you have is whether you are prepared to acknowledge that you depend on them and that they depend on you and to seize the opportunities when they come along to strengthen the connection with them. If you take everything on your shoulders you will stop others contributing and signal that you don't trust them. If, on the other hand, you can share some responsibility and tackle issues together, you make clear that you do respect your people and you connect with them more.

In our research, the most powerful way in which leaders and groups connected was by "getting real" about the context they were in – confronting the realities of the situation and talking about how they could turn circumstances to their advantage. In the next chapter we describe this process of developing the art of the possible, which is the second leg of *Living Leadership*.

* Building good enough working relationships comes before running operations or shaping the future. It's the necessary foundation for delivering results.

* Constant changes of leaders and organisations have led to a pattern of disconnection between leaders and the groups they work with:
  - leaders don't want to commit to the people around them for fear of being overwhelmed
  - followers see the leader as just "passing through" and wait for her to move on or be sacrificed.

* However, we found a strong wish for leaders to work *with* their people and stop doing things *to* them.

* You can respond to this desire by seeing yourself as in the middle and not just at the top.

* Trust, respect and acknowledgement of interdependence do not come from talking about them but from experiences of working together, when people see how you are and what you do.

* Issues that are not easily resolved and require the collective intelligence of you and your group provide a key opportunity to connect with your people.

* There is a pot of gold in connecting with the group around you, as a whole, and not just as individuals.

Thinking about relationships

Think about your working relationships with two key individuals and with the group, as a whole, that you work with most:

- What have been the moments recently when you had a sense of connecting well with these people?

- What have been the moments recently when you did not connect so well?

- What seems to help or hinder these relationships?

- What could you do more of or do differently?

Get real

Practise the art of the possible

When a management with a reputation for brilliance tackles a business with a reputation for poor fundamental economics, it is the reputation of the business that remains intact.

Warren Buffett

Leaders are often seen as standing apart and seeking to mould organisations. There is a widely accepted image of the leader having to "force change through" his organisation. The metaphor of a rodeo cowboy comes to mind, wrestling the steer to the ground, dominating it by force in order to impose his will. The underlying assumption is that the qualities of individuals determine the nature of the leadership and the context provides a stage on which the individual can shine.

In *Living Leadership* we turn the discussion around. We believe leadership starts with consideration of the context in which the leader works. The leader is interdependent with the business and organisational context. While recognising the role of individual abilities and qualities, we believe the context is more important. Context shapes the nature of the leadership that is provided – and it largely determines the results. Serge Tchuruk, the successful CEO of Alcatel, highlights how the role of the individual can be made to seem disproportionately important in the overall context: "In times of crisis, executives are seen as imbeciles, and in times of euphoria, they are seen as geniuses."[1]

---

1 Serge Tchuruk (CEO Alcatel SA), *Bloomberg*, 25 June 2002.

By context we mean not just the social and political environment. We also mean the business situation and the organisational culture – the patterns of "how we do things around here". But does context shape the results – can that be true? Surely leaders have more impact than that?

To say that contexts shape results is not to argue that leadership is unimportant or that leaders can do little. On the contrary, by recognising the importance of context, successful leaders begin to see where and how to focus their efforts. Like experienced yachtsmen, they don't complain about the weather or deny its significance. They don't see the weather as "the problem" and themselves as "the answer". They acknowledge that they may not be able to take the most direct route. They study conditions intently and are knowledgeable about the fine detail of the performance of their boats and crews and their achievement under a range of circumstances. They recognise that sometimes there is little they can do to move forward but they are ready to move quickly when opportunities present themselves. They are ready for storms and know what they will do to get through them. They don't try to conquer the conditions but think about where and how they can harness winds, tides and currents to take them where they want to go.

> by recognising the importance of context, successful leaders begin to see where and how to focus their efforts

Living Leadership involves valuing the art of the possible – and often being surprised by the results once the interdependence of the leader and their environment is acknowledged.

Relishing the possibilities

One person we worked with is a leader in Britain's National Health Service, one of the most difficult organisational environments that we know. People have to manage in the full glare of politics. In addition to frequent reorganisations, managers are subject to bewildering changes and reversals of policy. What is centralised one year is decentralised the

Making the most of what's more powerful than you

next. What is made into an internal market one year is abolished the next and then reintroduced, as politicians and top managers search anxiously for a structure and strategy that will deliver the all-important improvements in health care that governments see as essential for their survival.

In this environment, many senior managers naturally conclude that the best they can do is to survive. They aim to respond as effectively as they can to the twists and turns of central policy – but not to take the initiative or attempt to shape the future. Many managers opt out of taking any responsibility and are content to float with the tide. Alan is not one of these.

A doctor turned manager, Alan is passionate about his subject and full of energy to make a difference in the speciality that he leads. He took time in his early years as a manager to reflect seriously on himself and the changes he would have to make in shifting from the individualist and fact-based world of a doctor to the collective and uncertain world of a leader. He went on courses, sought help from friends and an executive coach and joined an "Action Learning" group. He is intrigued by the political manoeuvres around him and knowledgeable about them but a little detached. He doesn't take it all too seriously.

Alan avoids spending time developing long strategy documents (a favourite activity of his colleagues) but does have a clear sense of where he wants his service to get to and often talks about this formally at conferences and informally in small groups and events. He wants the UK service to be equal to the best in the world, he wants investment concentrated on the best institutions and he wants to break down the silos (the functional or professional groupings that people get trapped in) and the barriers between different hospitals and care providers. He has a clear instinct of how he wants the situation to be better but avoids mission or vision statements, communicating instead by story and anecdote.

To reach his objectives, he is opportunistic, seizing connections and new openings wherever they arise. One moment it is a colleague from the USA or Sweden with some interesting experience or data, at another time it is a manager in the NHS who can offer access to some previously hidden source of funds, then it is a new Information Technology investment that he can harness for part of his agenda. He is sociable and a good networker and a source of energy and encouragement for those he is with. He tries to organise his work so that he does what he finds fun and he finds highly competent help to do those things he doesn't enjoy. Despite the appalling rates of pay for administrative staff in the NHS, he has succeeded – after long efforts – in finding two very competent personal assistants. He is entrepreneurial, getting help from pharmaceutical companies – despite the reservations of colleagues about partnering with the private sector.

Confronted by a likeable and distinguished boss who had, nevertheless, gone into survivor mode, he resolved, after a time, to take on part of the job the boss should have been doing. He offered to organise meetings and write up action notes afterwards. This was agreed readily and a partnership was formed in which Alan began to do some of the thinking and looking ahead required of the boss.

Alan is fully aware of the complexities of the system and the difficulty of achieving his aims. One of his assets is a disarming candour about himself and others. When people are with him they have a sense that he is charmingly indiscreet. He talks vividly and openly about bosses, others and himself but he does not complain or moan. He does look downhearted sometimes when confronted by some of the people consequences of reorganisations. However, usually, he seems to revel in finding the opportunities that others can't see, in introducing people and ideas that others exploit, in being both a public face of change and an assiduous worker behind the scenes.

Somehow Alan manages to be both passionate and detached. His core identity is as a doctor and that is what keeps him calm when buffeted by the endless reorganisations driven by people who don't understand health care. At the same time he has now moved far from his professional life as a doctor. He has become a skilled leader.

Alan is also in a way suited to the times and situation. Because of personality and background he wants to be different, to stand out from other managers. The government wants the NHS to be different; he is able to receive the message and act on it. The environment is marked by continuous change. He relishes this. There are risks. Alan may be seen as too independent a thinker. But for the moment he flourishes.

The power of context

To say that objectives change and results differ from expectations is not as shocking as it may at first appear. It is part of a normal human process to dream great dreams, to work hard for them and find that what you create is not quite what you expected. The capacity to articulate your aspirations and the self-belief to want to put them into practice is essential to leadership, but so is the ability to adjust to reality and learn as your story unfolds.

We learnt in our research that contexts shape leadership. All the leaders in our research set out to achieve a transformation – a business turnaround, a fundamental change of culture or the development of a new enterprise. None achieved the result they originally had in mind – yet all but one of them were seen as successful by their organisations.

JOHN'S STORY

John was the head of a new Internet business unit set up by a giant utility company. His original dream was to create a new type of business and organisation, taking the best of an Internet start-up and of the utility parent. It didn't happen. After two years, some successes

▶

and some failures, it became clear that the culture of the parent was too strong. The safety-first, cautious, analytical approach of the parent won out. The collective memory of the organisation, of which John was part, told him you cannot just will things to happen. You always have to compromise between what you want and what the world lets you do and that is more than good enough. Some useful businesses were developed but they were add-ons to the parent business – not a whole new type of enterprise.

SVEN'S STORY

Sven was the head of Information Technology and Supply Chain in an international, European-led, manufacturing company. At the beginning of his tenure he hoped, with his boss, a main board director, to use IT to help change the culture of the whole company. They wanted the culture to be more Anglo-Saxon, more results and shareholder-value oriented, less obsessive about technical excellence and less comfortable. Over two years, Sven learnt that this change of culture was out of reach. Business turned down, IT budgets were cut and the transformational potential of IT had to be left for another day. It would be good enough to make IT a valued service to the businesses. A very old pattern reasserted itself – the Viking warrior went overseas and sought to make changes, achieved some things and then was welcomed back home and given an important new job in the mother company.

MAX'S STORY

Max was the new boss of a leasing business. His objective, constantly repeated, was to turn the company around. Once profitable and highly regarded by customers, the company had failed to invest over 10 years, lost its competitive edge and become involved in a desperate scramble to win and hang on to business so as to cover large fixed costs. The business was becoming more and more complex as managers did increasingly elaborate one-off deals with customers. Managers ran from one crisis to the next and had little time to "get off the fire engine" and see what needed to be done to save the business. After a year of hard work and bringing in a number of new managers, Max learnt that the parent company had decided to sell the business to a competitor. His dream of turnaround was abandoned and Max devoted six intense months to keeping the business afloat while planning the transfer of operations to the competitor. People in the company had a victim mindset and the story confirmed that they would continue to be victims, the objects of other people buying and selling companies, opening and closing operations.

all the leaders sought to fly high, and all were pulled back by the gravitational force of their contexts

All the leaders sought to fly high, to break free of the constraints of their situations and all were pulled back by the gravitational force of their contexts. The contexts did not determine the outcomes. We had the sense again and again that the story could unfold in different ways. But the context did determine the potential leadership that could be provided. Some sorts of leadership could resonate in the situation; others failed. If the leader is wise, he takes on one of the potential leadership roles and does not batter his head against the brick wall of impossible tasks.

In 1989 three leaders in turn visited East Berlin around the time that the Berlin Wall came down. First was Erich Hoeneker and the East German leadership to celebrate the 40th birthday of the communist republic. In the dying days of the regime the crowds came out – but as automatons, with no enthusiasm or feeling. A few days later Gorbachev arrived and was greeted with rapture. Russian leader, head of the Soviet Empire, in that moment he was the reforming hero, the beacon of hope. A few weeks passed and this time the crowds came out for Helmut Kohl and cheered. The standard-bearer for a peaceful transition to a prosperous, free and united Germany was with them. One context, three very different leaders, two roles that resonated with the moment and one that did not.

The elephant in the room . . .

Getting real is about facing and accepting things as they are, no better no worse – and ensuring that others do the same. It can be quite energising to hear a leader admit things are difficult – while retaining an optimistic view that they will find a way through. Organisations sometimes foster a climate where people say what they think others want to hear. This can be driven by fear (i.e. I am scared of the consequences of naming this issue) or political correctness (I must not offend anyone, appear negative or challenge the authority figure). In Chapter 11 we talk more about how leaders name the difficult issue, "the elephant in the room", to cut through time wasted in pointless, low energy meetings and conversations.

The dirty little secret of strategy . . .

Context also changes the goals to which leaders work. Perhaps one of the most uncomfortable findings of our research was to see how much people's objectives change over time. If you live with leaders you see that objectives shift and evolve. The idea of a steely-minded boss who pursues the same goal over years and arrives at his original objective is, in most places, a myth. Objectives change just as the means to achieve them do.

The dirty little secret of strategy (to adopt Gary Hamel's phrase) is that it is only clear with hindsight. There is so much talk about visions and missions, goals and objectives, strategy and implementation in the business world that it is easy to lose sight of what is really going on – the way in which organisations move forward with a mixture of intention and chance, good luck and bad luck, learning and wilful refusal to face facts. The way we make sense of our experience in many, varied organisations is that people start with some goal or intention and then – if they are effective – before too long they move to action and try some things. As they try to move forward, they bump up against obstacles. Conditions are not quite as they expected. So they try a bit more. Maybe they try harder and they overcome the obstacles – or they find that the obstacles are not easily overcome. Then perhaps they try to go around them – and, if they are lucky and determined, they find a different way through. Eventually they may make some progress and achieve some results. However, they are probably not where they expected to be. Even if they are very successful, the goal they reach is not exactly the one they originally aimed at.

Learning from mistakes at Honda

In *Strategy Safari*[2] Henry Mintzberg quotes a famous example of how the picture of managers involved in making something happen differs from those of academics and others who come afterwards and rationalise what has happened. It deals with the way Honda and other Japanese companies in the early 1960s conquered the US motorcycle market and pushed out the mainly British competition. Boston Consulting Group in 1975 produced a report on the story that became a classic, used for teaching in many business schools. According to the BCG report, "The basic philosophy of the Japanese manufacturers is that high volumes per model provide the potential for high productivity as a result of using capital intensive and highly automated techniques. Their marketing strategies are therefore directed towards these high volume models, hence the careful attention we have observed them giving to growth and market share."

Richard Pascale wondered about this account and flew to Japan to interview the managers who had made the breakthrough. They told a different story: "In truth we had no strategy other than seeing if we could sell something in the United States ... Mr Honda was especially confident of the 250cc and 305cc machines," the managers said. "The shape of the handlebars on these machines looked like the eyebrow of Buddha, which he felt was a strong selling point." (Bear in mind the market for motorcycles at the time was black leather jacket types. No mass market existed for motorcycles as everyday transport.)

One year after arriving in the US, a few of the larger bikes began to sell. Then, as the managers put it, "disaster struck". Because bikes are driven longer and faster in the US, the Hondas began to break down. "But in the meantime", they said, "events had taken a surprising turn. ▶

2 H. Mintzberg, B.W. Ahlstrand and J. Lampel, *Strategy Safari*, Financial Times Prentice Hall, 1998.

Throughout our first eight months, we had not attempted to sell the 50cc Supercubs. While they were a smash hit in Japan and manufacturing couldn't keep up with demand there, they seemed wholly unsuitable for the US where everything was bigger and more luxurious ... we had our sights set on the import market – and the Europeans like the Americans emphasised the larger machines."

"We used the Honda 50s to ride around Los Angeles on errands. They attracted a lot of attention. One day we had a call from a buyer at Sears (the huge US retailer). We took note of Sears' interest. But we hesitated to push the 50cc bikes out of fear that it would harm our image in a heavily macho market. But when the larger bikes started breaking, we had no choice. We let the 50cc bikes move."[3]

The rest is history. Sales rose dramatically. Middle-class Americans began to ride on Hondas, first the Supercubs, later the larger bikes. Whole new markets of customers who used bikes for regular transport emerged.

Does strategy always develop like this? Not necessarily. Every case is different. But there are some threads, which our research confirms:

▌ Managers *going into an uncertain new area* rarely end up where they expected. They may be successful but this is by reference to objectives that have also changed. Often managers lose sight of the goals originally set for an endeavour.

▌ Rationalisation after the event is very common. As one sceptical case study leader put it to us when reviewing two hard years of experience: "Revisionism is rampant. The main board has decided our business was a success and changed their view of the objectives to ensure that it was." In another case the leader, when reviewing two years of developments, said with complete sincerity that he could not recall any change in strategy. We thought we had witnessed an abrupt shift in strategy one year before.

▌ Managers start with some strategic intent, goal or ambition. However the strategy – the clear plan for developing and

3 Richard Pascale, "Perspectives on strategy: the real story behind Honda's success", *California Management Review*, Spring 1984, pp. 47–72.

maintaining competitive advantage – only emerges over a period and can be seen clearly when looking backwards.

▌ Opportunities emerge from time to time. What differentiates successful organisations is not chance events but how they respond to them. Are they able to be alive to the potential of the situation and seize the moment? Can they be opportunistic and, at the same time, consistent enough with their core direction purpose and values?

▌ Strategic learning emerges from enough variation, experimentation and failure. Unfortunately you can't shortcut the learnings, you can't wish your way straight to success, you have to go through the difficulties. In that sense leadership is like life itself. The transitions we negotiate in life are mirrored in leading change in organisations.

Viagra was developed as a drug by the pharmaceutical giant Pfizer to address certain heart conditions that were a strategic target for the company because of the size and growth of the market and the willingness of patients and health systems to pay high prices for effective treatments. Unfortunately clinical trials showed that the drug had no special impact on heart conditions – but it did have impressive side effects in dealing with erectile dysfunction. What was remarkable was Pfizer's reaction to this unexpected result. Instead of bemoaning the failure to create a product in line with the strategy, the company seized the opportunity to develop a quite different, new market and invested millions of dollars in promoting and selling the drug, with great effect.

> **what distinguishes effective organisations is how effectively they respond to the unexpected when it occurs**

What distinguishes effective organisations is not the capacity to foresee the future but how effectively they respond to the unexpected when it occurs. To adapt a phrase from our former colleague Patricia Shaw, strategy then becomes the *unfolding encounter between context, intention and chance*.

Execution power

We often see managers so concerned with PowerPoint presentations of the future in missions, visions, strategies and statements of values that they act as if they were already true. Some politicians act like this: they begin to mistake dreams for achievement. Or top managers become so preoccupied with effective communication of intention that they think this is the whole job. A manager of a leading multinational said to us that: "We produce communicators, brilliant managers of presentation, but not leaders." Managers in another international company laughed about all the "corporate slideware" that top managers use to describe the corporate strategy and that seems to take on a life of its own. One chairman of a housing association said to us, in a moment of candour: "I think that when it is written down, it's done."

In our research we saw how often leaders feel a need to focus on the future. The model of leaders as transforming heroes encourages people to live in the future, in the world of plans and targets, visions and strategy. Feeling under pressure to be transforming heroes, they gave priority to developing a vision of the future. The danger is that this picture of the future can become detached from current realities. In one case a chief executive held over 50 workshops with staff spelling out what they wanted their new organisation to be. The more they talked the more they fell in love with their idealised picture of the future and ran the risk of losing touch with the here and now real-life challenges facing the organisation. Indeed in many cases the graver the current problems the greater the temptation to will them away and focus on the wonderful future.

It reminds us of what can happen when reality becomes intolerable and the future the only safe place to be. Rather than engage with the real managers in the room, leaders can take refuge in a make-believe future. Things will happen, they tell themselves, if you will them enough.

When the elastic breaks

We think of a company where, in one division, the chief executive decided that the target would be to double sales from $150m to $300m in the next three years. The managers in the division felt that there had been no discussion. The figure was imposed top down as a "stretch" objective (and as we learnt later, in response to pressure from the group CEO to improve performance). The thinking of the divisional chief executive was that the figure would challenge the lethargy, the lack of "get up and go" among managers. It would force them to "think out of the box".

What intrigued us was the impact the target actually had on a group of managers who felt battered, overloaded with change initiatives, with little self-belief in their ability to bring about major change. In one workshop, we noticed the low energy and lack of straight talking. We asked several managers in a coffee break, "What's going on?" Eventually someone from outside the division who was attending the meeting said, "It's the $300m target. Everybody feels it's unrealistic but they can't say so with Dave (the divisional boss) in the room. They'll just get beaten up by Dave if they challenge the number." We were left with the impression that the target poisoned the atmosphere. It was a roadblock in people's minds. People couldn't say what they thought and refused to commit honestly to anything because the thought that was uppermost in their minds could not be raised publicly.

The cost for the divisional boss was that the target paralysed people. It deprived him of the resources that there were in the room. As one manager said to us:

In this company we don't have a vision, we have a hallucination

It's no wonder that companies like Nokia see their competitive superiority not in statements of future intent but in what they call "execution power", the ability to make things happen and translate ideas into results. They recognise that strategies are often easy to lay out and that they may differ little from one company to the next. The tough part is turning them into reality – and learning as they go that they don't arrive exactly where they first intended.

It is exactly this power not to be trapped by "alignment" processes and to persist in seeing the difference between dreams and real achievement that distinguishes *Living Leadership*.

Tolerating the lack of control

The hardest part for leaders in our experience is tolerating uncertainty. This is partially driven by external expectations of predictability and partially by the need for internal performance. Managers rise in responsibility and position in organisations usually because they bring matters under control. In the early stages of their careers, particularly, that is what they are paid to achieve. We don't think much of supermarket managers that don't get the food to the shelves when we want it, of IT managers who don't deliver on promised services, of airline managers who can't get us from A to B according to the schedules.

> the hardest part for leaders is tolerating
> uncertainty

As managers take on leadership roles, however, and as they are called upon to deal with the people issues that are at the heart of leadership, they find more and more uncertainty in their work. There often isn't a template or benchmark that gives the answer. Yes, there are ideas that other organisations can give you and there are useful techniques and tools. Yes, benchmarking and templates work for some tasks. When leaders are seeking to repeat what someone else has done before, they are fine. But benchmarking and templates don't work for everything. There is no certain answer when leaders try to change an entrenched part of culture of business practice. No-one has done it here before so no-one knows exactly what will work. There are many issues a leader has to deal with that are out of his control. He may be able to influence outcomes or he may have to recognise there is little he can do – but control, he cannot.

Thus it's one thing, for example, to put in a new payroll system. There is information about what makes for a good system under certain conditions and how to implement it. It's very different if you are planning a new product or new business in mobile communications. No-one has ever done it before. No-one can say exactly what will happen. The leader and all the team are making it up as they go along.

This is a painful truth for many would-be leaders. The pressure in the organisational world is to pretend that most tasks are like introducing the new payroll system. Managers are recognised and rewarded for bringing things under control. Add to this the natural human tendency to pretend that issues are under control because we are scared to face our lack of control and uncertainty. The consequence sometimes is a refusal to face uncertainty that is shown in a desperate clinging to espoused strategies and plans or being buried in day-to-day operations and activities and not allowing time for any longer term reflection. Daniel Vasella, the CEO of Novartis, gives an example of how it must be possible to resist the incessant demands for certainty: "I truly believe my ability to keep shareholders' faith in our company depends in the end not on whether I make the quarter but on who I am, what my guiding principles in life are, my behaviour. What counts is who you are personally."[4]

Implications for leaders

If this view of how success emerges in the real world is right, the implications for leaders are dramatic.

Leader as storyteller

The job of leading is not to foretell the future when matters are uncertain – as they usually are. It is to tell the story of the present and past. Leading involves making sense of what is happening to the group or organisation, finding a narrative that most people can accept and that works.

---

4 Daniel Vasella (chairman and CEO Novartis), *Fortune*, 18 November 2002.

By "story" we mean what the American philosopher Rorty describes.[5] A good story throws light on:

What situation are we in?

Who are we? What is our role in this situation?

How is the world changing? What impact does this have on us?

What threats or opportunities do we face?

What are our priorities?

To be effective, a leader seeks to extend the consensus or shared understanding of the story. To quote Max de Pree, the former chairman and CEO of Herman Miller, "The first responsibility of a leader is to define reality. The last is to say thank you. In between, the leader is a servant."

leaders seek a good enough consensus, a working majority

Organisations and groups will never be of one mind. There will never be full agreement. Leaders seek a good enough consensus, a working majority. A good story also enlarges the group's sense of what is possible. By imagining something it begins to make it do-able.

The idea of telling stories links to the notion that there is no objective world out there. People can only make sense of the world here and now. To articulate their perceptions is to define their world. That is their reality.

To be effective, the pictures have to be ones *that work* for groups and organisations – ones that meet some needs of individuals, groups and organisations. What we recognised in the research is that this sense-making between people is shaped by history and culture. Leaders are never working with blank sheets of paper. The inheritance of the past is always with them – and people's fears and hopes for the future. They are always in the room.

5 G. Calder, *Rorty*, Weidenfeld & Nicolson, 2003.

Working with current realities

In our research, leaders were effective when they dealt with the desired future *in relationship* to the capacities of the organisations and the dynamics of the group. They were able to hold on to their aspirations for the future and they were able to tell it like it is about current realities.

Adjusting to the small but vital differences

Goethe pointed out that "we see what we know" – people are only aware of the things for which their previous experience has prepared them. Leaders inevitably carry the hard-won lessons of experience from one role to another, from one setting and organisation to another. That's why they win their jobs in the first place. Yet contexts are subtle and constantly changing. We were often reminded in the research of how small differences in context can make or break success. What a leader does that works in one situation will fail in another. The leader needs to be on the lookout all the time for these small differences and be ready to adapt their approach.

We worked once with a capable and successful general manager who had moved from IBM to a large insurance company. Personable, astute and aware as this manager was, he had one unfortunate habit. He would preface many of his comments about the insurance company with, "Well, the way we used to do things at IBM was..." Predictably, it wasn't long before people, tired of being lectured, as they saw it, on the superior working methods of IBM, began to make fun of the "man from IBM".

Some of the case study leaders fell into the same trap – thinking they could repeat formulae and approaches that had worked for them in previous companies: "I have been in situations like this before, I know what to do." They were caught out if the characteristics of the organisations they were joining proved to be different enough to invalidate the repetition of past approaches.

Adapting to the fine grain of context

In her early days, the leader in one organisation did not appear to respond to the anxiety of her group. Instead she dumped her own anxiety on them. She tried to use a consultative process that had worked for her in a previous job. She assumed her direct reports were more capable at that moment than they were, and she ignored the impact of a previous tyrannical leader. Her consultative model at first produced a poor response. She complained, "I come from a provincial hospital. This is supposed to be a world-class organisation, yet they can't even produce decent input for a strategy paper."

When she took the work to Executive Management Board, she was criticised by her peers for its poor quality. When the attack was over, she received support for her approach from the Chief Executive, in front of those who attacked her. She was able to transfer that experience into her own executive group and change her own approach. Where previously she had given them the problem to solve and waited for results, and then found them wanting, she now decided to spend some time thinking with them, asking for their input while also producing some herself. She gave herself and the two assistant directors the job of editing the final paper. The changed process legitimised her authority, the team members recovered their sense of competence and the attacks on the "new kid" in the Executive Management Board stopped.

Working out: what's the magic in this organisation?

My first 100 days are all about listening and learning. The last thing you'll get from me is a grand vision in the first 100 days. You need to give yourself time to be a sponge.[6]

My job was to uncover what was going well. I think sometimes when a new senior executive comes into a company, the instinctive thing to do is to find out what's wrong and fix it. That doesn't actually work very well. People are very proud of what they've created, and it just feels like you are second-guessing them all the time. *You are much more successful coming in and*

6 Paul Pressler (CEO The Gap), *Fortune*, 18 November 2002.

finding out what's going right and nurturing that. Along the way, you'll find out what's going wrong and fix that.[7]

A crucial question for leaders is to seek out what makes an organisation special and seek to build on it. If leaders abandon the idea of shaping the world as they would like it to be and focus instead on what *is,* then they need to appreciate the possibilities in the organisation or unit for which they have responsibility. Organisations have grown and developed for some reason. They have achieved success. What is the underlying reason for the success? Why has the organisation survived and flourished when so many others have disappeared?

Many managers object that there is no magic in their organisations. Their energy and attention is so focused on what needs to change that they can't see what's valuable. Or they take for granted skills, knowledge and capabilities that to others seem remarkable.

Nokia is an example. Some parts of the success of the company, managers know, are related to a passion for learning and improvement, a flair for design and a deep technical understanding. Some are also related to aspects of the Finnish culture of management that is not easy for Finns themselves to see. For them their culture is just "how things are" – the company's collective will to succeed, the ruthless pragmatism and willingness to invest for the long term while also dropping products or businesses.

Take another example. We worked with one government agency that had been told so often that only the private sector does things properly that it seemed to have lost confidence in its own competence. Yet when people started to openly question this, they realised that there was an accumulated wisdom in the organisation about how to deal with their political masters, how to make policy and how to implement it. The first step in helping the organisation be more effective was not to threaten more change but to help people believe in themselves again, to see what they could do and where they did not need outside consultants and experts.

7 "Face Time With Meg Whitman", *Fast Company*, May 2001, p. 72.

* People are desperate to work in an environment that is more realistic about what is do-able.

* The success or failure of leaders depends more on the context (social and political, economic and business, organisation culture) than individual qualities and abilities.

* Leading can only be understood by reference to a specific context.

* If you give the context its due respect, you will be more effective as a leader; if you seek to fit the context into your vision, a lot of time and energy will be wasted.

* Leading involves having the courage to face the issues that everyone is aware of but no-one dares mention.

* Continuity needs leading at least as much as change. It's a major accomplishment to appreciate what works at the moment; it's an easy way out to dismantle and re-engineer at will.

* How should leaders be – and what should they do in a particular situation? It all depends . . .

So, effective leading happens between people and is shaped by the context. There remains the third leg of *Living Leadership*: how leaders need to bring themselves to their leading if they are to connect with others and understand the context. We explain how in Chapter 5.

REFLECTION

Thinking about context

For each element of your context:

1 the economic, political and social environment

2 the business situation

3 the culture of your organisation

Consider:

▌ What are the key features that shape the way you can lead?

▌ How are these features changing?

▌ What do you not understand and need to find out more about?

▌ What may be different from previous situations in which you have worked?

▌ What can you build on?

▌ How could you turn obstacles into assets?

Levels of influence

Brainstorm all the elements of your unit or organisation that you would like to build on or change. Then pick out the top three.

To what extent are these elements that you:

▌ can do something about directly?

▌ influence only?

▌ have to live with?

Get help

... and know when to give it

I've discovered the true secret of happiness ... and that is to live in the now. Not to be forever regretting the past, or anticipating the future; but to get the most that you can out of this very instant ... Most people don't live; they just race. They are trying to reach some goal far away on the horizon, and in the heat of the going they get so breathless and panting that they lose all sight of the beautiful, tranquil country they are passing through; and then the first thing they know, they are old and worn out, and it doesn't make any difference whether they've reached the goal or not.

Jean Webster, *Daddy Long Legs*, 1912

In this chapter we talk about the third leg of *Living Leadership*: leaders, coming alive in the moment and being able to use all their intelligence and intuition, feelings and emotions. This is enabled by having the humility to ask for help when you need it and having the courage to offer help to other people when you see they need it. We learn to know ourselves well through interacting with others, using feedback as a powerful way to increase self-understanding.

Living Leadership is subtle, contextual and involves working on a number of levels – rational and emotional, strategic and operational, task and relationships. Leaders cannot say in advance exactly what will be required in a particular situation. They have to be there in the moment to work it out. It is the capacity to bring all their faculties to bear that enables them to do so.

Cutting free from unreal expectations

We repeatedly found in our research that leaders knew more from their experience of life than they gave themselves credit for. There was a tendency to put the leading of people and organisations in a box labelled "business management and leadership" and act as if all their other experience of life was of no account. Yet, those with varied experience of life often had the wisdom required to lead others. Parenting, for example, was an extraordinary source of insight.

Leaders need to remember what they know – and be willing to keep learning. Much of the understanding they have about people and situations is what is needed, exactly because they have learnt lessons instinctively or intuitively and cannot spell them out in simple formulae.

Examples of the life experience we saw leaders use were:

▌ A French woman who had become used as a child to living outside France and moving from country to country as her father's jobs in a multinational changed. She was a very engaging, lively personality but also something of a nomad. She was very skilled at asking questions and finding out new situations – including the company and business she had come in to head.

▌ Another leader had been widowed twice. His determination to make the most of the moment and live life to the full – which was a huge asset in his leading – seemed to be related to these tragedies and the way he had responded to them.

▌ Another leader was a single parent with a young teenage daughter. She had learnt to juggle different responsibilities, to focus on what she was doing in the moment and to set clear expectations about what she could and could not offer in the different parts of her life. This capacity was a great strength when leading others at work.

▌ One leader had clawed his way up in the UK from a working-class, Irish family and now led people in an organisation where he was surrounded by people from privileged backgrounds and the best schools and universities. He had acquired a determination and persistence which was a large factor in his effectiveness as a leader.

Understanding the whole of yourself – good and bad

If leaders are to bring themselves to leadership, they need to be self-aware – conscious of what drives them and their impact on others. We all know that when you get a leader you don't get the ideal competencies that job adverts often specify. You get a package – good and bad, competent and less competent, strengths and weaknesses. What we saw in the research is that it's the imperfections that make leaders interesting.

Your demons – understanding what drives *you*

> A colleague noticed that a leader he was working with had a BMW 8
> Series, which seemed rather strange. The leader was a shy man and
> having a powerful executive car seemed out of character. "Why did you
> choose that BMW?" our colleague asked. "I bought it for my Dad," the
> leader said, "to show him that I am successful." "What did your father
> say?" enquired our colleague. "He said, 'Mercedes are better'."

Throughout our research we were conscious that an intense
personal drama was being played out for each of the leaders. It
was not simply a matter of professional life and work. The whole
"being" of the leaders was involved. Fundamental questions about
their competence, their identity and their purpose were exposed.
At times it was exhilarating. At other moments it was a white-
knuckle ride, testing them to the limit.

Each leader, it seemed to us, was engaged in a personal quest,
seeking to learn something about themself as they worked with
others. Often this took the form of a self-imposed test. They
seemed to be asking, "If I go into this new area or take on this new
responsibility, will I be OK? Will I be competent? Where are my
limits? Will I survive?" The leaders seemed driven not only by
how far they could climb up the career ladder; they were also
preoccupied with internal "agendas" that drove them to work
beyond the limits of their previous experience.

A key issue for the individuals we observed (and thereby for their
organisations) was how they dealt with their "demons" – that
nagging part of themselves that demanded attention or resolution.
Did they seek to suppress or deny these demons or did they seek
to accept and work with them? We believe that if people can
understand their demons and appreciate them for their positive, as
well as negative, impact, it helps them to be successful leaders.

Leaders – trying to fix something through work with others

We saw a powerful paradox in the leaders with whom we worked. They had an inner strength and security that made them capable of surviving in very tough conditions, of displaying the durability and resilience needed to be effective. They were impressive people. They had a self-possession and confidence that others warmed to and wanted to follow. They "held on" when many others might have been shipwrecked by the storms to which they were exposed.

> if people can understand their demons and appreciate them for their positive, as well as negative, impact, it helps them to be successful leaders

At the same time they had a drive and determination that was fuelled by restlessness, a sense of inadequacy, a drive to push and go further. They were driven to make up an inner deficit – a need to prove or demonstrate something. They were trying to fix something within themselves through their work with others.

Leaders are both ordinary and extraordinary. They behave just like other people but they are also attracted by a need to speak for and act for others as well as themselves. They want to represent and speak for a "we" and do something to, and with, a larger group. They want to be on the stage; or failing that, to play a powerful role behind it. If leaders perform successfully while on the stage, it is thrilling for them. It validates them and bolsters their sense of self-worth. To see a consummate performer with a crowd like Bill Clinton, who comes alive with an audience, is to see someone who is driven to prove himself and who finds himself when able to speak for and with a crowd.

The literature is full of the competencies and qualities a leader needs to be effective or transformational. What is explored much less is why the leadership role is so attractive to some people. Why do they want to be the "chosen one" who represents others?

We think it is the "inner drive" that is the key here, not the outer expressions of strength and competence.

The "demon" inside

In our view, every individual has "demons". These are issues or themes resulting from their formative experiences in life that they continue to work on as an adult. Sometimes these insecurities – and the behaviours they give rise to – are described in management development terms as "weaknesses". We believe they are much more interesting and important than that. They are the things that each individual finds problematic, qualities or attributes they would like to have, and problems they would like to resolve but feel they never can. They are the source of people's energy, drive and determination. Combined with an individual's strengths, particular abilities and experience, they are what make that person special. They give rise to a leader's potential to contribute to specific situations, groups and organisations. Take away the "weaknesses" and you would have neutered the leader. As was said about one of the women leaders in our research, "In a particular context and with particular people her defects became her strengths".

Examples of demons that we saw in the research were:

▌ The leader mentioned above who had made his way to the top in an organisation dominated by people from more privileged backgrounds. Our sense was that a lot of his motivation came from a feeling that "I'll show those ... what I can do".

▌ One leader appeared to be driven by the underlying need to gain the approval of his father and a sense that whatever he did was not good enough.

▌ Two of the leaders were coming up to 50. They took on risky leadership roles outside their proven areas of expertise that were like a "walk on the wild side" for them – jobs leading new organisations with people different to the areas they had managed before. It was as if they both had something to try out before they got any older and the opportunity was lost, probably for ever. The Germans call it *Torschlussangst* (the fear of the door closing for all time).

❚ One leader we worked with was particularly self-critical. He was never satisfied with his understanding of issues or with what he had done. He was always driving on, trying to do better. This led to criticism from his team for taking too long to make up his mind and focusing more on achieving a perfect understanding of issues than on achieving results. He was thoughtful and highly intelligent. He had taken time to reflect on his pattern of behaviour and its impact on others and the business. He made a conscious effort to tolerate not knowing the answer to the puzzles in his mind and move faster to action, without waiting for perfect data or a complete analysis. He was admired by his team for this effort, for making use of his "inner drive" in the service of the team when it came to understanding the corporate parent (and its expectations of time and perfection) but keeping it in check when that was needed to make fast decisions on potential investments.

Often leaders are self-critical, at least in private. It's part of what drives them on. One successful entrepreneur we worked with told us: "Every day, I expect to be revealed as a fraud." Other leaders display the "Groucho Marx" syndrome: "I'm not sure I want to join (much less be the leader of) any organisation that would have someone like me as a member."

Another common demon that we saw in leaders was the need for acceptance and the fear of rejection. This underlying drive was for many what sparked the need to speak for and act for others. It drove leaders to test themselves, to push themselves harder.

The point about these insecurities is not that they are good or bad. They are what they are. They are the "work in progress" that we carry with us and help to define who we are. They are like a recording in our heads that lingers there from formative experiences in childhood or adolescence. Because they are the issues that are unresolved, they give us energy. The parts of our identity that are settled don't give us energy, don't get us up in the morning. To a large extent it's the things that can't be fixed or completed that drive us on. For adults within a reasonable range, who are not mad, the demons cannot be sorted out or fixed but they can be lived with.

In his brilliant, award-winning children's trilogy, *Northern Lights*, Philip Pullman has a startling device which at first is very strange. In his fantasy world, every individual has a daemon (the spelling is deliberately different) – an animal which is always close to you and which embodies your essence, your soul, your inspiration. In childhood the daemon keeps changing its form but in adulthood it is fixed for each person and tells you what sort of individual you are dealing with, whether a panther or a snake, a butterfly or a cat. Some daemons are more unpleasant than others, some friendlier, but each symbolises the unique potential of every person. You are destined to live closely with your daemon: if you can't accept it you will be miserable; if you do accept it, you can flourish. To be separated from your daemon is the cruellest thing possible: it is to be torn apart.

In our world, Pullman says, the daemons are usually hidden. Only in moments of extraordinary clarity and self-awareness can we see them. Nevertheless, they are always there, symbolising the earthy, free, here and now, qualities that Pullman passionately advocates.

These daemons contain good and bad, beneficial and harmful potential. For Pullman, it is damaging to attempt to divide the world and one's self into good and evil, saints and sinners. The stuff of life, the source of individual inspiration and creativity, are the flaws, the "sin" that everyone has. He argues that what damages people are the higher, impossible, ideals that people can never reach and lead in practice to self-loathing, cruelty and repression.

> in most situations the inner demons help the leader to press on, to excel

Understanding your demons

We saw in our research that people cannot avoid their demons – nor can they vanquish or dispose of them. In most situations the inner demons help the leader to press on, to excel. Under pressure, however, the demons may demand excessive amounts of attention and cause the leader to function less effectively. Too much of her time is spent doing things to serve the demons inside, to the detriment of thinking clearly and operating most effectively in the service of the group she is leading. The leader's behaviour may become erratic or extreme as she strives for a form of self-perfection. In this state, leaders are merely "getting through the day", meeting their own immediate needs but unable to step back and think clearly about what needs doing in the bigger picture.

Just as the quality of relationship to others is key, so is the quality and depth of the relationship to one's self and one's own life story. Understanding the demons can calm leaders down and help them to think about the impact of their actions and avoid behaviour that is damaging – or perhaps even mad. Being familiar enough with their demons enables leaders to recognise their presence in moments of stress or difficulty: "Here we go again ... I know this place ... I must be under pressure ... I have regressed internally to a point where I need reassurance. It is time to step back and to acknowledge that I and the people around me are frightened, that I am anxious too but that, together, we can face what needs to be done."

A leader cannot suppress or remove her demons – but she can stop them leading to dysfunctional or even mad behaviour.

One leader was both fascinated by his group of reports and in fear of it. He was like a moth around a flame. When he tried to work with the group as a whole, he found it difficult. He generally worked one-on-one with members of his management team. Yet in discussions with us he kept coming back to the group. He expressed an apparently sincere desire to share responsibility with the group. He seemed powerfully drawn to what the group might offer him and, at the same time, incapable of sharing key issues with it.

In one company, the leader's position was difficult in the early months. He could not strike the right note with either his own team or the management team of the organisation of which he was part. An important moment came when the Chief Executive gave him the opportunity to talk about his "demon" – the passionate need he had as a working-class man to be recognised in an organisation he perceived as dominated by the elite – Oxbridge trained and upper middle class.

▶

The "drive" did not go away just because he talked about it with his boss but he had tested whether his authority figure could tolerate his true self and not demand perfection. The experience of acceptance made him able to be less consumed by his "drive" and free himself to think and act more clearly and wisely in the presence of those who needed to know from him that it was all right to be less than perfect and still be appreciated and do a good enough job. He was able to see how his current situation differed from previous ones he had been in and what he needed to do to be effective. He could work with himself and with the people he was depending on in a "living" and realistic rather than an idealistic and deadening way.

Contrast the competencies approach

This view of demons as central to people's potential is very different from the idealistic and cynical views we heard expressed during the research.

The idealistic view builds a picture of the competencies to which capable managers and leaders should aspire. There is a list, asserted in company after company, of the qualities and capabilities needed for success. The list of competencies is remarkably similar in many large companies: things like "drive for results", "relating to people", "leading change" and "customer focus". Introduced originally to make the assessment of people more objective, the list of competencies grows every year as consultants and HR managers try to produce ever more perfect lists to cope with the diversity of needs and situations.

In practice the end product of refining competencies is often an exhaustive and exhausting list, an idealistic model of management and leadership which no mere human can attain. The competencies-driven approach encourages "deficit" thinking – a focus on each individual's weaknesses or, more delicately put, her "development needs". Instead of appreciating the unique abilities of each person, the comparison is with a standardised template and the ways in which, inevitably, each person is lacking. As a consequence, individuals are exhorted to be somebody they are not and can never be – the perfect leader.

In the course of our research we heard one devastating attack on the competence-based approach from a leading headhunter. He told us:

> Management competencies are a "placebo" for middle managers. They keep them happy but they don't speak to the real qualities needed in leaders. Chief executives are among the unhappiest people I know. The idea that they are complete managers is dangerous nonsense. Often they have disturbed family backgrounds. These lie behind the qualities that they need to be successful. They have tremendous energy and focus. They are innately restless and dissatisfied. They are also ferociously anti-team and wilfully independent.

We do not agree with the implied view that leaders have to be detached and ruthless. But we do think the headhunter punctures an important balloon. For us, the path to individual and group development lies not through idealistic notions of what people ought to be, but recognising and valuing how they are and on whom and what they depend.

Unfinished business

One of the findings of our research is how much unfinished business there is around in organisations. The cases were like battlefields littered with the unexploded bombs from past conflicts – the unexpressed feelings about past experiences, many of them going back years.

In one company there was a powerful sense of anger and loss that had never been properly expressed at the tyrant who used to be boss of the company. He was perceived as an ogre – someone who had controlled every aspect of the business and not allowed any scope for managers (much less other staff) to contribute their ideas. The boss used to control which areas of the offices or factory people could visit. Years after this boss had left the company, his presence was still felt. There was also anger with the corporate parent, which had imposed this boss. People felt the corporate parent had bought a thriving business with a record of outstanding service to customers and then gradually destroyed it by the wrong appointments, the failure to understand the business and the incessant pressure for short-term fixes (as opposed to long-term investment).

In another company staff had been through a series of mergers – for some people, five mergers in 10 years. We were conscious of strong feelings about many of these past episodes – people made redundant and people retained, units come and gone, individuals promoted or demoted, skills and assets won and lost, leaderships and groups that were seen as victorious or defeated in the past. The feelings about different events could not be easily separated or identified. But there they were, ready to be reawakened by the disturbance of a leadership change.

Unconscious attractors

In their book *Families – and How to Survive Them*,[1] Robin Skynner and John Cleese describe the strange, largely unconscious process by which people often choose their partners. Frequently, it is not, they argue, common strengths or interests that bring people together but recognition of shared flaws or gaps in development – their unfinished developmental business. You warm to someone because you feel he will understand the issues that trouble you. What's more, they suggest, people can pick up the signals of shared trouble or pain across a crowded room, without ever saying a word. They understand the signals – a look, a gesture, a way of standing – intuitively.

It seems to us that organisations can unconsciously pick up signals about a leader who shares their issues. Just as people find each other in relationships, so leaders and organisations may find each other because they unconsciously recognise others who have the same flaws and weaknesses. These people have patterns that they know and are unconsciously attracted to work on. It looks like chance but it isn't. There are unconscious attractors. If the issues resonate, the leader and organisation will be drawn together.

---

1 R. Skynner and J. Cleese, *Families and How to Survive Them*, Vermilion, London, 1997.

This is not to say that the organisation and leader are necessarily good for each other. It is to say that there may be powerful attractors working beneath the surface and that the attractors may relate to shared "work in progress" of the leader and the organisation. The leader becomes available to the organisation to meet its own dissatisfaction with itself, to embody its omnipotent and perhaps scary dreams. Organisation and leader seem to need each other to provide the bit that they have come to think of, subconsciously, as missing, hidden and in need of acceptance or punishment in themselves.

Sometimes, however, the match is beneficial for both parties.

One leader mentioned earlier was distinguished by her rootlessness. She had spent much of her childhood living in different countries, following her father's international career. She was in revolt against her own nationality and candidly preferred the Anglo-Saxon ways of doing business. Her attitude to the past was dramatic. She dismissed history as of no use. She never visited museums, which she said reminded her of death.

In her childhood our leader's favourite game was to pretend to be an aristocrat ruling over a world of crabs. She had spent hours marshalling and organising the obedient and well-defended crabs. Although this story may sound strange, we were struck by the vitality, intelligence and self-confidence of this leader. She was remarkably successful in

▶

setting her own boundaries, saying what she would take on and what she would not. She was brilliantly successful in renegotiating the targets that head office placed on her business.

Thus, behind the success was an extraordinary hinterland. It was a hinterland that connected leader and company. The company was looking for a rootless missionary who would "convert" the French company and draw it into the international fold. It wanted someone who was "passing through", who would not make strong attachments to the local people but who would remain loyal to the corporate centre. It needed someone with a hard exterior, not bothered by the push back from resistant male French managers, and someone able to play, capable of winning over others by her vitality and intelligence.

In every leadership role there are hidden agendas. Different people at different times may have many views of the content of the agendas. What we noticed was the resonance between the inner demons of the individual leaders and the hidden agendas that emerged for organisations.

Implications for leaders

So what are the implications for individuals and for organisations if this view of demons and unfinished business is correct? We believe there is parallel work for leaders and organisations. Alongside the business task, there is another world to deal with, the world of your inner drives and of the group's and organisation's unfinished business.

With so much to think about and do, it is very tempting to "stay positive" and focus only on the task. Unfortunately the demons and unfinished business won't go away. We saw attempts to ignore them by drawing a line under the past or by fleeing into the future, only postponing the moment they would have to be addressed in some way. The demons and unfinished business came back to bite those who sought to ignore them. The good news is that there are realistic ways of working with them.

> the most important way forward is for leaders to be more aware of their demons and be willing to understand them

The most important way forward is for leaders to be more aware of their demons and be willing to understand them – not deny or run away from them. The demons are the leader's treasure (as well as her limit). It is the imperfections that make people useful as leaders, give them their drive and determination, their different way of seeing and doing things. When leaders are more aware of their inner drives and more accepting, the gain is enormous. They stop trying to be someone they are not and get on with the business of being who they are. They feel a sense of relief: "OK, it's out in the open, now. I have admitted to myself what's going on for me and it's not so awful. Now I can make the best of who I am."

The alternative is running away, denying the demons. We observed this in our research, and witnessed the huge amounts of energy it uses up. People beat themselves up for things they can't change. People can be so busy covering up who they are and how they feel that they have little time or space to connect to the people around them or to face the important and uncomfortable issues.

If people cover up their inner drive and pretend they are perfect, others cannot relate to them. It is like interacting with a stone. The admission of some vulnerability makes people worth attaching to as leaders. Asking for help is a powerful way of engaging other people in an important project, task or activity. Leaders should be aware of their own need for help, and whether they find it easy or hard to ask. They can also be of great service to people who work with them by spotting when these people need help but find it hard to ask.

Enough inner security to face your demons

The leader needs the organisation in order to work on something about herself and vice versa. The leader arrives in the hope that she can overcome her own sense of inadequacy, and realise her own more perfect ideal by joining the organisation. The organisation hopes that the leader will embody the more perfect idea it has of itself. However, neither the imperfections of the leader nor the insecurities of groups and organisations will go away.

The task is for the leader to understand that she is who she is, how she is. That is the resource she has to work with. Tolerating her demons opens her up to relationships and to the unfinished business of groups and organisations.

The task for the people around the leader is parallel to her task. When the group can let go of the idea of the perfect leader and tolerate the one they have, then they open up to effective working relationships and shared responsibility for shaping the future and managing the present. From being "too hot to handle", issues become workable. The strategic conversations that we described in Chapter 4 become possible.

If people try to avoid these issues and the uncomfortable feelings that come with them, the problems do not go away. The difficulties and disturbance accumulate. They may break out in a moment of stress. Opportunities to make connections between people are lost.

A bit of appreciative "betrayal" is often needed here. Someone close and respected has to say: "Look, the Emperor is naked!" and add: "Enjoy your demons. Don't look for magical solutions. You are who you are and it's fine – life itself made us all that way."

LESSONS FROM OUR RESEARCH

* The leaders we saw were extraordinarily resilient but didn't invest enough in self-care.
* Leaders need to be real, available and vulnerable for people to connect with them and work for them.
* What makes people interesting are their imperfections.
* Leaders are the people in each group who are more interested than others in the "we" and have a fear of rejection.

- Leaders fulfil a need in themselves to be "on stage" and meet a need in others for an authority who holds them together and helps them to get better at what they do.

- By meeting the needs of others, the leader satisfies some of her own needs.

- The inner demons connect with the unfinished business of the organisation.

Thinking about yourself

Living Leadership includes the habit of reflecting afterwards, trying to work out what feelings are yours and which belong to others (and giving feelings back to their owners if you conclude that they are not yours).

We suggest that after a critical meeting or incident, when you are feeling uncomfortable, when something bothers you or when you feel you have been praised unreasonably, you take a sheet of paper and consider:

- How did I feel? What was I thinking?

- What was really going on there?

- What are the patterns of feeling and behaviour in this group or situation?

- What is my "stuff"? What might relate to my demons?

- When am I able to ask for help (and not able)?

- How do I help others to ask for help?

- What is theirs? What are other people passing to me to work on?

It takes courage to slowly get to know your demons. Often private conversations with a trusted confidant are needed to bring important patterns to the surface and we will discuss this further in later chapters. However, some individual reflection is essential to greater understanding.

Surfing, sinking and swimming

Don't panic, you're only human

We worked with a group of managers in a well known multi-national. The group had a stormy time. There were strong-minded managers from many different cultures and backgrounds and the pressures to perform were intense. After some months the group had a review session. The Czech manager in the group said: "I really appreciated being in this group and have learnt a lot. I also never want to go through that again!" One of us said: "Oh yes you will go through it again – but it may be less painful because you will recognise the pattern next time. You will also know that you don't have to do it alone. You could pick up the phone."

A key conclusion of our research is that effective leadership does not happen evenly or consistently. Leaders will have periods when they feel they are surfing, others when they seem to be sinking and periods when they are swimming along fine. The idea that they can be competent, unfailing and effective all the time is another idealistic and burdensome fantasy. It is normal as a leader to have periods when you think you are sinking and others when you are just getting by; it is an inherent part of leading.

The choice that you have as a leader is how you respond and feel about going down. We encourage you *not* to be too hard on yourself. If you can avoid beating yourself up for falling off the surfboard and avoid panic, you can learn a lot. It doesn't mean you won't come off the board again and again. But it does make falling

You are swimming despite the sinking feeling

off less frightening – and enables you to improve your skills and to believe in your self more.

We found leaders in our research moving in and out of three modes, as shown in Table 6.1.

Surviving

Sometimes the response of leaders to seemingly unreasonable expectations and frustrating realities was to go into survival mode. By this we mean a state in which a leader is unable to form effective relationships with the people around him; an isolated position where the only thing that matters is surviving and complying with the wishes of the bosses. At its extreme, this becomes a refusal to attach to others. This was sometimes combined with a flight to fantastic ideas of togetherness and "team-working", an imagined world of shared purpose. There was an inability to hold the middle ground, of realistic connections with people, here and now.

Table 6.1 Surfing, sinking and swimming

Mode	Coming alive	Surviving	Coping
Feeling	Surfing	Sinking	Swimming
Characteristics	Well connected	Disconnected	Some connections
	Able to think clearly	Unable to think clearly	Defensive up to a point
			Moaning while coping
	Tolerates complexity and uncertainty	Simplifies complexity	Takes some responsibility and initiative
		Blaming and scapegoating	
	Tolerates disillusionment and reality as it is	Sees self as victim	Busy, busy but still able to think
		Trapped in the future	
	Able to use whole self, feeling as well as thinking	Over-dependent on bosses for survival	Struggles with finding the courage to stand up to the boss and the group
	Able to ask for and receive help	Getting lost in detail and losing the script	Complaining is the cry for help
		Can't ask for help but will send signals like "spilling the coffee over someone"; dependent on others to offer help	
Focus	Short and long term	Very short term	Short term

We all, at times, go into survival mode. We switch off from the people around us, we stop thinking and using all our senses, we focus only on getting through the day. We are reactive, we do the minimum to get by. We lose the ability to shape events or take the initiative. We lose sight of what is acceptable behaviour or conduct – so preoccupied are we with getting through the day without any further damage. We seem self-absorbed.

Sometimes it happens when we are tired or stressed or when we have suffered a personal loss. We feel hopelessly overloaded. There is just too much to think about and to do. The survival mode makes good sense as a coping mechanism. In a time of upheaval, the instinct for organisational survival can result in quite primitive behaviour. The incessant pressure for results, monitoring, constant progress checks, anxious pressure from above, the mistrust and the defensive paralysis in teams in reaction to the pressure, sometimes pushed leaders into this mode. The leaders may have felt uncomfortable about it but their physical and emotional resources were taken up by the struggle to respond effectively to the fluctuating demands of top management. They became skilled at surviving – at the cost of being cut off from their colleagues and losing a sense of adequate self-esteem.

When leaders were surviving, it was impossible for them to think clearly enough to ask for help. Sometimes leaders did send distress signals – irrational or strange behaviour – that others might pick up. However, those offering help had to tread very carefully. An offer of help could be perceived as an attack.

> In one case we saw a leader who was at times cut off from the people around him. He had just one confidant with whom he could talk openly about the issues facing the business. He was rather contemptuous of the rest of the people, saying they weren't up to the minimum standard of competence that he expected. The business pressures were intense. Although the leader put a brave face on things, it became clear that profitability was not adequate. A series of erratic decisions were made, without adequate research, first to give some types of business lower priority, then subsequently to give them high priority. Support from the leader's boss, which at first had seemed quite firm, became increasingly doubtful. Just as the leader wasn't there for his subordinates, so the boss was increasingly not available when the leader wanted him. The leader was not aware of all this until later. Indeed this is one of the characteristics of being in survivor mode. You are not aware of how you have been functioning until some change – or simply the passage of time – causes you to step back and reflect.

Surviving is the embodiment of the human capacity to cope with unbelievable amounts of stress and change. It has a high cost – to self, group, organisation and customer. For the self, the cost is additional denigration. You feel bad about yourself for being compliant and not being true to your feelings and thoughts – if you allow yourself to feel it. For the group, the cost is the inability to handle the strategic or operational issues effectively. For the organisation, the cost is the falsification of information that the organisation needs to be effective.

> "Max couldn't manage the people – so he managed the paper clips instead." (A manager in our research talking about a previous leader.)

Coping

Coping was a less dramatic way of dealing with the pressures. In this mode leaders struck others as somewhat defensive. They might react negatively in the moment to an idea or a comment but they were able to hear suggestions from others and might well act on them later. They could connect with some people, particularly those with whom they had long-standing relationships. They complained about other people and about the amount to do, but they weren't bitter. Their criticisms were qualified with some self-awareness and gentle self-mockery. They were incredibly busy but they gave you the sense that they weren't just reacting to others. They were also able sometimes to take the initiative.

A particular challenge for leaders in this mode was finding the courage to do the more difficult things that tended to get left for another day. Pushing back against the bosses was for some very hard. Others avoided challenging the groups around them and kept control of issues by dealing with questions one-on-one with individual reports.

In this mode leaders were able to accept help – from colleagues or friends, human resource managers or consultants. They could see the value of assistance and did not see offers of help as an attack. In the research we found that this stance was often good enough in reality. It only became bad when measured in terms of heroic leadership.

Coming alive

Coming alive is when leaders are able to use all their intelligence, senses and experience to connect with others and make sense of the context. They don't forget their life experience. They are able to acknowledge when a situation is different from ones they have experienced before and they need to pause and think again. They are able to tolerate the complexity of events and people and not rush to simple-minded solutions that don't make sense. Their focus is on both long- and short-term issues. They can ask for and receive help.

> We described the pattern of leaders surfing, sinking and swimming to a group of managers in one multinational. They picked up immediately on the idea and played with it for much of an afternoon, though they were suspicious that surfing sounded like too much fun. They weren't sure how much surfing they did as leaders. One manager commented that, for those who knew the sport, surfing had become much more demanding now in Australia. You're not supposed any more just to get up on the board and ride one wave as far as you can. You're supposed to get to the top, have a short ride and then jump to the next wave. Surfing has become wave hopping.
>
> This new style of surfing seemed like a metaphor for the absurd expectations placed nowadays on leaders.

Learning from the different modes

You can't be at your best all the time – you can't surf forever – but you can recognise the value of surviving and coping. They are essential if you are to learn as a leader – and if you are to get done all the things you need to do.

We encourage you to debrief the moment – to allow time to make sense, after a meeting, event or interaction, of what was happening. To review the task, your use of self and the dynamics of the group. Leaders need moments to review and see when and where they were blind, when they were blocked and when others helped them.

It is important to consider when and how it is realistic to step back. Can you debrief yourself – and take account of the stuff below the surface of history, time and culture? Does the moment feel right to go back over your experience and see what you can learn from it?

Can you reflect with others? Can you feed back your reflections at a moment when people can deal with it and not feel attacked? We talk more about how to review and learn in Chapters 9 and 11.

> we encourage you to debrief the moment – to allow time to make sense of what was happening

Healthy disillusionment

In our research, a key, if the leader were to come alive more often, was "healthy disillusionment" – letting go of an original dream, allowing it to be modified and adapted but avoiding too much bitterness, blaming of others or self-reproach. Finding the courage to disappoint and be disappointed was, paradoxically, a key to delivery.

Inevitably, all our leaders went through a process of disillusionment after the idealisation phase as their hopes and expectations came into conflict with chaotic and unpalatable realities. The cycle of dreaming, disillusionment and new hope is a natural process. It is dreams (hopes, ambitions) that get people out of bed in the morning and fire them up. What mattered was not that they lost their illusions but the way in which this journey was negotiated. Disillusion hurts – particularly for those who are self-absorbed. The trick was to leave a space for healthy disillusionment and for finding new dreams.

For followers, the "healthy disillusionment" often means coming to terms with the leader they have and letting go of the leader they might wish to have in some perfect world. Again and again we saw people dumping the problems of organisations on the leader. The transformational hero model encourages them to do this and it can be very comfortable. Followers say to themselves, "There is nothing we can do. The boss just isn't up to it. He doesn't have a clear vision of where the organisation is going, he doesn't inspire, he doesn't communicate clearly enough, he doesn't stick to the script, he doesn't empower, he doesn't give us a clear framework to work within." However, unfortunately, he is the leader and, often, he is going to stay as leader. The choice for followers is to work with him, as he is, or stand back and keep aloof.

For leaders, too, there is the process of letting go of the idea of the fantasy leader, of seeing that the ideal is self-destructive. If you stay wedded to the idea of the transforming hero, you end up, as a leader, focusing on the ideal instead of what's around you. For the sake of the higher ideal, you cut yourself off from the people you depend on.

If you can let go of the ideal, then it becomes possible to seize the moment and be a leader, here and now. In the research we saw again and again the opportunities to lead in the moment. We saw that when leaders do connect with others, get real about the context and develop their self-awareness – as they do their daily work – it strengthens the leader, develops the team and frees up energy for delivery and commitment.

The rest of the book looks at what it takes to apply these principles of *Living Leadership*. How do you cultivate your ability to lead in the moment? How do you come alive more often? How can you make best use of what you have to offer as a leader?

We start by identifying the choices that you make as a leader, moment to moment, about how you interact with others. These choices shape how you lead and the impact that you have on others.

LESSONS FROM OUR RESEARCH

- It's normal as a leader to have times when you feel you are just surviving or just coping with all the pressures but not moving forward.

- Don't beat yourself up for this.

- The moments when you are surviving and coping can help you learn how to be more effective as a leader – if you can make space and time to step back and reflect.

- Even when you have learnt and developed, there will still be times when you feel you are sinking.

- Dreams and plans always change when they come into contact with reality; the choice you have is how much you blame others – and yourself – and how much you can get on and focus on different aspirations.

Thinking about your experience

▌ Identify a situation in which you "came alive" with others, connected with other people, were able to face tough realities and used yourself well; and

▌ another situation or time when you felt you were sinking, disconnected from others, just getting through the day.

What were the patterns – on the one hand, when you came alive and, on the other, when you felt you were sinking? What happened? What did you do? What did others do? How did you contribute to your success – or your difficulties? What could you do, or how could you be, differently, another time?

Leading in the moment
Become more versatile as a leader

Successful leadership has little to do with having the right CV, a great job, or even how much overtime you put into work. It has everything to do with what you do with yourself. The use you make of your strong and your weaker sides.

One of the leaders in our research

Leadership is not something you can plan to do at an appropriate time in the future: "Ah yes, I will do a bit of leadership at 15.00h on Friday". We are often called upon to provide leadership when we are least prepared, and sometimes least willing, to give it. Something happens: a problem occurs or an opportunity arises providing the leader with a platform. Other people observe, and judge, how you behave as leader. You may step back to avoid the issue, hoping no one notices (unlikely), or you may step up and do your best. This is leading in the moment: having the self-confidence and awareness to believe your choices will be good enough.

Choice

As a leader, you make choices, moment to moment, about how you interact with others. These choices relate to the "in-between space" between you and other people. They shape how you lead and the impact that you have on others.

The areas of choice are like different dimensions of music. A composer in writing a particular piece of music makes choices about the key, the theme, the volume, the tempo. By moving around on these dimensions, he changes the nature of the music and its possible meaning or resonance for listeners.

So it was when we experienced the work of leaders. Sometimes leaders made music that resonated for the people around them. At other moments they made sounds that jarred. At some moments they made skilful use of the leadership dimensions and sounded notes with assurance. At others we weren't sure what tune they were trying to play, or a leader stuck with one note when we longed for him to play a tune.

These zones of choice first came up in our research as tensions or dilemmas. Leaders felt stretched as they struggled with seemingly incompatible pushes and pulls. "How can I do this – and that, at the same time?" they asked. However, over a period, we discovered that there are zones of opportunity. By moving around the zones and adapting to the needs of the moment, leaders could have more of the impact that they wanted to have.

It is important to remember that there is no one right answer – no one correct position or equilibrium in each of the zones. Effective leaders move around all the time, shifting their stance according to the needs of the moment. They are constantly discovering ways of satisfying both sides of each dimension. It is not a question of doing this *or* that but how to do this *while* doing that.

In our research, leaders, most of the time, made these choices unconsciously. They didn't have the time or a reason to reflect on the choices they were making. However, we encourage you to be more aware of these choices. By being more conscious of how you interact with others, you can be more effective as a leader.

We found it useful to think about seven areas of choice – spaces in which leaders lead, play and create.

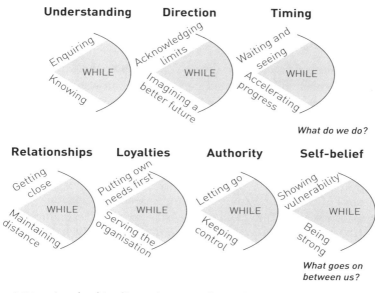

Exhibit 5 Leadership dimensions – making choices about how you relate to others

Understanding – *enquiring while knowing*

What was the leader's approach? To what extent did the leader present themselves as *knowing*: where to focus attention, how to work, with whom to work, and in which direction the organisation should go? And how far did the leader *enquire*: keep an open mind, tune in to the organisation and ask open questions?

▌ How far and fast should the leader take the lead and move to decision and action?

▌ When should the leader hold back and say more data or discussion was needed?

▌ When should he try to speed things up?

▌ And when to slow them down?

Leaders also have powerful lessons from past experience. It is natural that leaders roll out the formulae and processes they have learnt from experience. However, again and again, we saw leaders stumble because they didn't check to see if the well-proven formulae still applied in new circumstances. Leaders apply what they know. Often they have to be prepared to "unlearn" things but they don't find it easy.

An acute challenge for leaders is to deal with the anxieties of being a leader and find enough support to stay calm and remain thinking, feeling people. They need to admit to ignorance and be willing to enquire about how the situation they are in differs in subtle but critical ways from previous situations. They need to face ambiguity and mess and avoid trying to clarify everything, because very often it's impossible and the effort to tidy everything up will drive them to distraction.

Direction – *acknowledging limits while imagining a better future*

Leaders and others needed to confront the realities of the present and past while discovering their shared aspirations for the future. They needed a sense of history and to be able to look the present in the face while still, somehow, hanging on to their dreams for the future. Being positive was an essential ingredient of being a leader but taken too far it can lead to ignoring uncomfortable truths about the current position. On the other hand, too much dwelling on current difficulties can lead to hopelessness. People need to feel encouraged to voice their aspirations for the future.

Leaders were called upon again and again to make fine judgements about which stance to take. Often they did so on an intuitive or instinctive basis – sometimes leaning to one side, at another towards the other side and in some magic moments managing to strike both notes at the same time.

What we saw convinces us that it is essential for leaders to face the "negative". Powerful feelings of fear, anxiety, loss and anger are exposed by change in organisations. They have to flow somewhere. The attempts to ignore them and "always look on the bright side" didn't work and stunted the dialogue between leaders and followers.

We found that the more leaders could live intensely, in the moment, and let go of the anxiety to impose themselves on events, the more effective they could be in leading change – and maintaining essential continuity.

Timing – *waiting and seeing while accelerating progress*

What is the right time to table a key issue or decision? When should I start a new initiative? What can the organisation face now? What does it need to face now? Will we be in a better – or worse – position in one month's, one year's, three years' time?

We found in our research so much emphasis on the need to move fast and seize the moment that it was easy to lose sight of the age-old wisdom that some issues take time to mature. Yes, a sense of urgency was often a vital thing. However, often, we saw leaders and teams who were overloaded by trying to do everything at once. They pretended to deal with everything and ended up coming back to the same issues that had not been properly resolved. Sometimes the key job of a leader was to say "Let's be realistic. This is not the right time to address this issue. We will come back to it later." Or to say: "If we are to do a good job this task will take longer than planned." Often there was an intense

What feels like pulling you apart, in reality, connects you to people

sense of relief when leaders helped others take issues off their "to do" lists and leave them for another day.

Relationships – *getting close while maintaining distance*

It felt like a real struggle. How could they get close enough to others to have effective working relationships and get good information on the issues they faced *and at the same time* remain detached enough to see the "wood for the trees" and take tough decisions? Leaders needed to relate enough to others for others to attach to them *and* they needed to stand apart.

We found in our research that leaders were exhausted by the many demands they felt their direct reports made on their time and by the requests for more intimacy. They sought to balance competing demands. Is it right to let people get close to me? Are my people seeking to get close to me in order to win my favour or enhance their position in the organisation? Do I have an inner circle of managers who are closer to me? What impact will this have on others? Where do I draw my boundaries? How far should I get involved in my team's personal issues? To what extent should I disclose information about me and what makes me tick? Should I socialise more with my staff? Or should I keep my distance? How do I avoid them becoming dependent on me? And how do I keep in touch enough with what they are doing?

At times this dimension was experienced as an impossible dilemma. Yet we did see leaders being both intimate and detached, sometimes in quick succession and sometimes at the same time.

Loyalties – *putting your own needs first while serving your organisation*

Leaders felt they were navigating their way between two contrary pulls. On the one side was their commitment to themselves, to their own views, interests and careers. On the other side was their sense of obligation to their organisation or company and the leaders who had selected them (this was also described as "being a good company servant"). Sometimes good leaders didn't question too much; they just followed orders.

This dimension often came up in connection with the fraught question of how to achieve a better work–life balance. How could leaders do all that was needed at work and preserve enough life with family and friends?

One example was the difficulty the male leaders we worked with had in limiting their hours at work or taking their holidays. The women leaders were much better at this but the men succumbed often to the pressures to be "chop, chop, busy, busy" and much less often stood back to attend to their own needs and think through how greater leisure might make them more not less effective at work.

However, the choice about self and organisation goes wider than that. It embraced the setting of goals and objectives. Do I have clear enough goals for me and my team? Are my objectives realistic? The dimension included ethics and loyalty. Whose truth do I speak? The company's or my own? How far can I go in accommodating the values and priorities of the company? Am I prepared to give my organisation the benefit of the doubt? How much do I identify with the company? Whose interest do I place first?

We found in the research that leaders putting their own needs first was a precondition for effectiveness. Faced with pressures to do anything, any time, anywhere, leaders had to identify their own boundaries – "What I am prepared to give or do for the company? And what I am *not* prepared to do or give?" They had to identify reasonable boundaries about what they could and could not achieve, about how groups and organisations should work. It is easy to say perhaps; we found that in reality it's often very difficult and can't be done by leaders on their own. Leaders need people they can talk to confidentially about where to set their boundaries.

Authority – *letting go while keeping control*

All the leaders in our study talked about the need for "empowerment" of their people. They were acutely conscious that they had too much to do and that they needed others to take responsibility. At the same time, we often saw leaders who were reluctant to let go, who kept control by keeping key issues in their own hands or by intervening when issues became more sensitive.

Leaders needed to ask themselves: "Do I really need to do this myself? How can I develop more confidence in those around me to take on more responsibility? How can I support, coach, encourage others so that they and I feel comfortable that they can take on more? How can I keep in touch enough with progress to satisfy myself that things are on track and yet not give others the sense that I am interfering? What is it about me that stops me delegating?"

Self-belief – *showing vulnerability while being strong*

It is easy to see that leaders sometimes need to be strong for those around them – capable of holding the stress of the job, able to face the challenges and obstacles, confident that both he and the organisation will succeed when others doubt it. However, showing vulnerability also plays a big part in helping people connect with others. If you are too certain, too self-confident, people will hold back and say: "Over to you. You seem to have it all in hand. There is nothing we can offer to help." People identify often with others' insecurities, perhaps unconsciously, and connect with a leader because of a shared sense of failing or inadequacy – provided they perceive it as a genuine expression of vulnerability and not a sham.

Taken too far, "being strong" turns people away; while too much vulnerability repels people or results in a following among the disturbed. The trick is to learn how and when to do both, sufficiently but not excessively, over a period.

Making a choice

The sort of leadership that will work in a particular moment and situation often cannot be defined in advance. Leaders need to be there *in the moment* to sense what is needed. They cannot know for sure how the contextual, group and personal dynamics will play out until they are in the middle of them.

Working with these dimensions is a constant dance. In each leadership encounter, a leader takes up positions in the zones. What is the correct position? *It depends*. Different leaders have different preferences. They may tend to spend more time in particular places in the different dimensions. Sometimes leaders get trapped in playing the same notes over and over again, without regard for the needs of the moment.

You may have your own views of the areas of choice that are most important in your leading. We encourage you to test how far the choices that we have presented here are relevant in your context or whether other areas of choice exist for you. What we found is rooted in our research and consultancy experience. If there are for you other dimensions of leading in the moment, please include them. Listen to your experience; work out what it means and what it implies with those on whom you depend in your organisation.

We have used the diagnostic questionnaire on the next page with hundreds of managers around the world to help them to diagnose their preferred position or underlying preference on each scale. We have found that some organisations place a greater value on the right-hand side of the scales which suggests a more transformational style. In contrast to this, at an individual level the spread along the scales is remarkably balanced on all the dimensions.

What is perhaps most interesting for leaders is not so much their underlying preference as what helps or hinders them as they seek to move to what they feel would be the right choice (position) on a scale, in a given situation. The ability to move is influenced by external factors such as national or organisational culture, your boss's personal style, and the experience you have in a particular role. It is also heavily driven by personal issues such as self-confidence, control needs, need for clarity and willingness to take risks. We invite you to score yourself to see your own "starting point" or underlying preference and then to read further to see how you can be most effective.

Enquiring				Knowing		

I admit to ignorance and am willing to inquire about how the situation I am in differs in subtle but critical ways from previous situations. I face ambiguity and mess without trying to clarify everything

I like to move to decision and action. I have powerful lessons from past experience and want to roll out the approach and processes I have already learnt

3	2	1	0	1	2	3

Acknowledging limits				Imagining a better future		

I confront the realities of the past. A sense of history and an ability to look the present in the face is essential

Being positive is essential. I encourage people to voice their aspirations for the future

3	2	1	0	1	2	3

Waiting and seeing				Accelerating progress		

Age-old wisdom tells us that some issues take time to mature. Sometimes my job is to say "Let's be realistic. This is not the right time to address this issue"

A sense of urgency is vital. Time wasted can never be regained. You need to move fast and seize the moment

3	2	1	0	1	2	3

Getting close				Maintaining distance		

I get close enough to others to build effective working relationships and get good information on the issues they face. I relate to people enough for them to "attach" to me

I maintain the distance required to remain objective. I do not get emotionally involved with people, in order to have clear judgement and be able to take difficult decisions

3	2	1	0	1	2	3

Putting your own needs first				Serving the organisation		

I have a commitment to myself: my values, my health and my career. I work to achieve a good work–life balance and preserve enough time for my family and friends

I have an obligation to my organisation. Being a good "company servant" is essential. In reality I can't worry too much about time or personal values; I deliver

3	2	1	0	1	2	3

Letting go				Keeping control		
I have too much to do and need others to take responsibility. I have confidence in those around me to take on more responsibility				To achieve results and avoid mistakes I must retain control by keeping key issues in my own hands or by intervening when issues become more sensitive		
3	2	1	0	1	2	3

Showing vulnerability				Being strong		
Showing vulnerability plays a part in helping people connect with me. People identify with my insecurities, perhaps unconsciously, and connect with me because of the call for help				I need to be strong for those around me – capable of holding the stress of the job, able to face the challenges and obstacles, confident that I will succeed when others doubt it		
3	2	1	0	1	2	3

The trap of transformational leadership – overdosing on one side of the dimensions

Looking at the zones of choice helps explain why the transformational leadership idea is so damaging. The transformational picture of leadership corners leaders into thinking that they have to do it all on their own, standing apart and moulding their organisations into shape. It takes one side of the leadership dimensions and elevates it into a tyrannical template for all times and occasions – a "one and only" style of leadership.

The transformational model suggests that the leader should *know* the answer – who to have on his team, what direction to go, what goals to set, how to get there. We often found leaders who felt under pressure to pretend to know more than they really did and found it difficult to value the holding of uncertainty. All the propaganda about a critical first 100 days pushes leaders to adopt positions when they may not be ready to decide. Inside, leaders often feel they *don't know* but fear the damage to their credibility if they admit this.

The transformational model pushes leaders towards a preoccupation with the future, an emphasis on visions and idealised strategies and, often, a denigration or ignoring of the past. Paradoxically, the focus on setting vision and direction – intended to instil a positive, forward-looking mentality – could leave people feeling compliant and resentful or cynical and passive, waiting for the leader to move on to another role.

The transformational idea pushes leaders to accelerate progress. It makes speed the Holy Grail of leadership. It constantly intones: "More, faster, quicker." It suggests to leaders that they need to stay distant from their people in order to maintain control – when in fact leaders need to mix intimacy and detachment if they are to be effective.

The transformational model encourages people to have no sense of personal limits. The theme is "You can do it, if you try hard enough!" The leaders worked hard to serve their organisations. The objectives that they were working to were often not clear. Their bosses acted like Greek gods with contradictory, capricious, insistent demands to follow this or that direction and endless demands to restructure and reorganise. These demands posed a challenge to people's own boundaries. A key to survival was to find some limits to how much of themselves people invested in their work. Without clear limits people lost the capacity to think and act rationally and got trapped in reactive activism. The transformational picture encourages leaders to keep control and to be strong at all times. Leaders are supposed to know the answer. If necessary, they must compel their organisations to adopt this answer.

Transformational leadership suggests that you can avoid being contaminated by the mucky, people side of the leadership zones that includes intimacy with people, putting your own needs first, confronting uncomfortable problems, holding uncertainty, letting go, ambiguity and acknowledging limits. It seduces leaders, under pressure from their responsibilities and from events, into thinking that they can stay with the "good", clean, rational side of the dimensions.

Tapping the potential for leadership

We found that people were often very versatile. Rationally, instinctively and emotionally, they had the potential to stand in many different places in the zones at different moments. Throughout our research we saw able, experienced, highly motivated individuals in positions of power and authority who had a sure instinct for people and situations. We saw groups ready to respond – indeed in some cases more ready to take responsibility than the leaders. We experienced situations that cried out for leadership – often simple acts like calling attention to unacknowledged issues or the "bigger picture" or the needs of others.

> engagement with the "mucky" side of the dimensions is the necessary investment of leadership

The key to unlocking this potential, it seems to us, lies in seeing both the good and bad of organisations, individuals, groups and situations. Perhaps surprisingly, that releases enormous energy and enables people to be constructive and shape the future. The "contaminated" side of the leadership dimensions is, in fact, where all of humanity lives. Engagement with the "mucky" side of the dimensions is the necessary investment, the giving before taking, of leadership. Investing in relationships, current mess and uncertainty makes the tasks of the group or organisation do-able.

From their experience of life, people know that good and bad are wrapped up together. They know the bad feelings that may accompany major life events – births, marriages, moving house, changing jobs – and the tendency to resort to blaming. They also know that they have to work through these feelings if they are to make the most of their life changes.

Putting it another way, the pressures on leaders today are such that they are tempted to suppress instinct and feelings, sensing and intuition. Leaders are drawn sometimes into relying on their intellect alone and not making use of the understanding that their

You can't be at your best all the time

other senses give them. They fear that they won't be able to contain the feelings once they start, more explicitly, to rely on them. They may be sitting on powerful feelings about others, about the dynamics of groups, or about their organisation or environment. They sometimes fear what will happen once the lid on these feelings is opened. Isn't their job to bring events under control – not to expose themselves to the messy world of emotions and feelings?

In our research cases, it was frequently painful to observe the way leaders cut themselves off from their feelings and emotions. The irony was that when leaders did this, when they insisted on "a positive mindset", they deprived themselves of the energy and creativity that they craved. The cauldron of feelings was always there. If not tapped into, it was liable to explode in possibly damaging ways.

The mucky feelings and instincts may seem an uncomfortable resource for leaders to work with. After living with leaders for up to two years, we know that it is what leaders do anyway. What we are suggesting is to be more aware of them – to see the dimensions as a rich source of opportunity and dare to use them to the full.

A delicate dance

This story is about a multinational corporation, Atlas, and John, a team player within it who was assigned to set up a new subsidiary, Netco, to act as a focus for Internet business. John faced complex issues about how to manage the leadership dimensions. To make a success of his leadership, John needed to hold together two very different histories and business cultures: that of the global corporate parent, a utility company, Atlas, and that of the nimble, risky and young Internet start-up. John had a deep knowledge of the whys and wherefores of the "mother-ship", acquired over decades of work in several functions and territories. The people he recruited from the Internet world also had deep knowledge of their quite distinct world, which had thrown up a major challenge to the assumptions and established behaviours of John's world.

The success of Netco depended on the quality and currency of each of these knowledge bases as independent capabilities in their own right. Netco's standing within the parent company depended, to a large extent, on John's understanding of its culture and his adroitness in steering through it. Similarly, the value of Netco's start-up enterprises – largely in fields unrelated to the parent company's business – depended on the depth of understanding and knowledge of John's Internet people. Could John ever aspire to knowing as much as they, or even more, about the Internet? Could John's people ever achieve the depth of John's knowledge of the parent? The answer was indubitably "NO!" in both cases.

In the early days of Netco, John placed emphasis on not knowing, opening up the opportunities for creative thinking and action by acknowledging how much he did not know about the Internet world and about how a Net business might work. His capacity to hold difference and avoid moving prematurely to a conclusion looked like a major asset. He held the very different Netco and parent company cultures and business models. He was under pressure from his team to "make up his mind" and be more decisive, but he held back. He allowed the members of the team to discover the usefulness for Netco, at different times, of both cultures and business models. Instead of

▶

having a battle with winners and losers, he let the issue gradually diminish in importance as managers discovered the value of both approaches.

In our view, John held the uncertainty and the not knowing bravely, with intense stress, "close to his chest". He believed that Netco could succeed, but only if it could create what he called a "narrow ledge" on which both worlds could cohabit. That narrow ledge would necessarily be unstable. It would be frightening to the parent company because of the lack of knowledge available, and frustrating to the Internet people because of the slowness and exhausting thoroughness of the parent's ways. To parry the instability of the ledge, John worked hard, usually on a one-to-one basis with his direct colleagues or bosses, to find a solution in which both worlds' needs could be accommodated. John was largely successful in creating a ledge on which his bosses suspended their normal standards of knowledge and proof, and his Internet people would produce what appeared to them as unnecessary "bureaucratic" justifications for projects.

So, John created a middle ground, which could be held temporarily until some greater force pushed him and his colleagues off it. That greater force eventually came, in the shape of a decision by the main board to disband Netco and disperse the businesses around the operating divisions.

John was also preoccupied with the loyalty dimension. He worked hard to understand what the corporate Board of Directors and the system wanted to achieve – and to avoid. It was difficult for him to be clear about objectives when his bosses were not clear or disagreed, and there was chaos in the e-commerce market that went from boom to bust. There were several layers of complexity with which to be worked. He seemed to revel in the complex chess game of working out what the intentions of his bosses were; he was alert to the weaker signals and ready to respond instantly to a hint or change in tone from one of the main board directors. The game was exciting, the culture was his, he had grown up in it and understood it intimately. We cannot imagine an outsider, a turnaround or Internet expert being able to cope with staying in the e-commerce world while also understanding and protecting the parent company. John was supremely good at holding the tension between the conflicting cultures of the parent company and the Internet world – but it stretched him to the limit. There seemed to be little mental capacity left to deal with the demands of the group for a meaningful share in the strategic process.

We are not just talking about the quantifiable objectives here. We are concerned with the overall task for the leaders. In Netco, it only became clear after the event, with hindsight. Two years after Netco was set up – and with the unit now about to close – top management said that what it had really wanted for Netco was to explore what was "out there", what opportunities there were, and whether there was something the company was missing out on. It was not to maximise its position in e-commerce. The company wanted to make sure its competitors did not steal a march on it, while protecting its position and avoiding unnecessary risks.

Until the end, John and his team had no definitive statement of mission and objectives on which they could rely. There were general statements of direction, but they left wide room for interpretation. Various main board directors had different views, and in the close circles of upper management, these views were widely known and much discussed. Circumstances changed radically – the dotcom crash happened soon after Netco was set up – and the balance of power in the main board shifted, as a new chief executive emerged and the director who sponsored Netco was sidelined. The business climate changed with the onset of recession in the USA and Europe. Market analysts and non-executive directors put top management under increasing pressure to stick to the core business and avoid experiments like Netco. The result was that, as the old saying puts it, "the goalposts kept shifting". The best John and his team could do was to tease out in discussion with top management some interim and shifting sense of mission and objectives, to guide people in the business.

Kicking the table in frustration

The next story concerns an international team that had been meeting in Germany for two days.

One of our research team was kicking the table in frustration. "How can they go on with this PowerPoint festival any longer?" he asked. "Why doesn't someone lead and name the 'elephant in the room' – the things they are all talking about in the coffee breaks but ignore when they get together as a group?"

We researchers withdrew from the room and over an hour were able to work out how we felt, why we were so frustrated and what we could offer back to the group.

Next morning the leader of the group initiated a review of how the group had been working and we fed in our comments. Within minutes the group homed in on the issue of how they could work together more effectively and what type of leadership they wanted from their boss. It was, they agreed not a "schoolmaster" they needed but an "oil can" to help the team work and smooth its way in working with the rest of the corporation.

Not every situation is capable of such quick understanding and movement. Yet our experience was that often there were moments like this when a group or organisation was ready to move forward but required some act of leadership to help it. No-one can anticipate exactly when these moments will occur. Yet if you can bring yourself to your leading at these moments, and make use of all your experience and intelligence, feelings and instincts, it will work enough. It is the best you can do – and it is enough.

LESSONS FROM OUR RESEARCH

- ✱ There is no one right way to lead.
- ✱ The leading that is needed depends on the business situation, the organisational culture and the characters and dynamics of the people you are working with.
- ✱ The leadership dimensions identify the choices leaders make, moment to moment, as they interact with others and adapt to the needs of different situations.
- ✱ The model of transformational leaders provides a one-dimensional view of leadership that gets in the way of leaders being as versatile as they need to be.
- ✱ Once freed of the transformational straitjacket, many people have the ability to move around the leadership dimensions and adapt to the needs of different situations and moments.

REFLECTION

Thinking about your leading

▌ Think about the patterns in the way you lead others and how they have played out in a recent situation. Consider your own approach with regard to the leadership dimensions:

▌ What part of the dimensions came easily to you and worked well?

▌ Which parts did you underuse? What were the consequences?

▌ Which parts did you overuse? With what consequences?

▌ What will you experiment with doing differently another time?

part

How it works

In Part 2 we explore how the three big themes of *Living Leadership* – get connected, get real and know yourself – work when you are faced by the day-to-day challenges of leading. Apparently simple, these themes have dramatic implications.

The challenges that we examine are those that managers and leaders across Europe have identified in the course of our research. They are:

- **chapter 8 – bosses:** how to negotiate expectations that are realistic
- **chapter 9 – self:** how to be in good enough shape to lead others
- **chapter 10 – people:** how to select, and engage with, the people around you
- **chapter 11 – groups:** how to manage the dynamics of groups

- **chapter 12 – strategy:** how to set direction
- **chapter 13 – change:** how to encourage others to take responsibility
- **chapter 14 – development:** how to learn to be a better leader.

In each chapter we offer:

1 a way to address the challenge

2 stories of how leaders have worked with the challenge

3 suggestions about what you can do.

We do not pretend to offer a tool kit that will deal with all situations. That would be crazy. For us, leadership is a living experiment. As we stated earlier, there is no precise formula that will tell you in advance what to do in a particular situation, but we have outlined choices that exist in every leadership situation. Check what choices you are making and think about the impact on others and on the job you have to do. We encourage you to look to your own resources, to remember what you have learnt and what you know from all your experience of life, in order to adapt to the needs that emerge in the moment between you, others and the context.

The stories that we tell in the following chapters are slices of corporate life as they actually unfolded. They are not studies of excellence nor do they provide models to follow. They are the stories of competent managers and leaders in respected organisations across Europe. We hope that you will be encouraged by the stories and that they will confirm some of your own experience which, in turn, will give you confidence to trust your instincts more when you lead. We anticipate that you will also, on the basis of your experience, see and hear different things in the stories from those we have in mind. For us, that's great. Telling and reworking the stories is an age-old way of communicating meaning that is richer and more complex than that of any simple text.

Bosses

Manage expectations

One British manager put it to us, "We need top management to stop giving us more and more bloody jobs, on more and more bloody projects".

The first challenge that we explore is the one mentioned most often by managers and leaders we worked with in our research. How do you deal with bosses that set unrealistic expectations? When you are overloaded and your boss says, "Here's another project for you", how do you respond? When people ask you to transform your organisation, and do it by next Tuesday, what do you say?

A central job that leaders do is to manage the bosses. However high a leader is in the hierarchy, there is someone who sits above. For a chief executive it is shareholders or trustees. For senior managers it is the chief executive or main board directors. For politicians it is the voters. But always, in the end, there are the boss(es) – usually plural – to whom a leader is accountable and from whom he must take direction. And those bosses are themselves responsible to others in the long chain of accountability.

We saw often in our research that the bosses, seen from below, seemed like Greek gods – always wilful and capricious, sometimes benevolent and supportive, usually demanding and occasionally violent and cruel. The gods had their favourites and could be kind but they often did not return the loyalty of uncritical servants and

Appeasing the gods can be dangerous

threw them over with little restraint once their own welfare was in question.

The leaders had to interpret the Greek gods and find out their wishes. It was up to the leaders to identify from all the speeches, PowerPoint presentations or focus groups: what are the essentials that have to be delivered – without which I will lose my job? What is the meaning of the statements, actions and behaviours of the bosses? How can the concepts of grand strategy at the corporate level be translated into objectives and plans locally?

What we experienced in this area was quite shocking when compared to the textbook claims made over 30 years about management by objectives. The idea that leaders were set clear, coherent goals, which lasted for some time, was a myth. The identification of objectives was a continuing work. There was rarely a blinding flash of light when leaders could say, "Ah, I've got it – that's what we are expected to deliver." They had to go on struggling to negotiate and renegotiate expectations. There was no point complaining about this. It was a fact of organisational life.

It seemed to us that this lack of clear mandate was not due to a lack of competence on the part of the leaders' bosses, or that the leaders failed to do enough to interpret what their objectives should be. In our view, the lack of clarity was inherent in the situations tackled by the leaders and their bosses. Given the swirling mists of uncertainty surrounding the companies, the markets and the environments in which they operated, detailed objectives could only be clear for a moment. Then the mist would descend again, and people would stumble forward, having a general sense of the direction they wanted to go and trying to find occasional landmarks or signposts to guide their way.

The underlying task for leaders as they stumbled forward was to promise enough of what the gods cared most about – to keep them happy – while leaving enough time and resources to do what leaders and others felt was truly important locally.

We also noticed that successful leaders managed progressively – over months and even years – a "healthy disillusionment" of bringing targets and objectives out of the stratosphere and down to ones that could be delivered. They let go of initial dreams of transformation and adjusted to the more complex realities that emerged as they worked.

> successful leaders managed a "healthy disillusionment" of bringing targets and objectives out of the stratosphere and down to ones that could be delivered

A potential trap for leaders was getting too close to their bosses. In our research we found a preoccupation with managing upwards. At a time when there is constant organisational upheaval, when roles and responsibilities are often unclear and when leaders are asked to move mountains, it was not surprising that often the first concern of many leaders was to secure the good opinion of those above them in the hierarchy. In part this was a rational strategy – to hang on to the centre of power when all else seemed unreliable.

At times, however, the leaders became so focused on their bosses that they lost (or never made) their connection to the people around them – on whom they depended for delivery. The leaders identified themselves emotionally with the "top teams" and deprived themselves of the chance to engage fully with the people around them. Their executive groups were encouraged to lean back and leave all the responsibility with the leaders. Then the leaders couldn't deliver.

Overidentification with the bosses was damaging for the leaders themselves. In public some leaders made the case for objectives and plans passed down by the bosses while in private feeling that they were not realistic. They punished themselves for the failure to live up to the wishes of the bosses and felt bad about the split between their private and public selves.

Even more dangerous were the instances where leaders lost touch with reality and deluded themselves about what was possible. In several cases we saw that the leaders' demons caused them to swallow impossible dreams set by the bosses. They got trapped into promising the impossible. Sometimes this was linked to the leaders' sense of personal obligation – of "debt" – to the top managers who had appointed them. It felt disloyal or dangerous to question too much the visions or targets set.

Critical therefore to the effective leaders' success was an ability to hold some distance with regard to both the gods' and their own demons. Some scepticism and a thinking space – time and people to think with – was essential.

Our advice to leaders is: don't be a victim. By accepting the leadership role, you have taken on the job of adapting the targets to reality. Yes, you need to look after your bosses; but look after yourself and your people too. If you look only to your bosses, you will be deprived of the support from people around you that you need for delivery. As we said in Chapter 3, you are *in the middle*. Look both ways. Beware the illusion that attaching yourself to those who have power makes you safe. It can also destroy you.

> beware the illusion that attaching yourself to those who have power makes you safe: it can also destroy you

Pushing back with success

Our first story shows how a leader can take expectations management into her own hands.

Diane was the new boss of the French subsidiary of a US consumer products company. In her forties, charming, approachable, she came across as dynamic, and full of vitality. She was taking over what seemed to be a profitable company run by a competent management team. The initial mandate given to her by the European headquarters in Holland was to implement the company's new strategic orientation: a shift towards global product lines and away from local brands. This meant less power for the country managers and more for the international product line managers. She was asked to bring the processes of the company into line with those of the international organisation, recruit the right people to fill the vacancies in the organisation and maintain the financial results.

Headquarters had decided to put in place someone very different from Alain, the previous boss, who was much more a traditional French "patron". Alain had been a charismatic leader, an excellent communicator, someone who was close to his staff, but who could also be quite hard and showed his anger when the figures didn't meet objectives. According to one manager, "He is a man with real human qualities. When he decides to be with you, he can be really close, he is great with relationships and is capable of turning around a difficult situation. But he is focused on short-term profit. He is more a figures man than a process leader. But everyone supported him." He was considered particularly good with the sales staff, who appreciated his "leadership from the heart". However, he also had a confrontational relationship with the European headquarters and didn't give people much scope to manage in their own way. One person commented, "The whole organisation is impregnated with his personality and with a French ethos. He has developed a very strong culture here, notably the fear of the Dutch [bosses]."

This time, headquarters wanted someone with an international profile. Diane was French but had lived most of her life outside France. They were happy to have a woman to give a strong signal about the

▶

company's equal opportunities policy. Diane had a strong marketing background and was seen as a capable strategic thinker. She was also perceived as a strong and determined personality. The minus side was her lack of general management experience and her limited knowledge of the French retail business.

Perhaps surprisingly, most senior managers in the French company were prepared to see the change of leader as a positive move. Times had changed, they said. Alain, the previous leader, no longer had the support of the big bosses. He had been an effective salesman and business winner but he was not prepared to integrate the French company into the international company. People generally had positive expectations of Diane based on what they knew of her profile. She seemed to be a capable woman, with a strong international background and previous experience in a highly respected company.

At the same time Diane was conscious of the risk that she would be seen as the servant of the Dutch senior managers – imposing inappropriate products and processes on a successful French business. Diane spoke Dutch and had lived in Holland. Under her predecessor the relationship between the French unit and headquarters had been quite confrontational. There were lots of stories about the sessions in the Netherlands at which members of the French management team presented annual budgets and plans. French managers described themselves as "lambs going to the slaughter".

Diane's start with the French company was not auspicious. The handover from Alain was described as "a flop". The change of MD was announced in July, but with the holidays in August, Diane was not really seen in the company before September. The announcement of the change of leader was "weak" and it did not make much of an impact as people were busy ending the fiscal year, and some were away for the summer holidays. What is more, the whole company moved location during the summer. This move caused substantial disruption and reduced the impact of Diane's arrival.

From her first days with the company, however, Diane made very good first impressions. The managers who reported to her commented that she was "easy going", had a "strong character", is "courageous, decisive, warm and friendly" and "a woman of temperament, frank". They also remarked on her listening capacity, which enabled her to get a good understanding of her new environment. She was considered straightforward, efficient, with an "American style". Already people could feel she would bring something new: "She is active and rigorous, you can feel things are moving." People appreciated Diane's non-hierarchical, consultative style, considered more typical of American or Anglo-Saxon management. She appeared to be bringing about a real cultural revolution in the management of the company. For example, she changed the tone of relationships by using the informal "tu", instead of the "vous" that her predecessor had used. Though she did not seem at ease at large events, people warmed to her.

Most importantly, she involved and informed people in a way that her predecessor had not. According to one person, "Before, it was top down ... She started by looking at our situation, she asked people to take another look at their hypotheses, saying that she would present the results to the Group. It's a revolutionary change in our way of functioning ... People underneath perceive the new way of working, they have understood that business can be done differently. She actively sought out people's ideas on how to improve the organisation." "She asked me to make proposals based on how I would like things to work," said another manager.

Diane was also appreciated at headquarters: "She is very good, she defends her case and her people. She is open and straightforward, she says what she thinks of people and situations, and a problem is called a problem and not hidden. She is working to solve things in a structured manner. There is, of course, a natural fight (with headquarters): we cannot 'let the boat sink too much'." Another view was, "She is taking a lot of pressure, but handling it very maturely, learning very fast, even though struggling at times. She has proved she is the right person, a good turnaround person. She has argued the issues very well. She empowers people."

Meanwhile the business situation was deteriorating. The fragility of the company started to manifest itself during the last six months of Alain's time and a number of severe problems coincided with Diane's arrival: the departure of half of the marketing team, problems with supply leading to customer financial penalties, a drop in profits. According to some people, there was a form of blindness among the unit's managers about the underlying weaknesses. The headquarters too may have been unaware of the whole situation when they first described the company to Diane. The strained relationship between the Dutch directors and the French managers must have made it difficult to have any open discussions about the deteriorating business.

The financial objectives had been so high in the past that people wondered whether Diane would have the strength to bring them down, in order to take account of the difficult situation that had emerged. They wondered particularly whether she would be able to resist the pressure from headquarters, which had taken on almost mythical proportions in local perceptions, better than Alain had done in the past.

Diane herself feared that staff would associate her arrival with the numerous failings that occurred in the company at the same time. What made matters worse was that she also had to make the manager for a major product line redundant one month after her arrival. The decision had been made by her predecessor but was left to her to implement.

We sensed that there was a lot of anxiety around as Diane grappled with the business problems and the need to rebuild the business plan at the same time as she experienced feelings of uncertainty about her capacity to succeed in a role she had never had before. However, she never seemed highly stressed or overwhelmed. She managed to find ways of soliciting the help of others, asking advice of her peers in other subsidiaries and working in small task forces to undertake one task at a time. Whenever she felt close to being overwhelmed, she resorted to a technique of writing things down and working out priorities.

Diane was careful to preserve her family life, which she saw as a crucial means to find relaxation and renewed energy. Diane drew strict boundaries around her personal life. She made clear that she would not work on evenings and at weekends. She would work hard, but within ordinary working hours. She would take her full holiday entitlement. She limited her personal engagement with the people around her to what was manageable for her. Charming and full of life, she nevertheless also communicated a sense that she was "passing through", someone who would spend two or three years in the post and then move on. This sense of transience suited her. It was how she was used to living her life, always moving from one job and one country to another. She was playing a role she knew well. Whatever the strains and stresses of the business and the people she worked with, she was at ease in this role.

Despite the pressure to make quick decisions, Diane resolved not to do so until she had understood the situation better. She seemed to set up in her mind two levels of intervention: the first were priorities and/or basic interventions; the second were longer-term projects, such as major organisational changes. Diane's capacity to filter out unnecessary detail and to set priorities for her actions appears to have been crucial to her success. Her approach, based mainly on face-to-face relationships and management by small projects, apparently enabled her to create a clear map of the situation. She was able to reduce the context to a small enough scope to be understood.

Diane seemed to have an intuitive sense of the phasing of organisational change. She had a clear idea of how long she would need to complete the learning about the new organisation and business: she considered she required about six months to become knowledgeable and to judge whether she had any real chance of success. Given that financial results were expected after 18 months, Diane wanted to have achieved turnaround in that time, and then to use the rest of her three-year term for stabilising things.

Perhaps the most impressive short-term achievement, in the eyes of the local staff, was Diane's intervention at headquarters to reduce the financial objectives for 2001. Despite the Dutch directors' reputation for toughness, the European president showed himself open to the arguments put forward by Diane to justify the reduction of the budget. "I agreed to her proposal to halve the objectives as she made a proper analysis of the situation and was capable of explaining it to me. With hindsight, the plan for this year was too ambitious, given that the bases were not there and the results were inflated last year. Also, when you start doing things differently you have to expect a drop in results temporarily." His support may have been because he was relatively new to the Division and had a more long-term, process-oriented approach to business than his predecessor. Diane may also have benefited from greater leniency due to her recent arrival.

Given the history of submission to ambitious annual objectives imposed by the Group, staff in the French company wondered how she managed it. It was crucial to establishing her legitimacy in the local company. Many considered it a first and essential step to allow for recovery: lower the figures so that the company could reach its targets and thereby gain credibility, while allowing the company a pause during which the organisation and its processes could be stabilised and strengthened.

Diane was effective at getting the HQ on her side and developing a more trusting relationship, adroitly exploiting her knowledge of the Dutch language and culture. She consulted them repeatedly on her organisation design, flagged up difficulties with financial results at an early stage, and used her direct link to the Divisional president to seek advice about how to prepare for the financial review meetings. In that way, not only was she transparent, but she was also able to seek out further clues as to what was expected of her. She had the courage of her convictions and at each stage negotiated rather than accepted the terms or requirements expressed by headquarters.

It was a courageous approach by Diane. We were amazed, as you may be, by the headquarters' willingness to halve the financial objectives in the first year. Such a shift in expectations is not always possible. The context was very important, as was the skill Diane showed in using the cards that she had in her hand. She was confident about her own boundaries, well connected to the bosses and (in the promise to bring the French business into the fold) had something important to offer to them, other than the year's results.

JOHN'S STORY

The long-term play

The first puzzle that John, the head of the Internet unit, faced was to clarify the mandate the main board had given him. The mandate was "fuzzy": "Recruit some people, and with the backing of the Atlas divisions, go test if there is a viable Net business." John was aware that the mission he had been given was a compromise between one director's enthusiasm and other directors' caution. He could not be sure how the debate among the directors would develop: who might shift their view or which side might gain the upper hand.

Part of the initial mandate for Netco was to be a "thought leader", trying to work out an approach and decide how to "drag the Atlas divisions forward". However, John was criticised by colleagues for spending too much time on research and planning in the early days. Some felt that John was long on ideas but short on delivery.

In October 2000, six months into the life of Netco, John presented to the board. It was what he called the "low point" in the life of Netco. John presented his thinking and plans so far and got a firm rap on the knuckles. "You are trying to do too much, be too ambitious!" he was told. "Select a few priority areas and make them happen." The idea of waiting till divisions of Atlas were ready to make Net investments was dropped. Netco should go ahead by itself – setting up new ventures – and seek to mobilise the divisions by example.

Clarifying the mandate

Much of the strategy emerged as Netco bumped up against real problems. A key debate was about the pay structure for the people coming into Netco. About half the managers in Netco were recruited from Internet companies; the other half were from Atlas. The two groups had different expectations. The externals were used to share options and other forms of profit share. The internals were familiar with salaries and discretionary bonuses. John and his HR manager decided that to be competitive for high-quality Net people, Netco needed to offer a percentage of the value created in the business. This was very contentious. The Atlas board had fought shy of giving employees a direct share in value-added. Nevertheless, eventually, the board accepted the idea as the price of participation in Net business.

"I was astonished that the board of a large corporation should find time at several meetings to discuss the remuneration of managers in a small unit," said the HR manager. "However what came out of the debate for us was very positive. For the first time everyone in Netco had an agreed and shared objective – to create value by the end of 2003. It gave us a focus and a sense of real urgency."

All Netco staff were given a share in the one scheme. For some members of the team, this was a crucial step in focusing staff on one shared objective. However, it did not end the debate about objectives.

"I did get frustrated with the main board director I reported to," said John. "He operated at the level of big concepts – 'we need to do something about the Net' – or operational detail – 'why isn't this or that happening'. He didn't engage with all the stuff in the middle." He didn't help John with the all-important thinking about how to translate broad objectives into results.

"Eddie was only intermittently engaged with us," John said. He had many other divisions for which he was responsible and could only give Netco a small part of his time. John complained about the difficulty of getting access to Eddie and of finding enough time to talk issues through with him. "He could be motivational but at other times he slumped back and seemed depressed. I began to feel there was no point transmitting my problems to Eddie. He didn't have time to help. He was in reactive mode [to pressures from above]. I could not predict where he would be on a particular issue. This uncertainty slowed down the building of Netco."

A "narrow ledge"?

Netco was tasked with creating value for Atlas – and in businesses that were "strategically relevant" to Atlas. But how could managers tell what this meant? It all depended, according to one team member, on your sense of what the main board directors would see as strategically relevant at the end of 2003. There were bound to be shifts and turns in the interpretation of strategic relevance all the time up to the end of 2003.

Even when plans were agreed with the board, there were different interpretations of the strategic intent. Some in the team emphasised that Atlas businesses should be different from Atlas's current ones. For example, one of the key projects was to create a business to aid the learning of individuals in Africa. At other times, team members stressed the need to create businesses that the Atlas divisions would relate to and understand.

John came to the view that the mandate Netco had been given was defective. "It contained some wishful thinking about how Atlas operates," he said. "Netco could only be successful with the cooperation of the Atlas operating divisions. However, access to the divisions was not sorted out. Netco was too small to negotiate over such a broad front as all the operating divisions." He added: "I realised with a shock about nine months into the life of Netco that we were no better positioned than operating divisions to address Internet opportunities in their areas. The operating divisions had a solid base of understanding, networks and customers to work from. Though we were new to everything, we gradually learnt. They had part of the puzzle. We had another part. The challenge was how to put them together."

"There was another strategic challenge," John went on. "The fact that Atlas had 'deep pockets' created limits as well as opportunities. We could not afford to expose Atlas to possible litigation." Atlas could become a target for litigation for some companies it might deal with. "Some areas that might have been attractive for a company without a rich parent were off limits for Netco," said John. "This was very puzzling for some of our people. In the end what we did had to be aligned with the needs of Atlas. We were operating on a 'narrow ledge', just beyond the scope of the current Atlas businesses," he said. Just what constituted this "narrow ledge" was not always easy to see.

Netco begins to take shape

Behind the constant and exhausting whirl of activity, one year after John started work on Netco an organisation and business was starting to emerge. The many disparate projects that Netco was involved in were grouped together in three sections: Consumer, Business and Venture Capital. The teams working on Consumer and Venture Capital were felt to be working well together. A number of projects had been set up and some were beginning to show results.

Repeated judgement days

When the dotcom crash came in spring 2001, it was at first, paradoxically, good news. It meant the unit could recruit good people who had until then been locked in to other companies by the steeply increasing value of their share options. Instead of huge amounts of money chasing any halfway plausible business ideas, the world became more rational. Netco, with the resources of Atlas behind it, became, relatively, a more attractive business partner and investor.

Gradually, however, during 2001 the mood changed. Main board directors were asked questions by non-executive directors about the direction of the company and its new businesses. Analysts asked if its Net activities were a "hobby business". The telecom bubble burst.

▶

Marconi came near to bankruptcy. September 11 shocked the world. Then came Enron's collapse. Now the pressure from outside was to retrench, to cut costs and to focus on the core. Was time over for Netco – just when it was beginning to be effective?

The impact of these changes in the outside world was initially muffled within Netco by the focus on making progress on agreed plans and projects and the mass of activity. The changes eventually made their presence felt through the Atlas planning process. In the late summer and autumn of 2001 and the winter of 2001/2002 there was hardly a moment when the future and direction of Netco were not in question. There were three reworkings of the Netco scope and direction as strategy, business plans and budgets were agreed. A new director took responsibility for Netco and Eddie moved to another role. The new boss, under pressure from the non-executive directors and conscious of the "contracting Zeitgeist" (as John called it) asked for another fundamental review of Netco. Each time there had been hope that would bring stability for a while and each time that hope had been disappointed. John said about the latest examination of purpose and direction that: "We are involved in another rethink before the ink is dry on the last plan."

We saw John come alive when working out how to handle the Atlas system. It could be depressing – as when recently formulated plans were pushed to one side and another review requested. Nevertheless, John often gave us the sense that he liked the game of move and countermove. Once, when we met him, he said: "The situation has become deliciously complicated."

John seemed to pride himself on his knowledge and understanding of the Atlas world. At one board meeting, at the end of a satisfactory strategic review, one director said: "Well of course, any spending on Netco is discretionary." That one word, from a powerful director, spoke volumes for John. It signalled that Netco's future was hanging by a thread, that the key political sponsorship of Netco was no longer there. It was imperative to take the initiative, to offer a revised, slimmed down Netco, responsive to the "contracting Zeitgeist".

Closing down and moving on

In June 2002 the decision was announced to close down Netco. The main board director who had pushed for Netco's creation moved to another role. The board had finally concluded that Netco had done its work and that in the much more difficult business climate then prevailing Atlas could not afford to devote valuable managers and resources to an experiment separate from its core business.

John supported the board's decision. His last presentation to the board had been: "Expand us or dismantle us". The board accepted that this was the choice and opted for closure. The "salami cuts", slimming down Netco, could continue no further. Netco could not survive, John said, "... once the decision was made not to let the narrow ledge become wider".

The successful parts of Netco that had developed in partnership with business divisions were moved out to those divisions. Many of the Netco staff were found jobs elsewhere in Atlas. John himself was given a more senior job at corporate HQ. The unit was wound down slowly in order to maximise the prospects for the continuing businesses and the chances of Netco staff finding jobs in Atlas.

An insider, who had worked for the corporation for many years, John played his role with great skill. He seemed to revel in the complex chess game of working out what the intentions of his bosses were. He was alert to the weaker signals and ready to respond instantly to a hint or change in tone from one of the main board directors. The game was exciting, the culture was his, he had grown up in it and understood it intimately. We cannot imagine an outsider, a turnaround or Internet expert, being able to cope with staying in the e-commerce world while also understanding and protecting the parent company.

John had an acute sense of the possible – how far he could go in teasing out a clear message from his bosses, how the message was changing as the context changed, what he could and could not do. He was supremely good at holding the tension between the conflicting cultures of the parent company and the Internet world – but it stretched him to the limit. There seemed to be little mental capacity left to deal with the demands of the group for a meaningful share in the strategic process.

▶

In the end our reflection was that the corporation acted intelligently in placing one of its own in charge of Netco. John was there to ensure that the interests of the corporation were protected. He was a safe pair of hands who could be trusted to represent Atlas on a dangerous voyage of exploration and bring the ship safely home.

RANESH'S STORY

A leader protecting his people to allow them to get on with "the real work"

Ranesh, the director of Environmental Services in a large local authority, was faced with a dilemma. An engineer with high standards and an instinctive focus on the needs and wishes of local residents, he was, nevertheless, sceptical of the quality programme that he was asked by his bosses, the local politicians, to put in place. He liked the idea of a systematic approach to quality but he worried about imposing a quality bureaucracy that seemed to be separate from the people delivering the service.

How could he deliver the day-to-day service that residents wanted at the same time as completing all the paperwork needed for this new quality assurance programme? How could he avoid overburdening staff? "We mustn't lose sight of the need to keep filling in the potholes while we develop a quality system," he said.

After discussion with people inside and outside the Council, Ranesh decided to appoint a consultant to prepare the quality documentation. The consultants would prepare the required paperwork with the help of a link person from each service team. That would leave the operational managers free to go on managing the service.

The approach worked and gave the department kudos. They had got their act together faster than other departments of the Council. The politicians were delighted to see a large department win the quality badge quickly. Everyone was pleased that Ranesh had kept the service running to high standards.

It seems to us that leaders are often called on to do deals with "the system" or with the bosses. They have to meet some expectation or fulfil a goal which is not essential in their minds – while protecting their people and giving them time and space to get on with what they feel is most important. Ranesh did it unusually openly – prioritising operations over the latest "flavour of the month" initiative from his bosses. Do you face a similar dilemma? Could you do what your bosses need, while allowing space for "the real work"?

Negotiating realistic expectations

When discussing our experience with many different groups across Europe, people have sometimes said to us: "What you say makes sense but leaders have to live in a world where they are expected to transform organisations. The financial markets expect it of chief executives. If you don't offer transformation, you won't get – or keep – your job."

The same can be said of leaders in many places, at many levels. They are caught up in promising transformations that they (or some part of them) do not quite believe in. Chief executives promise transformations to investment fund managers. Senior managers promise them to chief executives. Front line managers promise them to top managers. And investment fund managers promise them to their customers. In the public sector, politicians promise transformations to voters and civil servants and senior managers promise them to ministers. The cycle of commitment and pretence seems unbreakable.

So how can leaders deal with the pressure of inflated expectations and ever-shortening time-scales to produce results?

What you can do

Allow yourself an "inner review"

It's important to make time and space from time to time and reflect:

▌ What is do-able?

▌ How does that compare with the objectives and targets?

▌ How might my "inner demons" lead me to agree to expectations that are unrealistic?

▌ How can I begin to chart a course between the expectations set by bosses and what I feel in my heart can be achieved?

▌ What will I do if the expectations do not become realistic?

You have to believe there is "life after death" – that this job is not the only possibility and that there is potential for you if this job does not work out. Otherwise you risk losing your critical faculties and being seduced into accepting crazy expectations. As one leader in a health organisation said to us: "When the frustrations get too great I say to myself: 'If all else fails, I can always go back to being a doctor.' That way I keep my sense of proportion about the issues."

Get support

Try to talk through what is realistic and how to go about modifying expectations.

Effective leaders are constantly sounding people out and testing what can be achieved and what can't. It's unlikely that you will be able to form a clear picture without reviewing the issues with some confidants.

Consider:

▌ What is challengeable?

▌ What is not challengeable?

▌ How could I take the initiative and begin to shape more realistic expectations?

Consider how to change expectations. It is often a group event – you don't have to do this on your own.

▌ What can I best work on privately?

▌ What should I work on with my team?

▌ What should I work on that involves different levels and parts of the system that requires alliance building?

▌ When is the best time to influence key expectations – now or later?

Have a dialogue with your bosses about what is realistic

If you challenge your boss, just as John and Diane did, then over a period – sometimes months or years – you can help to reshape expectations. Confronting the boss can be a dangerous game. Often the boss has to be seen to pressurise you and you have to be seen to be going along with it. He needs time to let go of dream-like targets; so does your team. However, making smart challenges will give respect at top and bottom and increase your chance of survival. The bosses will never respect you fully unless they experience you as more than their servant. Paradoxically, the bosses will respect you more if you stand up for yourself. Asserting your own authority within the hierarchy will also motivate your executive team to work for you.

> making smart challenges will give respect at top and bottom and increase your chance of survival

Consider:

▌ How could I initiate the process of managing expectations?

▌ What are the issues we could handle now?

Don't start with the huge issues. Start with something you and the bosses can handle, topics that you believe will leave you both in a better place.

Play the long game

Throwing yourself against the bosses does not work. It takes time. Get some support around you. Let the boss hear the issues from others.

Be patient – wait for the moment when it feels right to challenge and shape expectations.

Consider:

▍ When are there opportunities in the process to modify expectations?

▍ Could I gain "first mover advantage" by being the first to challenge something that others do not agree with but are reluctant to confront?

Invite challenge in your group!

This is how you practise receiving challenge. Learn how to frame challenge by seeing what you think and how you feel when others challenge you.

Ask yourself:

▍ How and when can I invite challenge from others that will be credible – and useful to me?

Self

Practise "healthy selfishness"

We shall not cease from exploration
And the end of all our exploring
Will be to arrive where we started
And know the place for the first time

T.S. Eliot, "Little Gidding", *The Waste Land*, 1922

One of the strongest findings of the research was that leaders need to look to their own needs if they are to survive and be effective. Leaders are most effective when they come alive, when they remember what they know from their experience of life, and when they can use all their faculties and senses. That requires them to look after themselves. The question leaders need to keep in mind is: *how am I going to lead others if I am not in good enough shape myself?*

Paying attention to your own needs is a prerequisite of effectiveness, not (as it is sometimes presented) a slightly self-indulgent whim. Unless leaders can gain some distance from the inevitable anxieties and confusion that come with a leadership role, they will not be able to act wisely or see what makes sense for them, for the groups around them and for the wider organisation.

In the current organisational world there are more and more pressures on leaders and managers to speed up and lose sight of themselves and what they really want. The endless e-mails, the

Putting your heart into holding yourself together

insistent mobile phone calls, the incessant travelling add to the "chop, chop, busy, busy" pattern of working lives. When do you have the chance to stop and think? How do you maintain your sense of self, who you are and what you most want? How do you keep yourself intact against the pressures from bosses, colleagues and outsiders?

The term "healthy selfishness" comes from Luc Vandevelde, the Belgian former chairman of Marks & Spencer. He described the importance of looking after number one, which he discovered as key to good leadership. He encouraged his managers to adopt the same practice. For example, when as boss of the company, he went to visit a store in one city it was natural that managers in other stores in that city would also want him to visit. They felt left out if he did not go to their stores. Vandevelde told them firmly he couldn't visit all the stores in a particular city. If he was going to do a good job, understanding customer preferences and staff feelings *and* conserve his own energy, he needed to focus on just one store. The disappointment of other managers at not being recognised by a visit from the boss was something they must manage, not something he could take on, if he was to look after his own needs.

By healthy selfishness we mean:

▌ identifying your personal boundaries – on issues like the hours you are prepared to work – and sticking to them;

▌ knowing your limits – what expectations you can reasonably take on and what you can't;

▌ ensuring the necessary personal support at work – resources like an effective personal assistant and other support staff;

▌ paying attention to your feelings and allowing yourself to see them as useful data on what's happening;

▌ not being afraid to offend people when it's necessary;

▌ having people to talk to honestly and openly about the issues that most concern you and taking time to work out what you want for you and for your people;

▌ developing "thinking spaces" – places where you can stop and reflect on what's working and what's not working so well, express your feelings, without damaging key working relationships, and identify how to move forward.

We saw the difficulty for leaders in finding space and time to think. When there are always a hundred e-mails to respond to, a mobile phone ringing and another flight to catch or car journey to complete, what chance is there that you slow down long enough to think? To ask questions like, "What am I trying to achieve?" "What is most important for me?" "How can I do more of what I want?" "Are my actions having the impact that I want?" "How do I keep myself intact?" More and more, the immediate and tactical and responsive has squeezed out the long-term, strategic and creative.

As Pedler, Burgoyne and Boydell say in *A Manager's Guide to Leadership*: "Leadership is a deeply personal matter; you can only influence and offer it when you believe in what you are doing. What is it that you want for yourself and your people? What you can offer depends upon who you are, what is important to you, how you see the world and how well you can learn."[1]

1 M. Pedler, J. Burgoyne and M. Boydell, *A Manager's Guide to Leadership*, McGraw-Hill Publishing Co., 2004.

Stage fright is normal – as is needing help

We found many leaders rushing on, reluctant to step back and consider these questions. They were slow to give their own needs sufficient priority. The rhetorical question was, "Isn't it the business of a leader to be strong, to look after others?" Acknowledgement of their own needs could seem a sign of weakness or self-indulgence when there were so many organisational priorities needing attention.

We often saw this reluctance of leaders to put their needs first. Being a leader is tough in current circumstances and made doubly difficult if the leader feels unable to ask for help. In our minds it is related to their demons – the need of leaders to take on leadership roles in order to "fix something" within themselves. Sometimes the sense of inadequacy that drives leaders to want to achieve more and more leads to a tendency to blame themselves when things go wrong. These are familiar patterns in leaders. They can make it difficult for the leaders to acknowledge to themselves, let alone others, that they have pressing personal needs. There may be a fear that if they admit some needs, the whole edifice of self-esteem will crumble and nothing will be left. Better perhaps to admit nothing and carry on regardless, lest those upon whom you depend expose you as the fraud you sometimes believe yourself to be.

Leadership does not have to be lonely

It has often been said that leadership is a lonely activity. Who can you talk to about the things that concern you most? Questions like: "Who can I trust?" "How should I handle my boss?" "Should I be doing this job at all?" Often leaders feel they cannot discuss these questions with those closest to them. They may not be able to talk to colleagues because the colleagues are the subject of their concerns. They may not be able to talk to their bosses because they don't feel the necessary closeness or trust. They may not be able to talk to spouses because their partners won't understand the context. In the absence of people to talk to openly, a pressure cooker can build up. More and more worries, more and more anxieties – some of which, at least, could be relieved if only the leader had someone to talk to openly.

We were made aware of this pressure cooker as we undertook the research. We offered an outside ear and we often became the recipient of leaders' confidences. In this context we think of one leader who was always madly busy. Getting in to see him was a struggle and there were sometimes people queuing at his door in the hope of a discussion. Yet several times, once we got to see him for a "quick 20-minute discussion", the floodgates opened. A few open questions like "How are you?" or "What's the latest news?" led to an outpouring on a range of topics. More than once, it was we researchers who, after an hour and a half, said that we had to leave because of other commitments.

In our minds there is a choice for leaders. The loneliness of leaders is not an act of God. It is associated with the transformational hero idea – the notion that the leaders stand apart and seek to work on their organisations as an object. If, on the other hand, leaders let go of the transformational hero idea, they see that they do not have to be distant from the people they work with. If they can see themselves as *in the middle*, they can begin to see the resources that are available to them from the people around them and other colleagues in the organisation. If they do *get connected* the burden of loneliness is much lighter. Leaders can begin to tackle some of the issues that exercise them most with their colleagues – and not bottle them up or take them to secret places like outside coaches or friends.

We suggest that leaders find ways of discussing things with others (both within and outside their team) on a regular basis. "A bit at a time when it feels right" is more helpful than allowing things to fester. Naming the issues, describing how it makes you feel, acknowledging the limits, are all helpful steps. This is not a complicated process but it is very difficult to do alone. Leaders need to initiate relationships that allow the process to start.

From self-help to mutual help

For each leader there is a balance between what they can bear alone and what they can only bear with a trusted confidant. Having the courage to ask for help widens what a leader can bear and what they are able to contemplate as a task for themselves and their teams. Tom Gilmore offers the "paradoxical advice that leaders – even as they feel beleaguered, torn apart and overloaded – need to stay open, take in more intelligence or more relationships until there starts to be some larger gestalt that makes sense of all of the information".[2] Allowing yourself to depend on, to trust another, enables you to bear much more.

The alternative is to be unselfish – and not ask for help. Paradoxically that exposes leaders to what they fear. The unselfish end up lonely and open to attack.

Self-care comes from connecting with others

We encourage leaders to give themselves permission to look after themselves and to do so *with* others – to live out their own social natures. We suggest you sometimes ask for help from those around you. This will help you to connect with others and find a shared meaning in all the apparent chaos. Having a good experience with this will demonstrate that asking for help is a strength, not a weakness.

2 T. Gilmore, "Leaders as middles", unpublished paper, Center for Applied Research, Philadelphia, June 1997.

And, as we all know, caring for your self is a work in progress. You never arrive. What matters is the quality of the search – which is associated with the confidence to tolerate the uncertainty of not knowing what the whole answer is – not knowing for certain what will enable you to stay in good enough shape to lead.

> allowing yourself to depend on, to trust another, enables you to bear much more

The act of leadership is to be selfish enough to ask for help, to connect and thereby set a model for others in your team to do the same. Pick up the phone when you're stuck.

Putting your own needs first

A leader had recently arrived in a high-profile role. Her style was unassuming and direct but extraordinarily demanding and tenacious. She asked a lot of others and of herself. Her predecessor had been a charismatic leader, a loner skilled at working with senior stakeholders but who had neglected the internal organisation. The new leader found she had very little support from her immediate staff. The personal assistant she inherited was unresponsive and demotivated. There was no-one internally able to help her to prepare for discussions with investors or push forward strategy.

The new leader's tendency was to take care of those around her, to "mother" them. But who was going to look after her? In the early days she ended up working very long hours doing things her personal staff could have done for her. Despite many evening commitments she got into the habit of getting up at 5am every morning to read papers and prepare for that day's meetings. She did take a holiday at Christmas but said just three days after returning, "I feel as if I never went away".

A moment of truth happened when the leader allowed herself to put her own needs first. After much agonising, she sacked her personal assistant, arranged for a new one to be appointed quickly and negotiated the immediate loan of an experienced investor relations manager from a sister company. She described the assertion of her own needs as the "most difficult thing I have done". Yet it was also a turning point. The leader was pleasantly surprised to find that other

▶

staff strongly supported her decisions. With a new personal assistant, whom she respected and trusted, she was able to get through the work in half the time.

Becoming more aware of what drives you

We worked with Manfred, the German boss of a telecoms company in Belgium. He had a difficult relationship with his boss, the chief executive of the group of companies. The boss was his sponsor and had selected him for the job and continued to support him. In many ways they worked well together and Manfred played the part of "junior partner" to his boss's "senior partner" role. However, at times, Manfred found the pressures from his boss intolerable. The industry was going through a desperate period with competitors going bankrupt and an urgent need to slash costs. Manfred felt imposed on by his boss. There were more and more jobs, Manfred felt, that belonged to the boss, yet he ended up taking them on. If something did not change, Manfred was contemplating resigning from his job.

In discussion with an outsider, Manfred brought up his problematic early life. His mother had died when he was young. He had to live with his father who had until that time been a very distant figure – heroic and frightening. After the mother's death, the father continued to work long hours but from time to time tried hard to be more available for Manfred and the other children. The dual role proved too much for the father and he transferred some of the burden on to Manfred, who was the eldest son. Manfred got used to being sometimes the son, sometimes the brother and sometimes a mother and father substitute. He too, then, was overburdened but had learnt to live with it and cope with role complexity.

When Manfred became aware that he was repeating at work the pattern from his childhood, he stopped blaming the boss for all the difficulties and took on some of the responsibility himself. He decided that he didn't have to take on the jobs and roles that his boss left undone. He could begin to empathise with the weaknesses and foibles of his boss and not just attack him for them. He could sometimes seize moments for a "man to man" talk with his boss to renegotiate tasks between them and see what was in the overall interests of the company.

A leader who lost himself in trying to please others

Our next story concerns the newly appointed head of Supply Chain in a major European multinational.

Getting into the job ...

Pierre was a "high flyer" with a successful track record stretching back over more than 10 years with the company and its predecessors. On his appointment he became the youngest Senior Vice President in the company. He had come to the notice of top management by helping with the rationalisation and divestment of parts of the businesses that had been brought together in a recent merger. His task, he was told, as Head of Supply Chain, would be to break down the barriers that existed between three "silos" in the company: Sales and Marketing, Manufacturing and Research and Development.

Reactions to his appointment were mixed. A number of his peers and reports in Sales and Marketing were pleased. His new colleagues in Manufacturing were critical of his lack of industrial and supply chain experience – despite the fact that he had worked in distribution and general management in addition to his early financial roles. Some were openly hostile, "Jaws hit the ground in some places!" a Supply Chain team member told us. His old boss, in the Sales and Marketing division (who had been sure Pierre would not take the job in the Manufacturing division) felt "betrayed". It seemed that the company really was three organisations in one: a "minefield" of political relationships to be negotiated with extreme caution.

Into the lion's den

The Supply Chain team faced some major challenges. There were short-term challenges, of improving product availability and reducing costs, and longer-term challenges of creating a new Supply Chain model and bringing about major organisational change.

Pierre's overriding feeling, in his early months, was one of too little

▶

progress being made, too slowly. In his mind, a number of people in the supply chain team continued to block the development of a clear agenda for change. As a consequence of this, and because he felt the necessary expertise was just not available "in house", he decided to bring in outside consultants to launch a major project. "I could not afford to wait, I knew they were not the right people." This decision effectively to circumvent his team had two major consequences. As one of the team members said, "It allowed Pierre to wrest the initiative away from the people who were blocking him but it alienated other members of the Supply Chain team who felt ignored and excluded." This set a pattern of behaviour, which was to continue throughout his leadership, of Pierre taking decisions in a way that was fairly detached from his team.

Restructuring his team

After a few months in his role Pierre restructured his team, in line with the change in structure elsewhere in the Manufacturing division. A level of hierarchy was removed and the regional Supply Chain managers brought directly into his team. Some of the dissenting members of Pierre's group disappeared and he brought in some new recruits with significant supply chain experience, for example to lead the Stretch project. At this point Pierre felt he had managed to create a team with which he could work more effectively, with only two remaining members of the original team. Although it was now quite a large group, Pierre felt the level of direct contact would be beneficial in terms of communication, particularly given the scale of change that was needed in the overall Supply Chain organisation.

A high level of ambiguity

It became increasingly clear to Pierre that Supply Chain was not only central to the company's success but that his was also a politically sensitive position because of the number, and nature, of connections needed to succeed. He felt that part of the difficulty in achieving a significant change was that there was no shared Supply Chain "philosophy" at the highest levels of the company. All the top managers agreed it was critical; however, questions of where the balance of power should lie and what the measures of success should be, were not answered. For example, there were conflicting views about the importance of inventory levels – was it more important to have products available where they are needed or to have low inventory levels?

A review

Once this new team structure had been in place for a few months, a review involving most of the members of the team highlighted a number of key issues and concerns.

Many team members felt that the objectives of the team and individuals were not sufficiently shared and understood. This reflected the broader organisational context where no particularly clear definition was apparent. It was, however, also clear within the team that there were different views as to how much clarity and shared vision existed and was needed. Some managers were frustrated by the lack of "vision, which we can use to set our objectives, determine our priorities and organise our work".

Our impression was that Pierre was working hard building networks around the company to support the development and implementation of change, but that he had become somewhat removed from his own team. He was perceived to lead by setting objectives and demanding that people achieve them. He appeared to show little interest in discussing with people how they might work towards the objectives. Some team members said he was autocratic, seeking to impose his will by telling people what to do. The members of the team said it felt a bit "rudderless".

The discussion demonstrated the difference in views both within the team and across the broader organisation on key questions. The power and politics of the broader organisation were very much in evidence as people spoke. For example, the discussion around the title of a new role to be called a "site leader" or a "site co-ordinator" reflected the broader organisational power issues of reporting lines and authority. It was clear that to achieve the desired goal of "end-to-end product responsibility", which the Supply Chain group was aiming at, major change was required in parts of the organisation outside the responsibility of Pierre and his team.

▶

Dark clouds gathering

Nine months later pressure was continuing to build that would ultimately knock Pierre and his team off track. Although some (business) regions were very successful, the overall performance of the company continued to be under budget and forecast. At the top level the share price was too low, and dropping; and operational results were not as good as anticipated. Increasing pressure was filtering down through the organisation to improve short-term profitability with year-end targets in mind. The spotlight was turned fully on to inventory and very demanding targets were established for stock levels. In this context Pierre asked his team to let him have accurate, detailed information on current and predicted stock levels.

Early in September it was apparent that the issues around performance measurement were beginning to have serious implications. Some very senior managers (the Head of Manufacturing in particular) said they were unhappy with the Supply Chain management team's inability to provide sufficiently accurate data about inventory movement and throughput. This put Pierre under increasing pressure – causing him to revert to his autocratic style of leadership.

An organisational restructuring

In November, Pierre's boss told him that a "restructuring" of the Manufacturing division had been decided and that Pierre's job would effectively disappear.

The new structure gave the clarity of focus, and appropriate responsibilities to enable the changes Pierre and his team had been working on for the past 18 months. Ironically, Pierre had been consulted about this restructuring, but had been left jobless as a result. He supported the logic of the restructuring, but was unhappy with the way the new structure had been introduced and his own position not considered. He felt that he had done many things to prepare and support the new system, but would get no recognition for it. In short, he felt he had been abandoned after having done a good job in difficult circumstance for nearly two years. He said he felt like a manager who has effectively cut the branch on which they were sitting.

In our view, Pierre allowed himself to be caught in a very difficult political situation. He spent a lot of time trying to manage his bosses but because of the way the job was originally offered to him, lacked strong sponsorship from any of them which could protect him when results from his area were poor. His inner demon, his driving need for recognition, caused him to take a job that afterwards looked like a poisoned chalice. He became the "fall guy" and suspected later that he had been set up to fail by his boss who was determined to show that only Manufacturing should be allowed to control supply chain.

At the same time his failure to connect with his bosses mirrored his inability to connect with his team. The more time and effort he put into managing his bosses, in a treacherous political environment, the less time and space he had for the team on whom he depended for performance. They complained often about the difficulty of getting Pierre to slow down long enough to have a proper conversation with him. They felt imposed on by him. And when Pierre ran out of credit with his bosses, his team abandoned him. His inability to keep an eye on his own needs meant, in the end, that he only began to notice that he was isolated and disconnected, without help in fact, when it was too late and he had lost in the survival game. He failed to practise healthy selfishness; he had not realised that it often comes before caring for others and the company.

What you can do

Get the personal support that works for you

We encourage any leader – even before thinking of others or of their organisation – to give priority to securing the personal support that they need. It could be the key to your effectiveness. It may be practical support to help you get done the things that you have to do. It may be emotional support – to provide an outlet for all the pressures and feelings that come up at work, to work out what they are telling you and how you can respond. It may be help to think issues through.

> what practical and personal support is essential
> if I am to be effective as a leader?

Consider:

▌ What practical and personal support is essential if I am to be effective as a leader?

Develop thinking spaces

Thinking spaces are vital – places where you can step back and think through what's most important and how to achieve your objectives. This can be:

▌ a drink in the pub with a friend;

▌ a quiet time with a trusted colleague in a car or on a plane;

▌ a session with an executive coach;

▌ meeting an old colleague or friend.

We saw in the research that "Awaydays" and "Strategy Days" often did not work as well as "thinking spaces". Often the days had over-full agendas and "PowerPoint festivals" that filled up the time but left little or no time for people to think. Some "Awaydays" mimicked the "chop, chop, busy, busy" pattern that they were apparently set up to avoid.

During our research we often had the impression that operations and performance, strategy and culture change were held in separate containers and seen as discrete activities to be performed at different times. What we found was that these dimensions were present all the time and that each meeting presented an opportunity to work on all of them. What is needed is to provide some resting places in the chaos to look again at what is important – to have a strategic conversation. You have no choice but to work with the disturbance. You can't avoid it. We're not adding something. It's there, whether we like it or not.

Our suggestion is to keep some time at "Awaydays" for people to get beyond operational issues and deal with whatever comes up in the moment. That involves trusting a group to identify the issues that it is timely and important to address. In the research, that direct experience of trust was repaid. The majority in groups did identify the issues that the organisation needed to address.

Consider:

▌ What "thinking spaces" do I have and how well do they work?

▌ How could I make better use of the time allocated to current meetings to generate real thinking spaces?

▌ How could I develop thinking spaces *with* my colleagues on a regular basis or even in every meeting?

Use your network!

What struck us also was the range of networks built up by effective leaders. Some leaders took key issues round a network of colleagues, friends and consultants and used the advice of some to calibrate the support of others.

Consider:

▌ What network do I have?

▌ How can I develop and make more use of it?

Define the boundaries that you need to be effective

The women leaders in the research were much more successful at defining boundaries than the men. With greater responsibility for childcare and family, they had to limit working hours and take holidays. Interestingly, it seemed to make them more, not less, effective at work. They were more focused, more disciplined in their use of time, more clear thinking about what they wanted to achieve and how.

Think about:

▌ What are my non-negotiable boundaries?

▌ How can I keep to them?

Practise following your feelings

We saw often that leaders had key information available to them from their feelings but were reluctant to use it. They deprived themselves of key data they needed to connect with others and see what the context demanded.

Consider:

▌ What could be a low-risk experiment in making more use of my feelings in meetings, in one-on-ones and chance encounters with useful allies in the organisation?

Get support but don't become dependent on it

Most of our leaders had developed support mechanisms but they were of various kinds and had different consequences for their relationships and performance. Some used Human Resource directors and managers inside their organisations. Others had a few trusted colleagues inside their organisations – or outside. Yet others used coaches or other outside consultants. Some used all these.

One leaned heavily on an internal HR manager for advice and support. This seemed to work well in terms of allowing the leader to sort out his ideas and identify how to achieve more of his objectives. Over a period, however, it also left the leader excessively dependent on the HR manager. The manager was involved in organising the agendas for meetings and facilitating them. The leader's authority with his management team increased when he took over these jobs.

In another case the leader talked through what was on his mind with an insider group of managers – people like him who were new to the organisation. This worked well in relieving the pressure on the leader and helping him think through his strategy. However, it also meant that the team was divided into "us" and "them" and limited the perspectives to which the leader was exposed. What he heard from the insider group mainly reinforced his own prejudices and instincts and meant that he did not take other views sufficiently seriously.

Think about:

▌ Am I at risk of becoming too dependent on some colleagues?

▌ Is there an "us and them" dynamic?

▌ How could I use my team more for support?

Get feedback

Getting good quality feedback about your impact on others is a challenge for leaders. Many leaders suspect that people only tell them what they think the leaders want to hear.

> ▌ consciously foster people and places who will
> ▌ "tell you like it is"

We suggest you consciously foster people and places who will "tell you like it is". It is priceless information to help you.

Consider:

▌ Where and how can I get feedback as a leader? Whom can I invite for a frank talk about their perceptions of the situation?

Be willing to offend others

Some leaders are driven by a need to please others. If you are going to put your own needs first, you must be prepared to offend others – and not mind too much.

Think about:

▌ Do I fail to give enough attention to my own needs because of fear of offending others?

▌ What, realistically, do I want to do about this?

Make use of your "inner demons"

We stated earlier that self-awareness is the key to leadership development. We suggest you should be selfish enough to "own" your inner demons and make use of them. They may not be comfortable but they are what makes you special. Exploit them!

Consider:

▌ How could I make more use of my "inner demons"?

Let go of trying to change the world

In each of the case studies there were magic moments when leaders stopped trying to change the world and settled for working with it as it is. Those, paradoxically, were the times when they became most powerful. There was such a surge of relief, of energy locked up in trying to pretend that everything would be OK, that the leader and those around them felt a new sense of self-belief and purpose.

Think about:

▌ Am I trying to do too much?

▌ What issues can I pick up now that will make a difference to performance as well as team cohesion?

People

See if they will trade with you

An experienced female leader told us: "Any management team is composed of the yes sayers, the no sayers and the don't knows. I used to focus on the yeses and the nos too much. I have learnt that the don't knows are the crucial element. You have to engage with them."

Few issues preoccupy leaders as much as the choice of people. They are often the most difficult issues a leader faces. Who should I have on my team? Who is competent? Who can I work with? Who can I trust and rely on? Do I work with those I inherited? Do I need new people with different experiences, ideas and perspectives?

For the people around a leader, the issues of selection and engagement also often loom large. Am I happy with my role? Can I persuade the leader to make any necessary changes? What does the leader think of me? Can I work successfully with him? Do I respect him? Does he give a lead on the things I think are important? Is the leader good or bad for my career and prospects?

People often talk about the executive group (those who report to the leader) as if it is a construction site. People talk about team *building*. They discuss organisation *structure*. They suggest adding or removing individuals as if they were components of the building. And directing events is the leader as an engineer, pulling the pieces together.

Trading keeps you connected with the people around you

In the light of our research and the themes of *Living Leadership*, an alternative picture makes more sense to us. It is that groups work on the basis of mutual exchange. What holds them together and makes them work is mutual obligation. "I give you this, and you give me that and then we begin to acknowledge our interdependence and to attach to each other. I recognise that I depend on you for A and B, you depend on me for C and D." In anthropological terms, it is like South Sea Islanders exchanging gifts – in order to mark their interdependence and avoid war.

Examples of when we saw leaders in our research "trading" were:

▌ A new boss of an international division who, as he went round the world meeting local managers, gave his reports small projects to do. The projects were tasks that the managers could do over a few weeks and provided insights into the state of the business in different countries. But they were also an explicit effort by the new leader to say he wanted to "trade" – he was willing to enlarge their roles, promote them, offer investment in return for support for him and the emerging new direction for the company.

▌ A leader with no financial experience allied herself with a very experienced financial manager in her team. Though very different characters with very different ways of working, she recognised she needed the financial manager to "protect her back" in an organisation with tight financial controls. He valued her leadership and recognised he needed her support to negotiate the constant restructuring that was happening.

▌ The leader of a new venture recruited a very experienced and successful manager from outside the company to set up a separate part of his division to make investments in other companies. The leader gave the manager a free rein to run the investment unit, without interference from him, in return for clear information to report to his bosses and an emerging record of results in making investment.

▌ The leader of a team of nurses had two deputies. They did a lot of the analysis and planning needed in her job in return for her listening to their advice and publicly appreciating their contribution.

The idea of exchange leading to mutual obligation explains why so many leaders over a period bring in new people to help them run an organisation. It may not be that the newcomers have greater skill, ability or insight than those they replace. Rather what distinguishes the newcomers from the old team is that they are obligated to the leader for their jobs. The leader knows that the newcomers depend on him and will be loyal. In return he trusts them and favours them – with more interesting roles, rewards and praise.

However, you don't have to change the whole team to develop this sense of obligation. You can experiment with those who are already there and see who is willing to trade.

The challenge for leaders is to start trading and to establish an environment in which others are trading too. It takes time to find out if others are willing to trade, how much and in exchange for what. Repeatedly in the research, we found that it was important that leaders took their time to find out for themselves what others were willing to offer and receive. We saw appalling waste when leaders made snap judgements and wrote off whole groups of managers – who seemed to us keen to trade – because of their background or previous experience.

Living Leadership is a continuing process of recombining the people you have available to meet the demands of the task. We often hear consultants say that structure comes before people and that you should decide on the proper organisation structure and only then decide if you have the right people to fill the roles. We think a more realistic and effective approach is to put people before structure – to start with the people you have and consider how to negotiate with them relationships, roles and responsibilities that will bring out the best in them.

People changes – a magical solution?

Sometimes the changes of people were an avoidance of underlying issues – that were still there after the new people took over.

In one case a leader was tasked with turning around a business that for many years had been on a downward slide. Once a profitable and growing, privately-owned business, it had been taken over 10 years before. A new boss was put in who was regarded by managers as a tyrant who tried to control every aspect of the company's business. He was notorious for installing locked doors around the plant which managers and staff could not pass through without his permission.

Meanwhile the structure of the industry had changed. The place in the value chain that the company had occupied was eroded as powerful retailers took over some of the jobs that the company had formerly done. Cost cutting was the order of the day and there was a failure to invest in new products and services. Valuable customer relationships were damaged by short-term decisions on prices and product availability.

Into this very difficult business situation came a new boss, coming from a related but different business. In the early days, he often said: "This is a simple business" and suggested that it would not be difficult to turn around. Quickly the boss became frustrated by the managers that he had inherited. "They are always talking about the history of this place. It's time to move on and look to the future." He became convinced that the managers were not very competent.

Each time we visited the company, we experienced a sickening feeling when we heard from the boss: "There have been a few changes since your last visit." This signalled that key managers had been asked to leave and new ones brought in as an "old guard" of experienced managers, who were felt to be blocking change, were weeded out. Considerable energy was expended on assessing and then replacing individuals. Over 12 months a more cohesive team, who all owed their positions to the leaders, was developed.

The focus on changing the managers detracted from other, perhaps more important activities, including guiding the development of the same people. Deeply embedded knowledge and understanding about the business was lost without a second thought. The new managers were not experts in the business they were leading, so they spent months learning the basics. With their lack of insight into the business, the newcomers found it hard to assess the expertise of their team members or coach them. Great feelings of insecurity were engendered by the uncertainties about jobs and roles and by the feeling that the leader was gradually removing all the old-timers.

After 18 months head office intervened. Performance was reckoned to be inadequate and the business was sold to a competitor.

Perhaps it was too late for the business when the new leader arrived. Years of poor management and strategic mistakes could not be reversed in 18 months. Yet what saddened us was the failure to face the underlying issues or seize the opportunities the business did have to improve performance. Instead of tapping into the understanding and loyalty of the older managers, the new boss got caught up in a primitive game of "us – good; you – bad". Deprived of the support of old-timers, the new team made obvious mistakes and changed direction several times on key issues like pricing and setting priorities for different customer accounts. Our sense was that the writing off of the older managers and their rapid replacement did not contribute to saving the company but rather hastened its downfall.

We are not suggesting that leaders should not change any of their team members. Often some new individuals are needed to bring in new perspectives, skills or experience. We do say it is helpful to resist the initial desire to make a clean sweep of existing managers and staff.

From zero to hero

A few years ago one of the big international accounting firms was seeking to make its audit partners into business consultants. The market for audit, it was agreed, was unattractive. There was increasing competition, buyers were becoming more powerful and discriminating, and fees were falling. The work was increasingly done by systems checks and by junior staff. One senior partner stood out against the trend. He criticised the move to consultancy. He said auditors didn't have many of the necessary skills. They risked losing sight of their purpose in life – to ensure the quality of financial and other information for investors and third parties – and undermining both their skills and their professionalism as auditors. He was attacked for this stance, and seen as a "dinosaur" who looked backwards to a past golden age.

Then came Enron and the other scandals. Suddenly the partner's stance seemed remarkably far-sighted. The role of auditors was essential. Their skills and approach were valued. In a few months, the partner went from zero to hero in popular esteem.

The partner had seen an important truth that others did not want to see. The firm was wise enough to keep him when he was seen as a maverick and not ask him to leave. It turned out he wasn't a Neanderthal as some had presented him.

We encourage you to think about trading with those whose views do not follow the received wisdom of the organisation. Is it possible that they too could turn out to be intelligent dissidents – whose views may be seen as insightful when the context for your organisation changes?

> think about trading with those whose views do not follow the received wisdom of the organisation

Mutual appreciation

Sven, the leader of the Information Technology team, came across in his early months in the role as anxious about his lack of in-depth IT experience. He had led an IT group before but he had never worked in IT himself. He tried to learn furiously and had discussions with members of the group about the latest technology. The impact on the group was to make him seem lacking in self-confidence. They thought Sven was competing with them in their understanding of IT and it appeared to diminish his standing as a leader.

One year later – it does take time – the picture was different. Sven no longer had debates with his team about aspects of IT – though he did sometimes ask questions. The group said publicly how it valued Sven's role in making the link to top management and to other parts of the corporation. They valued his political skill, his relationships and his knowledge of key players. They had no sense that he was trying to keep up with them in IT. He appeared to relax, to admit they would always know more about IT but that he still had a solid foundation with them on which to lead.

Our view was that in the early months Sven was too defensive about his own value as a leader. He didn't quite believe that he could have enormous value for the IT team because of his power, his relationships and his political connections to the directors of the company and leaders of the business divisions. He was anxious about having less understanding of IT issues than his team. Once he had settled in, he could admit his ignorance of some IT questions, confident in the knowledge that the team needed him to be their "oil can", as it was put in one meeting – helping them make things happen across a complex international organisation.

Leaders learn how to give and receive gifts

The shift of thinking and approach that is needed is from construction and destruction of the team to exchange within the group. Exchange develops the sense of mutual obligation that is a key to leading. If we take gift exchange not too literally and include the giving and receiving of information, ideas and support, we can see how this interaction can set up a system of mutual obligation which binds a group together and helps shape status and authority within a team. In simple terms it implies a shift in mind set in the leader from saying "Why haven't you done that yet?" to "Would you do that for me and the team?". In the follower the adjustment is from "Before I can do that, you must make sure that . . ." to "As you tackled a problem for me the other day, I will help you out this time".

So, we suggest that you develop a sense of how far you can trade with people. Differentiate between people who are open for trade and those who currently are not. Be open for exchange yourself. If you are able to receive gifts from those who want to exchange, they will be able to connect with you and work for you. If you are lucky, those who rejected your initial advances might even get jealous enough to want to join in the game of being obliging to each other.

What you can do

Think about what sort of team you need

It is important to think about the nature of the executive group that you need. Some years ago our colleagues David Casey and Bill Critchley pointed out that the nature of the teamwork that you need depends on the context. They asked the simple but alarming question: "Do you need to be a team?" and suggested that to answer that question, managers first need to ask "What work do we need to do?" The nature of the work a group wants or needs to do shapes the degree to which it needs to function as a real team.

To quote David Casey:[1]

> Here is a very simple and powerful idea: the more uncertainty surrounds a problem, the less amenable it is to solution by the application of specialised expertise. For example there are no techniques for determining the future ... so it is in all organisations. There are mind-boggling problems, especially concerned with the future which by their very nature are outside the reach of all known specialisms. For these divergent problems the best we can do is put together the wisdom, experience, feelings and aspirations of that group of managers charged with running the organisation ... and require them to work together as a real team, sharing all they know and all they *are* as well.
>
> ... the corollary to this is equally important: it is particularly stupid to waste the energies of the full team, with all its power, to crack simple puzzles which rightly belong within the responsibility of one or two members of the team ...
>
> So here is the clue to why many so-called management teams do not work well in team mode – they *avoid* work charged with uncertainty. Instead they fall back safely on work they can cope with, work they have done before successfully, work with low risk – for which they do not therefore need to be a team.

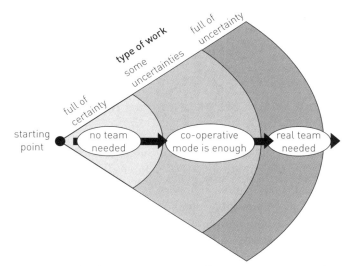

Exhibit 6 Relationship between the type of work and the need for teams

1 D. Casey, *Managing Learning in Organizations*, Open University Press, 1993.

One job of the leader is to help to assess which zone the group is in – or needs to be in:

▌ When are you dealing with the known, which can be dealt with one-on-one or by individuals or small groups?

▌ When are you dealing with the genuinely uncertain, which needs the group as a whole, working as a true team?

Set up experiments

We suggest that leaders try trading with others. Set up some experiments. Give people short projects to do – with encouragement and support – and see what they come back with.

We suggest fostering an environment in which people can trade successfully. Some clear hierarchy helps to set the necessary framework for trading – some signals that the leader is willing to take responsibility and use his authority.

Think about:

▌ What experiments could you set up, with whom?

▌ How can you set them up to maximise the chances of success?

▌ How you can use projects to link parts of the team or open the boundary between different sections of the organisations?

▌ How can you weave together the connections between the key players on whom you depend?

> ▌ the exchange of obligations is much easier
> ▌ when people feel valued by others

Show you value their expertise – and your own

The exchange of obligations is much easier when people feel valued by others. In the research we saw again and again the importance of letting people know that you appreciate their contribution and value. It isn't enough to appreciate others; you have to make sure that others know you appreciate them. Some genuine appreciation goes a long way (we were struck by how many leaders get trapped into emphasising that the glass is half empty rather than celebrating that it is half full).

Find a valued colleague with whom you can explore, in an open and appreciative way:

▌ What's my special value to the group or organisation?

Ask the group that you work with most closely:

▌ What do you need from me?

Consider the people around you:

▌ Have you told people when they do things you really appreciate?
▌ Have you raised frustrations you have quickly, in the moment, so that they don't fester and get in the way of your relationship?
▌ Are you giving people enough credit for what they do well?
▌ Do you sometimes have the courage to explore the meaning of your role for your people and ask them how they want you to fill your role as an authority?

Focus on the executive group

Focus on developing a web of mutual obligation with the group around you and let go of the anxiety to make an impact everywhere in the organisation all at once. As we said in Chapter 3, the executive group is the key. If you are "on song" with that group, the messages will spread by osmosis throughout the organisation; if not the discords will also be heard and felt widely.

Engage with individuals, pairings and sub-groups and resist the temptation to see the group as a (probably hostile) mass. Take the initiative with those who don't approach you. Your best friends in the long term may not be those who overwhelm you with ideas and attention in the early days.

Consider:

▌ Are you burdening yourself with trying to reach everyone all at once?

▌ If you focus on the group around you, what would be a priority to develop greater shared understanding?

▌ And what would be a first step?

▌ How can you extend the working majority in your group?

Foster enough common ground and enough difference

A judgement the leader is asked to make is how much common ground there should be in the executive group and how much difference. Too much difference and the group will not be able to work together. Too little and there will be "group think" on issues and important assumptions or possibilities will be overlooked.

We suggest you try tolerating more difference than you would usually. In the research the nuggets of insight often came from exploring the viewpoints of those who expressed a different and uncomfortable perspective.

> nuggets of insight often came from exploring the viewpoints of those who expressed a different and uncomfortable perspective

▌ How much real common ground is there in your executive group and how much difference?

▌ Is this about the right mix?

▌ What is a good enough working majority for you to engage enough people in extending the boundaries of what you can achieve?

Start with yourself

Some self-awareness on the part of the leader is essential. The most common reason why leaders wrote off others who might have made a contribution was the leaders' own anxieties. In one case the leader's perfectionism meant that in the end what he did was never good enough in his own eyes. Over several years he projected this sense of "never quite good enough" on to each member of his team in succession and sought to change them. Another leader was anxious about his lack of understanding of the business he had joined. His fear that he would be found out made him unable to value the expertise of those who had been in the business many years. He wrote off all the long-standing managers as "unprofessional" and "incompetent".

We suggest that leaders ask themselves:

▌ What is it that I am not comfortable with myself that I may be projecting onto this person I am not happy with?

▌ Why does that person get under my skin?

▌ What does that tell me about myself?

▌ What does the "irritating" person express for the other people?

▌ How can I find a response that is connecting and moves things on?

Let go

If the experiments are to mean something, the leader has to let go enough to allow the other person to do things in his own way. Leaders who are parents know what's involved in helping their children to learn to ride a bike. You know there is an awful moment when you have to stop supporting the bike and see if your child will be able to balance by herself. It's an uncomfortable moment. The child may crash. But she will never learn unless you do let go. Then there's the magic feeling when the child (and you) discover she is riding by herself. What had seemed like a daunting task suddenly becomes easy.

In the research we saw how difficult it can be for leaders to let go. When the pressure is on them, it is easy to lose sight of the need to let go. We suggest you think through the following:

▌ What are the opportunities for low-risk "letting go"?

▌ What are the small steps that, with support and guidance, will build confidence both on your side – and on the side of the person to whom you want to delegate?

Groups

Work on and off the table

Lou Gerstner describes a strategic meeting he chaired after he took charge at IBM in 1993. Managers sat at a large conference table with scores of assistants behind them, all listening to a PowerPoint presentation and engaging in little or no discussion. Gerstner was so frustrated by the lack of dialogue that he turned off the overhead projector, with what he calls "the click heard around the world". Managers everywhere heard that the new boss was determined to have an honest conversation about the challenges facing the company.

Harvard Business Review, February 2004, p. 85[1]

How often have you sat in a meeting and asked yourself: "What's the point of this meeting?" "What I am doing here?" "What's the value of all these PowerPoint presentations, all this talk?" Have the number and nature of the meetings you have to go to sometimes frustrated you? Have you wondered why the discussion doesn't tackle the issues that are most on your – and possibly other people's – mind?

In the research we found that opportunities for leadership came up frequently *in the moment* – moments when groups or organisations needed leadership if they were to seize an

1 Reprinted by permission of *Harvard Business Review*. From "How to Have an Honest Business Conversation About Your Business Strategy" by M. Beer and Russell A. Eisenstat, February 2004. © 2004 by Harvard Business School Publishing Corporation; all rights reserved.

"I'd rather talk about the weather . . ."

opportunity or tackle a difficult issue. What was needed was not looking wider and wider, not introducing more issues and initiatives, not burdening people with ever-longer action lists. It was focusing, at the right moment, on what was in front of their noses, the one or two issues that were just off the table but needed to be brought on to it.

We also found that these opportunities were often not taken. As in IBM, so-called "strategy meetings" often became "PowerPoint festivals" with no real discussion in the meetings and the interesting conversations happening by accident in the coffee breaks. Management meetings were often anxious affairs in which managers were burdened with ever-longer action lists and more issues and initiatives. The leaders themselves, who in private were sympathetic, thoughtful characters, often became one-dimensional taskmasters in management meetings, saying things like, "Why haven't you done this, why haven't you done that?" and "Here's your assignment for next month". All the while it seemed, from the coffee break conversations, that there were issues in everybody's minds that were blocking progress but they were not mentioned in the public sessions.

We call these issues the "elephant(s) in the room" – big, smelly and uncomfortable – questions that everyone is aware of, at some level, but no one dares name.

On several occasions when observing team meetings, we remember banging the table with frustration. "Why doesn't someone tackle 'the elephant in the room'? It's maddening. The team won't make progress till it is sorted out." Our sense often was that there was a shared waiting game. The group looked to the leader to raise the uncomfortable issue. The leader was waiting for someone in the group to name it.

What exactly do we mean by the "elephant in the room"?

Our view, based on the research, is that there are usually one or two issues that are just "off the table" that need to be brought on to it if the leader and the group are to take some shared responsibility for influencing the future. If they are to avoid casting themselves as victims of people and forces beyond their control, they need to talk about the key issues that are in their minds but not yet openly expressed.

Examples from the research were:

▌ recognising that a chief executive and finance director were being competitive and giving conflicting signals on priorities;

▌ facing a rapid decline in sales in the USA and consequent reductions in budgets;

▌ acknowledging that members of a nursing team each had two bosses – the Head of Nursing and head of each medical speciality – and therefore two lots of targets and objectives;

▌ recognising that the boss of a German subsidiary did not want to participate in a strategy review and that his participation was essential;

▌ acknowledging a challenge to the leadership of a group;

▌ facing the division in a management team between "us" and

"them" – managers who had been in the business some time and newcomers.

> there are usually one or two issues that are just "off the table"

Once the "elephants" were named, it became possible to work together on tackling them. Sometimes the appropriate response was obvious, even if unpalatable. The decline in sales and budgets, for example, meant that activities would have to be scaled down. The "two bosses" issue meant that it was imperative to have a plan for influencing the line bosses if the functional team was to be effective.

Other issues took sustained work over weeks or months for progress to be made. The problematic relationship between chief executive and finance director became worse before it became better. Both individuals did contemplate life without the other and each concluded that he needed the other person if the organisation was to succeed. There followed a bumpy road over several months of ups and downs – over the course of which they discovered more effective ways of working together.

What stopped the leaders dealing with the "elephants in the room"?

Our sense was that a number of things were happening. First the leaders were newly in position. They were too anxious about their positions, too concerned about developing their authority with their teams to take the risk of confronting these issues. Paradoxically, the "elephants" were a litmus test of the authority and legitimacy of the leader. The biggest thing they could have done at these moments to enhance their authority was to confront one or two uncomfortable issues. Nevertheless that is not how it felt to them.

Then there was the pressure of events. So much to do, so many targets to hit and projects to run. Our sense was that confronting the "elephants" felt like overload and that the leaders said to themselves: "We'll never get through the meeting if we open up that issue." It seemed often that managers feared that once the "elephants" were confronted, there would be a bottomless pit of problems and complaints. Would every dark and unpleasant issue, lingering in the back of managers' minds, have to be put on the table? No, thank you!

Sometimes we sensed that it was lack of experience that stopped people. When you are used to managing projects and people, getting things done, pushing forward, it is difficult to change gear suddenly – to slow down and start opening up the uncomfortable issues just below the surface. Managers were not sure how to do it. It raised questions like, "How would I do that? What would I say or do? Should I start with a statement of my views – or with questions to others? What questions could I ask?"

Leaders often said they wanted to keep the discussion positive. They were fed up with managers complaining and "moaning". How could they open up unspoken issues without getting into a painful and unproductive "bitching" session? Better, it seemed, to stick to the positive and constructive than allow room for the unresolved concerns to be addressed, however valid they might be.

We guessed that leaders also felt they would be expected to have an answer to the uncomfortable issue. How could they table it, if they had little idea how to deal with it? It often became clear later that the group didn't expect an outcome; what they wanted was a leader with the courage to raise the issue.

The costs of *not* confronting the "elephants"

Sometimes the cost of not tackling the "elephants" was high. We saw groups sitting back and leaving the leader on his own to tackle key issues. We experienced the erosion of the authority of the leaders, the implicit rebuke that "If you can't tackle the tough issues, what use as a leader are you to us?"

We saw the energy needed to tackle issues draining away and topics coming back repeatedly for review because they were not really resolved.

What it takes to lead in uncomfortable moments

What was remarkable was that when leaders did confront the "elephants in the room" their fears were not justified. When they did seize the moment, they found it wasn't as hard as they had feared. When they noticed the issues "off the table" that were blocking progress – and had "the bottle" to name them – relationships in the group opened up. "Getting real" about key issues brought people together – not everyone sometimes but at least a working majority. When leaders could avoid seeing the raising of concerns as a personal attack, their authority was increased. When they trusted the group to identify the one or two key issues that needed to be tackled, the majority agreed to limit the discussion and prioritised the important questions and were not side-tracked by every individual complaint.

> when leaders did confront the "elephants in the room" their fears were not justified

Our passion, following the research, is to encourage leaders and executive teams to seize more of these leadership moments.

Leaders using all their senses

Leaders do negotiate their way through these dynamics, whether they like it or not. It is important to reflect sometimes and consider how these dynamics may be playing out. It is like a washing-up bowl – though you can't see it, you know there is a knife or fork in there somewhere. You fish around till you find it – or you don't.

To help your search, you need to hold together the rational world of strategies and plans, roles and responsibilities with the messy world of feelings and emotions, individual and group dynamics. You need to work in both if you are to seize the moments to lead. Taking the risk will enhance your authority and increase the chance that the people around you are loyal to each other and to you.

Voicing fears make them less frightening

A colleague worked in a special school for disturbed young people. One day a child climbed on to the roof and threatened to throw himself off. Staff and pupils were terrified and for a moment did not know how to approach the boy. After a while a psychiatrist appeared. From the ground he shouted up to the boy: "I am very frightened. Are you?" This broke the spell. The boy came down.

This is an extreme case. But we need some of that courage to stop meetings becoming empty exchanges.

Making time and space for the unspoken issues

The chief executive of a telecoms company faced a collapsing market, huge uncertainty and the need to cut costs fast to stay alive. Despite all the millions of things to do, he organised a monthly, one-day retreat with no fixed agendas to enable senior managers to step back and think and to talk to each other. He said his objective was "To share stories of chaos. Chaos is how it is and will be. We need to see how to link up the dots. We need to keep managers responsive, flexible – with enough sense of responsibility but not too much."

"The best management team meeting we've ever had"

In one company the management team were divided into "us and them" – those who had come in from outside to "modernise" the business and those who had worked in the company for some time. The boss of the company was feeling under some pressure. He knew head office needed better performance. It was the sort of organisation where "you are as good as your last quarter's results". Management meetings were rather tense affairs. We had a sense that people were sitting on a lot they wanted to say but dared not.

At one meeting, with our encouragement and after the formal part of the meeting was complete, the boss initiated a review of how the team was working. Perhaps to people's surprise, the boss was quite open about his frustrations with the business and with the team. Two of the older managers spoke up and said how unhappy they were with the

▶

way a decision had been made to prioritise one customer at the expense of another – contradicting what the group decided just six weeks before. The formal meeting had been low key; now managers were leaning forward in their seats and speaking with feeling. A key strategic issue about product development was identified and next steps agreed.

Afterwards as we left, the boss said to us: "That's the best management team that we've ever had."

Facing up to a "hub and spokes" pattern of working

In the Internet company Netco, members of the executive group all expressed a desire for the group to take more collective responsibility and to shape its future together. Those who came from the Internet world said there needed to be a powerful executive group focused on making clear decisions on priorities and driving operations. They saw their boss John as too "process oriented, not practical enough". They wanted a "Chief Operating Officer" to work with John to make things happen and complement his strengths as a strategist and interpreter of the parent company.

The managers who had come from the multinational parent focused on the need, as they saw it, for a strong team to come together to handle all the uncertainty that Netco faced. If Netco was to succeed, it needed, they felt, all the intelligence of the management team working together on the strategic issues – not John processing all the data through his own head and deciding on his own. Both sides expressed frustration with what they described as the "hub and spokes" reality of the executive team, with John as the "hub" and everyone else working to, and with, him in one-on-one relationships.

This fitted with what we observed. Executive meetings were muted events, lacking energy or bite. John determined the agendas, without much apparent input from others. There was a lot of focus on delivery, the current operational tasks to complete. Another focus of discussion was management of the Atlas leadership. The purpose of many items seemed to be to pass on information from John or test John's ideas.

John used the meetings as a sounding board and kept back important decisions for his later and private review. Team members also felt John dealt with all the important issues one-on-one with individuals. There wasn't much sense of shared responsibility for plans and targets, nor collective awareness of the main issues Netco faced. People worked in "silos" and knew only a limited amount about their colleagues' areas of responsibility.

Team members said roles were not clear enough. One person argued that John delegated tasks but not roles. For some there was a pattern: John kept responsibilities unclear so that when an area became critical – whether because of business changes or interest from John's boss – John could intervene.

John disagreed. Where individuals had demonstrated their ability to deliver, he was happy to give them a lot of responsibility. In some areas, the managers concerned had proved their competence. Then, he said, he was only too happy to let them get on with it. In other areas, which were more problematic, it was right that he should stay more closely involved.

This felt to us like a classic dilemma for a boss – how to give people scope to perform when you don't yet fully trust them and how to supervise operations that managers are responsible for without undermining them. What struck us was the resonance that the phrase "hub and spokes" seemed to have in the group. There was a contradiction between the teamwork that most said they wanted and the reality of divided responsibilities.

The hub and spokes issue came into the open as a result of two review meetings that we held with the management team in late 2001 and early 2002. Once a couple of people had described the pattern, the team agreed that it was an accurate description of how Netco worked.

In both meetings it was not clear initially that we would have time to hold a review. The meetings were running late and it seemed that team members had pressing commitments elsewhere. Yet team members insisted on having the review. The discussion started slowly and fitfully after we positioned the review as focusing on John's leadership of the group and asked an opening question. Yet, both times, there was real passion in the room. Once the conversation got going, people leaned forward and engaged, in a way they hadn't in much of the prior discussion. While some members of the team talked as if it was all John's responsibility, others acknowledged their own part in the pattern and wondered aloud what they might do to shift it.

John expressed surprise at the hub and spokes pattern. He said it was not what he had intended. At the second review meeting, he said that he hoped the pattern had shifted and that his revised format for management team meetings had made a difference. John was told bluntly by a colleague that the pattern had not changed. The Venture Capital manager said that he did not know what the purpose of management team meetings was. They didn't help him with his part of operations nor did they help him take responsibility for the whole. There wasn't a remit for the management team that he could understand and support.

John demonstrated great openness. He enquired into views that others held. He asked for proposals and suggestions about how to improve the working of the team and his relationship to it. He offered ideas himself and shifts in his own behaviour.

Yet all the time we had the sense that this was a difficult process for John. He was tense and tight-lipped. He said afterwards that the experience had been "powerful but uncomfortable". He had found it "quite painful". "There was an element of reproach," he said, in what the team had said about the way the team worked. He did not manage the meetings to make time for the reviews. He allowed other opportunities for group reviews to pass. In October the team agreed to hold a one-off meeting to look at the role of the management team, with us in attendance, but the meeting was never held. There was never an opportune moment.

After the first review, we were elated. It seemed to us that in a very short time the group had named the critical issues facing it. Our judgement was that some taking of collective responsibility, some greater drawing on the resources and insights of the group was essential if Netco was to succeed in such an uncertain and difficult context. We assumed that once named, the issue would have to be addressed.

We were wrong. There was some shift to greater openness, we were told. The team operated on a more collegiate basis in the months that followed. However, the main pattern remained unchanged. There was no follow-up discussion to decide what the group might or would do about the issue. John responded to the review by coming up himself with changes to the pattern and nature of executive meetings. John handled a strategic review as he had previous ones, pulling in individuals as and when he needed them, processing everything through his own head till he had an answer with which he was comfortable.

The limited response to the discussion about hub and spokes only made sense to us afterwards when we knew the wider story of the business. In the following weeks the team was working flat out to deliver on the business objectives while, at the same time, undertaking a strategic review. John knew that the board was considering closing down Netco and passing the successful projects and businesses to operating companies. It was not the time to rethink the way the management team operated.

John dealt with issues one-on-one with members of his team so that he could remain the protector of the parent company interests. To have involved the other members of his team would have been "irresponsible". They could not understand the history and culture of the parent. They did not fully know the purpose of the business in which they were working. It was therefore impossible for them to make the right, informed decisions: the answer – in John's mind – was for him to keep all the decisions firmly to himself.

leaders sometimes need to do what is right in the context and not what is fashionable

Reflecting afterwards, the moral of the story, in our minds, was that leaders sometimes need to do what is right in the context and not what is fashionable. It takes courage to push back against the accepted wisdom and do what you feel is correct in the circumstances. For John, *not* changing the way of working in the team was the most sensible thing to do.

For the group it was important that the issue had been tabled, even if the pattern of working did not fundamentally change. Not everyone was satisfied but a majority were happy that the issue had been raised, that they had had a chance to express their views and that there were good reasons for John's choice of direction.

What you can do

Don't be a hero

The first ingredient is to let go of the belief that as leader you have to know the answer before you can tackle an issue. If you feel you ought to be in charge and control exactly what happens, you will get lost. If, on the other hand, you are prepared to trust yourself and the group and believe that together you will find the answer, then probably you will. If you let go of the idea that you have to come up with the answers, it's so liberating.

Think about:

▍ Am I trying to be a hero – and sort out a difficult, uncomfortable issue on my own when I could reasonably take it to the group around me?

▍ How valid are the reasons I have given myself for not taking it to the group?

Follow your intuition and check it out with the group

Allow yourself to follow your intuition to identify the one or two "undiscussables" that may need to be addressed if the group or organisation is to make progress. Here and now, condensed in this very concentrated moment, reflect on what is not working for you (if something isn't) and try to articulate, as best you can, what that is:

▍ Is there an unspoken issue now that is getting in the way of your group making progress?

One of the most important interventions can be to say: "Something is stopping us working properly. I am not sure what this is about. Does anyone else experience this right now? Does anyone have an idea of what is stopping us?" It may be to say:

▍ What's happened in the last hour that has not been properly tackled? or

▍ What's been left unsaid?

Sometimes you may need to offer a hypothesis about what's happening and interpret events and feelings; sometimes just ask the question.

Look for the signals of discomfort

Allow yourself to notice all the non-verbal signs that give away people's state of mind and use them as data to understand what is happening in the group as a whole. Someone doodling is not an accident or a personal failing. Other typical signals include:

▮ people arriving late;

▮ moving the chair back from table;

▮ coffee break conversations;

▮ people making jokes or playing the fool.

These are all symptoms of a lost connection between issues on and off the table. They are a signal for you to take note of an unconscious wish in the group, that you as leader take up the reins, step back and think about what is not being said and what is being avoided.

> ▮ notice all the non-verbal signs that give away
> ▮ people's state of mind and use them as data to
> ▮ understand what is happening

Think about a recent meeting or interaction:

▮ What did I sense that was unsaid but important?

Avoid judgement

It is essential to hold back, as far as you can, from judging those who challenge or fidget or give other signs of discomfort. Don't see the signals as either an attack on you or as a personality fault of the other person. Consider if the other person might be a messenger for the group.

Instead of thinking, "You are wrong, you don't see the whole picture, you don't take responsibility, you are at fault", try asking yourself:

▊ What's the key message here?

▊ What does it tell us about the group and about the organisation?

▊ What's the underlying issue?

Allow time for reflection

Stop the pattern of overloading meetings. Set a realistic agenda and don't persist with the agenda if it becomes unrealistic.

You will also need time for reflection and, probably, someone you can talk to openly about what concerns you:

▊ Am I clear enough about how I feel?

▊ What could be causing my discomfort?

▊ Can I raise the issue in a way that's constructive and that will be heard by others?

Try some low-risk experiments

It is important to be able to move from a focus on action and results to emphasising reflection and learning – to move, if you like, from action manager to learning leader mode – and back again. It is only a small part of your meetings or activity that will need to be devoted to confronting "elephants". About 95 percent or more of the time you will, of course, be getting on with the ordinary work. If you are not experienced in helping groups step back and learn, try some low-risk experiments. Pick a forum or situation where you feel reasonably comfortable and try the questions and steps described earlier:

▊ What situation or forum might be an opportunity to develop my skill in confronting the "elephants"?

Judge when confronting "elephants" helps – and when it doesn't

Be prepared to judge when stepping back is needed and when you feel you can handle it. We are not suggesting that you tackle every issue that gnaws away in the background. Your judgement as a leader is critical.

Consider:

▌ Which issues or concerns need to be tabled now?

▌ Are they blocking progress?

▌ Are there key opportunities you are not taking?

▌ Is now the time?

▌ What do your instincts tell you?

The important thing is that the people around you learn that, when it is required, you can handle going deeper and that, when it's not needed, you can leave it alone.

Strategy
Nudge it forward

The dirty little secret of strategy is that it's only clear with hindsight

In the research we saw a pattern. Many leadership groups at the top of companies felt that they had a clear strategy. But they were frustrated by the difficulty of getting middle managers to take responsibility for making the strategy become a reality in their areas. It was one of the reasons for many leadership development programmes in large corporations. These programmes often have the task of answering the question: "How can we get them (the middle managers) to 'buy into' the strategy and provide a lead in implementing it?" – and the implicit rider: "How can the programmes protect us, the top managers, from any further discussion of direction?" The strategists at the top felt that they had worked on that and sorted it out. What they needed was commitment, urgency and local leadership in implementing what was already a clear direction.

The chief executive of a bank said to us: "Not more than 20 percent of our energy should go into formulating the strategy. At least 80 percent needs to go into implementing it effectively. That's what makes the difference between success and failure."

When we talked to middle managers we heard a different story. Often they "didn't get it". What seemed obvious to top mangers was not clear to them. Often middle and junior managers said that they didn't feel the company had a clear strategy; they didn't understand the vision and didn't feel a sense of direction. The top

Making sense through stories

managers' slide presentations came across as conceptual ideas and
slogans, not a clear strategy. "What does it mean for my area? How
I am going to translate that into plans and objectives for my team?
Is the declared strategy consistent with the actions and decisions
of top managers?" the middle managers asked.

The difference led to frustration on both sides, wasted energy,
mutual incomprehension and a failure to take responsibility.

Part of the problem lay in the different meanings attached to the
word "strategy". Some understood a detailed road map of what to
do, how and when. Others wanted a general sense of where to aim
at and some sense of how to get there. Yet others wanted a
rigorous, analytical assessment of areas and markets to prioritise
and a clear definition of competitive advantage.

Discussions about "strategy" are often very confusing because
managers use the word in such different ways and are thinking of
different needs. In our research, when people said "We don't have
a strategy", it was vital to probe further and ask: "What do you
mean by this? What is it you want a 'strategy' to provide you with?

Are you saying you are not clear about the organisation's direction? Is it the organisation's purpose and identity you are not clear about? Or is it what to do next – what your priority should be now?"

The difficulties are exacerbated by the tendency to personify the different roles in strategy: senior managers define the strategic intent, it is said, and middle managers implement it.

These different interpretations are symptoms of an issue that goes to the heart of management and leadership. As we discussed in Chapter 4, we challenge the view that leaders develop visions and strategies and then organisations go and implement them. In most cases, that's the cleaned up, rationalised version – good for a case study in a business school classroom, not much use as a practical guide for managers who have to make things happen. The reality when you are part of it is much more like a blindfolded man who wants to cross a room. He has no map or guide because his organisation has never been this way before. He can't see ahead but he can feel his way a short distance in front of him. He has an idea of where he wants to get to; he believes the door is over there. So he moves forward and makes some progress. But then he hits some furniture, so he goes sideways or, if he is very brave, he climbs over it. Now he is moving forward again but then he hits another obstacle. This one, he guesses, he can't climb over. So he goes to one side. He hits another blockage. If he is smart, he is beginning to learn the nature and difficulty of different obstacles and how to overcome them. So he goes backwards sometimes, sideways at others. If he is lucky and skilful, he makes progress. Eventually he reaches the far side of the room and discovers that his objective, the door, is not quite where he expected it to be. If he is persistent, he moves on until at last he finds it. And if he goes through the door, he finds another room beyond ...

If this view is right, then the role of leaders with regard to strategy is very different from Moses coming down the mountain with the tablets of stone. Except in the most stable environments and businesses, there are no tablets of stone. Leaders are learning along with the rest of the organisation. Yes, it's important for them to describe a direction or overall objective but it's important to recognise that this may change as the organisation finds out more about its environment, itself, customers, competitors and partners. It's also dangerous to have too much of a master plan. As shown in Chapter 2, when leaders try to be the architects setting out a master plan for the development of their enterprises, they nearly always fail – and in failing often do great damage.

Following Mintzberg and others,[1] we suggest a different way of seeing how leaders work with strategy. When they are most effective, leaders are the storytellers of their organisations. They help the people around them to make sense of the chaos and complexity of daily work. They listen attentively – as good storytellers do – and notice both the fine detail of what is happening and the broader patterns. They come alive when they talk about what the organisation has done or needs to do. They have a gift for articulating an emerging trend or challenge in the context. They engage with others because they speak some truths in compelling ways. Often it is not the formal speeches or presentations that matter but the short conversations with one or a few people. When the conversations strike a chord, they are quickly relayed around an organisation.

> when the conversations strike a chord, they are quickly relayed around an organisation

The leaders enable others to tell and retell stories. In so doing, the others change the stories, take meaning from them and invest something of themselves in the tales. Over a period, a tapestry of stories develops that carries the organisation's view of where it has come from, where it is now, what it needs to focus on and where it is going (if anywhere).

The stories deal with strategy – and with a good deal more:

The purpose and identity of the organisation (What are we for? Who are we? How would people miss us if we didn't exist?).

History (Where did we come from? How did we develop?).

---

1 H. Mintzberg, B. Ahlstrand, and J. Lampel, *Strategy Safari*, Financial Times Prentice Hall, 1998.

Context (How do we relate to others? Does the world help or hinder us?).

Intention (What do we want to be?).

Direction (Where are we going?).

The stories are at two levels: individual events and people – and the organisation as a whole. The individual stories add up over a period to the story of the organisation as a whole – multi-layered and constantly evolving.

The stories that we have in mind function, perhaps, like the ancient myths in preliterate societies. The function of a myth is to reinforce the way things are organised and done around here and the sense of "who we are". It derives its effectiveness not so much from personal authorship but from being memorised, internalised and passed on across the organisation and from generation to generation. Like a myth, the strategic story of an organisation is only alive when it goes on being recounted and is adapted in the retelling. The retelling in turn is influenced by the context and local needs. Sometimes a department or unit uses the story not just to reaffirm its loyalty to the company but also to legitimise its own unique subculture within the overall system. Memory, oral tradition and a sense of history are what makes a company myth and its strategic story vital, flexible and adaptable. To tell and retell the story, to confirm the identity of the company and adapt its function and intent to changing needs, within and without, is not an exercise that happens over a few weeks and months and is then complete. It is developed over a long period.

GORDON'S STORY

A leader who took his time and was prepared to say "I don't know"

Gordon was the newly-appointed managing director of the UK division of a US manufacturing company. The previous boss had been sacked. Head office in America felt that he had been too slow to move on the competitive challenges faced by the division. The division was still making money but there was a sense that it was living on borrowed

▶

time. Low-cost competition from the Far East was eroding its position. Action was needed quickly if the division was to survive more than a few years ahead.

Gordon had worked for the corporation most of his career. He knew the big bosses in the States well and had a strong link with the Chief Operating Officer who had once been his boss at another division. Gordon's natural style was consultative. He believed deeply in taking people with him. A private and thoughtful man, with a strong interest in strategy, he was also very unassuming and approachable. He was a very loyal company servant who on several occasions had been prepared to uproot his family to move to new jobs.

Gordon did not know the business he was coming into. He had worked for the corporation around the world in a number of divisions but never before in this particular sector. Members of the executive team he inherited were sceptical. Though not strong supporters of the outgoing boss, they were worried about the intentions of head office and knew of Gordon's links to the COO. Was Gordon going to be the COO's hatchet man?

Early on Gordon decided to involve not just the executive team but other managers around the company as well in defining the challenge the company faced and deciding what to do about it. One manager in the executive team was almost openly hostile to this approach. He asked how a strategic review would help. The problems, he said, were well known. It was time to act. Other members of the executive team were cool but nevertheless willing to be involved. It looked as if they were taking their time and getting the measure of the new boss.

Gordon established a number of small groups looking at different aspects of the strategic issues: customer needs and wants; internal competencies; supply chain capability and costs; product development. The small groups included a mix of managers from different functions and levels and managers from within the company did all the work. Outside consultants were only used to help with the process and not the content of the work.

At first the work started slowly and Gordon felt discouraged. He organised a meeting of all the groups – about 20 people in total – and the energy seemed low and people reluctant to take the initiative. Within a few weeks, however, people began to report on significant progress. Managers found that important data and insights were available but had not been shared because the previous boss never brought people together to look at strategy. Managers relished looking at things from a company perspective. We also guessed that managers were beginning to feel that Gordon was "for real"– that the process was not a charade and that Gordon had already decided what to do but that he was listening, asking very good questions and determined to get an objective picture of the issues.

All the time Gordon was receiving phone calls from the COO asking him when he was going to close the UK factory and move production to China. The COO was a powerful figure, very clever and enormously ambitious. He knew the answer. Our view was it took some courage from Gordon to push back and say he needed more time before he could decide what was right for the business.

After three months the strategy groups came together for another, two-day meeting. The atmosphere this time was very different. Engaged, energised, the managers participated in passionate discussion. Despite protests from the Marketing Director, Gordon had insisted in inviting some customers in to the meeting, to hear "from the horse's mouth" what was most important to them. It was clear the company wasn't doing enough to meet customer needs and that there was a great opportunity to improve service. Managers became enthusiastic as a pattern emerged: the same issues and possible ways forward had emerged from several sub-groups. What had previously been unspoken was now firmly on the table for all to work with.

It became clear that the case for moving to China did not add up at that moment. The challenges of providing prompt service to meet different customer needs in Europe were too great and the cost of transport of the company's equipment from Asia were too high. In the medium term production would remain in the UK.

Six months later, the COO asked Gordon to become boss of another, larger division where the boss had suddenly died. With some regrets for a "job half done", Gordon moved on.

> courage and willingness to be an authority in the presence of others and in relation to the boss and customer are vital parts of surviving

The implication is that Gordon's courage and his willingness to be an authority in the presence of others and in relation to the boss and customer is a vital part of surviving in today's context of permanent transitions. Gordon was at ease with doing it his way. Remember he built up his confidence step by step – so can you.

The story about the business that came to make sense to Gordon was different from his boss's. Gordon saw at least a medium-term future for UK manufacturing based on the realities, as he saw it, of serving customers. His boss focused on the cost numbers and was impatient of any story other than the shift of all production to China. Gordon worked expertly to develop a shared story with his local team and to gain time and space from his boss to look at the facts.

SRDJAN'S STORY

Involving others in developing the story

Srdjan was a thoroughly international animal. Born in the old Yugoslavia, his parents had moved to Australia when he was eight and there he went to school and college. Graduate school in America and first jobs in Germany and the UK meant he had a truly international outlook as well as fluency in English, German and Serbo-Croat.

Trained originally in computer science, he had briefly been a reluctant programmer before going on to be a business analyst and manager. After an MBA at Wharton, he had tried his hand at running his own business and showed a strong entrepreneurial streak. However, his own business had not worked out as he hoped and he had become a senior manager of a small software house specialising in products for the financial services industry.

It was from this small company that he was head-hunted to be chief executive of Scart, a well-established software business with strong links to many of the largest financial institutions in the City of London. The previous chief executive of Scart, Geoff, had been skilfully and quietly levered out by a chairman who concluded that he did not really have a grip of the business nor enough rapport with the people to be an effective leader. Geoff was an Englishman, a brilliant but introverted mathematician who had earlier spearheaded the development of products.

Scart was an unusual enterprise. Built up over 20 years by an earlier, visionary leader, the company allowed teams focused on different market segments a lot of autonomy. People stayed with the company for years because they liked the strong, people-centred culture and scope to "do their own thing". The picture managers had of the company was that they would be left alone provided they achieved their business objectives.

At the same time, many people inside the company felt the organisation had become too inward looking and reluctant to change. Historical success, a well-regarded brand and strong client relationships at the operational level had made a cocoon, they argued, in which the organisation had failed to adapt sufficiently to changes in the marketplace. "We have been like the proverbial ostrich with our head in the sand," said one director of the company. One of the key business lines of the company – providing clients with a customer management tool – was felt to be in trouble. Many people inside the company felt the product was out of date and that the market had moved on. The managers of the area disagreed. The problem, they argued, was a cyclical dip in the market. The business would come back when the market recovered. The managers also denied that their profits were as bad as others argued. The way in which central overheads were allocated, they said, gave a distorted picture of their performance.

Srdjan made a positive first impression on most. With his international background, relative youth – he was 15 years younger than his predecessor – his energy levels and his American way of expressing himself, he was clearly very different from the previous chief executive. He talked a lot about marketing – because this was his passion – and about action. He said that Scart was a great company but had done a poor job of selling itself to the world. Not enough potential customers knew about the great work that it did. He quickly changed the marketing manager and approach. Where the previous chief executive had emphasised cost cutting as the way to restore the company to health, Srdjan talked about the need to increase sales. "In such a high fixed cost business as this," he said, "what matters most is the top line [sales]. Almost all the increase in revenue will feed through to the bottom line."

Six weeks after joining, Srdjan initiated a strategic review, with the purpose, he said, of getting everyone's ideas on how to improve performance and getting people to look with fresh eyes at the issues the company faced. By e-mail he quickly assembled five groups that were to look at different parts of the strategic picture and gave them three months to come up with "one side of a flip chart on what we should do to improve performance – short and long term". Managers would work in these task groups as well as undertake their normal work. There would also be "Town Hall" meetings on the General Electric model – designed to get everyone involved and make them aware of the situation faced by the company.

Despite the occasional cynical comment about strategy reviews – the company had a history of reviews that were all talk and no action – the strategy exercise created quite a buzz. Srdjan's direct, action-oriented style and effort to draw in people who hadn't been involved before made it feel different from previous exercises. Some managers complained about the overlapping remits of the groups. Srdjan said that he wasn't bothered.

There were ups and downs as the exercise proceeded. There was a lot of gossip about the reorganisation that Srdjan had talked about with some managers. He wanted, it was said, to set up a matrix structure. Some argued that he knew already what he wanted to do and that the strategy exercise was a smokescreen. Others were excited by the questions and issues that emerged as the strategy work proceeded. "At last we are able to say what we really think and get some change around here," said one manager.

Srdjan attended the "Town Hall" meetings. At one session he kept quiet for most of the time. Participants were examining the company's product lines and how far they met customer needs and wants. The discussion became most animated when participants talked about the need for internal cultural change if the organisation was to be more innovative. It was a classic Scart discussion – people spoke with passion about what they saw as deep-seated, cultural problems without being clear about what action would follow. Srdjan burst out just before the meeting closed: "I am not interested in this. What we need from this group are suggestions about which products to stop and which to start. We need to know how we are going to sell more next year. That's what matters." Srdjan's words were very un-Scart like. The abrupt tone, the impatience with what he saw as "navel gazing", the pressure for results created quite a stir.

The strategy exercise concluded with two meetings at which all the groups reported back informally. The meetings went very well. It was apparent that despite their different focus, the groups saw the same issues as key to the company's future. There was a buzz around a new sense of the magic of the company, a real sense that the company was different from competitors in a way that had huge value for customers. The groups identified the same key issues that needed to be worked on if the company was to capitalise on its magic. These included far more encouragement to innovation, a change in measurement systems to focus on profit, not just revenue, new modular products that would be tailored to the needs of particular customers and a move away from following the strategy of competitors. Srdjan didn't have to tell people what the direction should be; they were telling him – and in ways with which he generally agreed.

Following the strategy meetings, Srdjan went ahead with his reorganisation. This did not go well. Presenting the new organisation to a meeting of managers, Srdjan did not speak well. He talked for an hour – without the energy and excitement he had when talking in smaller groups. He confirmed the cynicism of some managers by introducing the matrix organisation that had been so much talked about but was felt by many to be unnecessarily complex. He met stony silence and uncomfortable looks from the managers from the business group that was in trouble.

Srdjan was criticised for having favourites, one or two managers he spoke to frankly while keeping his distance from others. People also wondered, "How long will he be around? Is he just passing through on his way to greater things?"

One year in and the jury was still out on what his long-term impact would be.

Srdjan started changing the story of Scart from the moment he first made contact with staff. He supported part of the story he heard – the technical strengths of the company, committed staff and client relationships – but he changed others. He said "Don't compete with the software big boys" and "We have a different sort of product that provides unique value for customers". He urged Scart to lose their defensiveness, to be proud of the company's achievements – and he encouraged them to be much more businesslike and action–focused. Not just by his words but by his early promotions, his interest in some projects and topics and not others, and by his attention to different people, he began to shift the story that Scart people told about themselves.

Leaders need to keep working on developing the strategic story

We saw that effective leaders like Gordon and Srdjan held strategic reviews without pretending that they had "arrived" and the strategy was now set in concrete. They made it clear that the strategic exercises were directed to clarifying particular issues or choices that the organisation faced. They organised the processes well enough so that a working majority came together in each case for the choices that emerged. But they recognised also that the strategy process was only a step on a long road. Their job as leaders was to go on listening and talking and shaping the story that enabled the organisations to make sense of the road they were on.

What you can do

So how does strategic storytelling in organisations work? How can leaders do it well?

Engage with people – don't go up a mountain

The first point from the research is to avoid the trap of building up expectations in your early days, as a new leader, that you will come up with the answer. One of the risks of all the exaggerated talk about new leaders having 100 or 90 days to prove themselves is that leaders get boxed into this expectation. It also often happens when leaders are consultative. They listen to lots of people and give the impression that they will, after due consideration, come back with the tablets of stone.

Given the expectations about transformational leadership, leaders often have to work hard to lower the temperature and reduce expectations. There may be some specific decisions or questions that urgently need to be addressed. But the whole direction of the organisation? We encourage you to bring expectations down to the level of what is within your capacity to achieve.

Ask yourself:

▊ Are the expectations people have of my role in strategy realistic?

▊ What can I do to shift expectations to make them more realistic?

> bring expectations down to the level of what is
> within your capacity to achieve

Pose the classic strategy questions – but don't look for final answers

We suggest you hold the strategic questions in mind and push yourself and others to consider them carefully – but don't drive yourself mad believing you will find the answer. You won't.

Questions that we have found very useful are:

▊ What's the magic of this organisation? What has made it special? What has caused its success?

▊ What's the current reality of our position today? What challenges are we not facing up to? What opportunities are we not seeing?

▊ What key trends are shaping our world? How will it be different tomorrow from today? How should we respond?

▊ What critical assumptions are we making about our environment, ourselves and others?

▊ In which markets or areas should we focus our efforts?

▮ What will be our competitive advantage in our priority areas?

▮ What's our "big bet" – the big move that will secure our future and which requires 110 percent of our effort?

▮ What's our "Plan B" – what will we do if the business, the industry, the world does not turn out as we expect?

▮ What continuity do we need to be successful in the future? And what change?

The point about these strategic questions – and there are many, many other good ones – is that there is rarely a definitive answer to any of them. You study the data, you ask other people, you try things and seek to learn from them – but you never arrive. It is only when looking back that you may – perhaps – be able to say, "Yes, that was the key" (just as historians come up with many different interpretations of the same events).

We encourage you to be realistic about what strategy reviews or processes can produce. Often people are disappointed because they join strategy reviews in the honest expectation of defining or changing the strategy or direction of the organisation. Help participants to see that coming up with answers to particular questions may be very valuable – and certainly good enough.

Consider:

▮ What are the most useful strategic questions to work on now?

▮ Why these questions? How will the responses help you?

▮ Are the expectations of any strategy reviews realistic?

▮ What could you do to make the expectations more realistic?

Bring in different voices

Much discussion in recent years has focused on uncovering the assumptions that people in organisations make about the world they are in, about their organisation and other ones. The history of business and organisations is littered with stories of those who were blind to some change and whose enterprise suffered – or collapsed – as a result. Encyclopaedia Britannica assumed they were in the book business and then saw their 250-year-old business destroyed in two years by competition from CDs. The airlines assumed the low-cost market was only for a few students or tourists and are now all suffering as a result. The mighty Nokia assumed it knew what customers wanted and failed to develop in time enough clever, colour screen, clamshell phones and is seeing its dominant position challenged as a result.

The challenge for leaders is how to broaden the strategic conversation in an organisation and bring in people with different voices who might alert people to trends or changes they do not see. This is the zone of *knowing ... while holding uncertainty.* You have to act on the basis of some assumptions. And you have to keep part of your mind open to the idea that some of those assumptions may not be true. How much you need of each depends on your situation, your context. Do you feel you are getting the mix about right?

We encourage you to be *knowing* in finding smart questions to ask (and new people to ask) *while* remaining open to the bliss of *not knowing* until you have involved the key players in the organisation in stretching your imagination on what is possible and do-able. Only after that point is it important to be directional – until the next point of uncertainty arrives.

Consider:

▌ What "new voices" could we involve – people who will have a different way of seeing the issues?

▌ How could we involve them in ways that will help them to be heard by those inside the organisation?

Connect the thinkers and doers

To develop a story that draws on many voices and adequately reflects the complexity of your situation, we encourage you to bring thinkers and doers together. Serious strategic thinking bridges the big ideas, up in the clouds, and the fine detail, on the ground, of how things work today. Make sure your strategic conversations involve those at the coalface who know how things really work. Otherwise you may end up with a strategic story that is all hot air! Making the connection between the thinkers and the pragmatists is up to you. Your responsibility at this point links to our picture of the leader in the middle, pursuing the aim of leading by working in-between those parts of the organisation that might pull apart without a helping hand.

Think about:

▌ Are "thinkers" and "doers" both sufficiently involved when you work on your direction?

▌ Is there enough thinking?

▌ Is there enough doing?

▌ How can you improve the mix?

Think about "timing, timing, timing"

Timing is critical. What issues is it timely to move forward? In our experience, there are usually a few key issues that are important and urgent. Helping people to identify these issues is one of the particular contributions a leader can make and is often more important than providing the answer.

We strongly caution against tackling all the issues at once. Usually this only leads to superficiality. Better, usually, to identify the vital few questions for now and work through them thoroughly – to satisfy the key players and find responses that will be sustainable. Limiting what you and others can do at any one time might dent the ambition to be an all-conquering hero, but it unburdens everyone involved enough to make realistic progress on changing things while providing the continuity needed to care for the existing business.

Consider:

▌ What are all the strategic issues on our agenda at the moment?

▌ Of these, which are the critical few that we can, and need to, make progress on now?

Identify the key choices your organisation is making

It is vital to try to identify the key choices the organisation is facing and focus the strategic conversations around these. Generally some choices are clear. However, often organisations – like individuals – are not aware of the strategic choices they make at the time. "Things just happen" and organisations discover later that they have chosen to be in or out of certain markets or technologies, to serve or not to serve certain customers, to develop or not to develop certain competencies. The job of the leader is to help to clarify:

▌ What are the important choices facing us now?

▌ When and how will the choices be made?

▌ Are there other choices that we are making – without being aware of them?

Allow for healthy disillusionment

We talked in Chapter 6 about "healthy disillusionment" – the process that some of the leaders we saw in the research go through. It meant separating from their early dreams and coming to terms with reality. An important job for leaders is to articulate the dangers they sense in a direction or proposal, and to keep the need for sufficient continuity and stability in mind during periods of change and turbulence. You are almost certainly not alone. Get real. Don't worry about "damaging morale", as the message that not everything has to change at once is heard as a relief and will, we predict, make those around you more likely to engage in change with you. Work with others on what is a do-able scenario.

Consider:

▌ Which aspirations – that motivated us in the past – do we have to let go of because we realise that they are not realistic?

▌ What are our hopes and dreams now?

▌ What aspects of our organisation and strategy need continuity, not change?

Draw into the strategic conversation those whose commitment you need

A story emerges from many conversations and is constantly evolving. The leader needs to judge who to have the conversations with. Who are the key opinion formers and actors whose views he wants and whose full commitment he needs?

It's often been said that if you want people's real commitment to something – as opposed to just lip service – you need to involve them in the developing of the "something".

The leader also has to decide what it is reasonable to expect managers to sign up to as good company servants – in other words, what he can expect people to follow without having to think through all the pros and cons for themselves. He has to consider what will be a good enough "working majority" for any decisions or directions that emerge. It is unlikely that everyone will agree (and probably unhealthy). But there need to be enough of the key players on side to make things happen.

The nature of the process varies very much from one business context to another and one organisational culture to another. What is workable in a consultation-minded health organisation would seem impossibly slow and indulgent in a sales-minded, financial services firm.

The choices for leaders are therefore:

▌ Who are the key players you need to involve?

▌ What ground to cover?

▌ When?

▌ How? Using what processes?

Guard against "group think" – or fragmentation

The tapestry of stories will contain some common ground and some difference. An interesting question for the leader is whether more common ground, or more difference, is needed:

▊ Is the organisation engaging in "group think" and not sufficiently aware of threats, opportunities and different ways of working?

▊ Or is there too little common ground, too fragmented a view of the organisation and the world?

Trust in small steps

In the picture outlined earlier the blindfolded man takes small steps, as far as he can feel his way ahead. He does not leap into the unknown. We encourage you to trust to the power of small steps. Over a period they add up.

> we encourage you to trust to the power of small steps, over a period they add up

Consider:

▊ What are the small steps, now or later, that will help us develop our strategic story?

Be prepared to "unlearn" what you know

Most challenging of all, the leader needs to keep in mind the difficulty of "unlearning" things that he and other people know. The really tricky part of any strategic shift is letting go of ideas, priorities and ways of working that people have learnt in the past. We all find it much easier to learn new material than give up things that we have – often with difficulty – learnt before.

It is likely that parts of what is familiar will have to be consigned to the past, other parts will be retained and some new elements will have to be taken in and integrated.

A leader can help by holding up the mirror:

▊ In what areas might the understanding and knowledge of people in our organisation no longer be valid?

▮ What might be alternative ideas, skills and ways of seeing issues?

▮ How does our strategic story have to be retold now in the changed circumstances of today?

▮ How can we bring in the new without losing the essence of our strategic story?

Change
Be part of it

13

A major international bank was interviewing short-listed candidates for the role of Chief Operating Officer. For the first time in years, the bank had decided it needed to look outside for suitable candidates. Towards the end of the discussions, the Human Resources Director asked candidates if they would seek support from an executive coach if they were appointed. She said afterwards: "If they said no, I vetoed the candidate because I knew they lacked the self-awareness required for this job. Anyone coming in at that level to the organisation has a lot to learn and needs all the help they can get."

Leaders often express frustration with the amount of effort it takes to lead change in organisations. They say they are fed up with having to drive through change. They feel as though all the energy for change is coming from them. They are frustrated by what they feel is the inadequate pace of change. Why can't others – be they colleagues, front line workers or middle managers – take the initiative and lead? To the top managers, it feels that, however hard they push, change still does not happen fast enough.

To use the language of marketing, top managers are desperate to develop some "pull" as well as "push" – to find ways of provoking or encouraging others to take responsibility for change.

But how do you encourage others to behave differently – particularly when it seems they have good reasons not to change?

The only person you can really change is you

> the effectiveness of change processes and the
> effort required was tied to choices that the
> leaders themselves made

What we found in the research was quite startling. We saw that the effectiveness of change processes and the effort required were tied to choices that the leaders themselves made. There were three important choices:

1 How did the leader see her role in the change process?

Did the leader see herself as apart, knowing the answer and *doing to* others? Or did she see leading as happening *between* people – with herself in the middle of the process of change? If the leader saw herself as *doing* things *to* the organisation, then change took huge amounts of energy and did not happen as the leader hoped. The people around leaders played back the leaders' own assumptions: "If you're the hero, you make it work!" Leaders changed people, structures, roles, responsibilities and systems and yet still the organisational culture remained stubbornly resistant to change. The leaders got compliance, people paying lip service to the new ways of thinking and behaving, but not the change in hearts and minds that they sought.

If, on the other hand, leaders saw themselves as *in the middle, part of* the process of change, then others also shifted their thinking and behaviour. There was a one-to-one correlation between the approach of the leader and response of the people around her.

We experienced this, empirically, in the research cases. In some of the cases we followed, leaders saw themselves as part of change from the start. In other cases it took 12 to 18 months before leaders were really prepared to accept that they were part of the issue. But, in all cases, leaders had to be willing to shift assumptions, thinking or behaviour, if the unit or organisation they were responsible for was to change its thinking and behaviour.

Exhortation of others to change did not work. Participation in the process did. If leaders wanted real change, they had to change themselves.

Leaders and followers learn and develop together – with reference to the context they find themselves in – or they don't develop. There is a critical shift when the leader sees change not as something out there, for the others, but something in which she has to participate. The leader has to be prepared to *not know*, to suspend her sense of order and certainty if she is to enable others to learn. She has to demonstrate the willingness to learn that she proposes for others. Exhortation alone is unconvincing; it merely creates false compliance and silent resentment and aggression. Thus, in a transition, the leader must see herself and the others as part of a collective process of learning.

The "stuckness" we observed in one case among the team mirrored the leader's well-defended position. She was very difficult to get to know and shrugged off the need for change as an issue for "them". The team blamed her and others and did not really believe that they could have a role in shifting the way the management team worked.

In another case, the leader became isolated. There was too much pressure, too little support from bosses and other managers. The leader got into a defensive position, unable to change herself or help others to change. By contrast, the cases where the team really developed mirrored significant shifts by the leader, changes in perspective and thinking, and letting go of cherished notions about individuals, the company and leadership.

2 What was the leader's stance with regard to change and continuity?

An important, but often neglected, parts of the stories that we talked about in Chapter 12 concern continuity. As part of the transformational mindset, leaders were often preoccupied with change. They sometimes got trapped in it. They wanted to make their mark quickly. They saw their role as bringing about fundamental change. Their energy was focused on what was wrong with their organisations, not what was right.

Continuity, however, needs leading, just as change does. Indeed it can sometimes be harder to achieve and more important than change. Often accumulated knowledge about customers and markets, products and processes was lost without anyone realising it had gone. Valuable skills and experience walked out the door when people moved jobs or retired or were made redundant. New structures eroded informal systems and processes that were barely visible but helped to keep an organisation working. Teams were broken up and the insight they had accumulated about how to achieve results was lost.

Managers have to deliver on the day-to-day business of organisations. That too can get forgotten if all the attention goes into change.

There was also a subtle interplay between change and continuity. The people in an organisation needed to feel appreciated for what they did and had done. A leader saying "all change" was heard as denigrating what had gone before. An appreciative view of the present and past enabled a leader to be more convincing about what needed to change in the future.

"All change" was, we found, part of the transformational mindset, the belief that you can reinvent your organisation and the people in it. It was not realistic and it was often very damaging.

3 How did the leader work with the negative?

Another choice was how to work with what is often called "resistance to change" and other expressions of negative feelings about change. Could the leader tolerate expressions of dissent and see the reserve of energy and commitment tied up in "negative" views? Could she bring together a "can-do" attitude and determination to make progress with hearing and getting value from people's doubts and concerns? Or did she insist on "alignment" the whole time and dismiss those who had doubts as "resistors" and "cynics".

We saw leaders who tolerated only positive views. They got trapped in a future further and further away from change in the here and now. Nothing useful could emerge in discussion because it was stigmatised as not aligned with the vision and strategy, not positive.

We suggest: work with the negative. It is easy to mistake compliance for change, easy to appreciate compliant subordinates. However, compliant managers are secretly resentful and find it difficult to be independent and responsible.

| work with the negative

Get to know the "negative" part in you and you will be able to work with these feelings in others. Remember the rush of energy, the release you experienced yourself when someone finally granted you the space in which to unburden yourself, to express your frustration and your desire to be heard. When you recall this experience of needing to be heard, before being willing to move on, you will reconnect to the fact that organisational change mirrors life events like death, illness, birth and marriage. You will know that in these life situations it is counter-productive to close down the space for expressions of grief, distress and disorientation. Better to let the distress out so that it can lose its hold over people and they can recover their capacity to dust themselves down, put the difficulties behind them and start all over again – only this time more conscious of their own responsibilities and creative opportunities.

We saw in our research that change through positive thinking alone revealed itself as a mirage. We saw that underneath the culture of compliance and alignment there is an unexplored world of passion and potential commitment – a reservoir that can only be tapped when a space between leader and group exists in which it is safe to bring the whole of the self, and the entire range of thoughts and emotions connected with the situation. Suddenly it's no longer only the leader pushing change but the many who are taking the initiative.

So, change starts with you, compliance is not change; you are more likely to change things with others when you open a space between you and the group that is safe and free enough to bring the whole person, good and bad, into the exchange designed to find the way forward.

Changing yourself as others change

SVEN'S STORY

Confident beginnings

We researchers first met Sven at the Lindtholm headquarters in Sweden soon after his appointment to the role of head of Global IT and Supply Chain in the newly merged company. Swedish and German family companies had come together in the hope that they could lead the industry in their sector. In a smart restaurant with spacious, wood-panelled rooms, bookshelves and cigars – more like a London club than a conventional restaurant – Sven talked about his background and why he had joined Lindtholm. His ambition was to move on from finance and IT roles and take operational responsibility for a business. For this he needed to broaden his CV and to gain experience of leading change in an international company. It would be the second time he had taken responsibility for IT. As someone who was not an IT expert, there would be much for him to learn but it should not be a disadvantage. He knew enough to identify key concerns and he would gain from not being too immersed in technical and operational issues.

Sven talked a lot about Lars, his boss and a main board director, and about the plans they had made together. For him, Lars was clearly a big figure, clear thinking and incisive, with a compelling picture of the change he and Sven would bring about. IT in the new company was not strong. It was barely doing an adequate job of supporting operations. There was an urgent need to integrate the fragmented IT systems and install ERP ("Enterprise Resource Planning") throughout the worldwide operations. Sven would have the job of co-ordinating global IT activities with the aim of developing a shared focus and approach around the world. There would be a new global IT team with a mix of Americans, Swedes and Germans to mastermind the changes.

For the first time in the company it would be a real global IT team – a group able to put aside their business group and national loyalties and work out what was needed in the interests of the company as a whole. Yes, there would be local bosses to whom the IT team members would report, but, with Sven as co-ordinator and Lars supporting it, it would be a genuinely international effort focused on the good of the company as a whole.

The change in IT was to be part of a wider culture shift. Lindtholm's way of doing things was very deliberate, consultative and respectful of people. It was only with great difficulty that the company had laid people off in the last recession. The atmosphere was very ordered. Meetings and events were planned well ahead and everything – down to the time of arrival of coffee – well organised.

Some of this, Sven said, he and Lars would change. There needed to be more directness in tackling problems of which everyone was aware. Things needed to move faster. The old conservatism and complacency would be challenged and a new, more genuinely international organisation developed – able to take on the best companies in America, Europe or Japan.

A number of the Americans in Sven's group of IT managers had a harsher view of the priorities. They believed that the merger 10 years before between the German and US parts of the company had never worked properly. There had never been the necessary facing up to different beliefs and ways of working. With the new merger it should be different. There was bound to be a power struggle between individuals, beliefs and values. As another American put it, "Let's get on with it. Let's get these issues sorted and then we will be able to focus on the IT."

Many people mentioned the culture in the group of "walking on eggshells", of failing to name and confront challenges of which everyone was aware. One person said, "If I really speak up, I might not be safe." The group norm seemed only receptive to good news and it was difficult to bring in challenges, setbacks and frustrations. Heinrich, the one German in the group, presented himself as "a lone troublemaker". "They don't like the reality I give them," he said, "I should be more careful. They don't listen to me. It's a pain for me to sit for three days hearing all this good news and Californian sunshine." In fact, when Heinrich did speak up, he expressed, albeit more directly than others were comfortable with, concerns that several others felt.

The group was also fragmented. People focused on the negative aspects of other cultures. Lindtholm – the Swedish part of the company – was perceived as "fat and happy" (it was implied that they were due some pain); the German part, Werner, as "lean, mean and baronial", with no adequate group IT function; the US part, Hunter, was seen as full of management religion but short on delivery and trustworthiness. The Europeans saw the Americans as obsessed with the need for a "John Wayne" type of management – "Let's have a shoot out and see who's boss around here". The Americans saw the Europeans as slow and indecisive, waiting for someone further up the hierarchy to give them orders.

Seeing with new eyes

Fifteen months later, the global team came together for its regular quarterly meeting, this time in North America. Several interconnected dramas played out in this setting. The context was increasingly difficult for the IT group. The downturn in the business was accelerating. US sales were falling faster and the recession had spread to Europe. The dilemma that the group had discussed before had become much more acute. How could they recruit people, build the infrastructure, make a whole new IT service, comparable to leading companies, when their budgets were being savaged?

Customers within the company were dissatisfied with the service IT was providing. Sven had just come from an international meeting with Sales and Marketing in which there had been criticism of IT's performance. Among themselves, some members of the IT group agreed that IT had not produced results that managers in other areas would recognise. Long-promised projects had not delivered. In some areas movement was backward, from the point of view of users, as previously available services were withdrawn so that they could be improved or put on a more secure basis. As one manager put it: "We have to calm the organisation down by delivering on the immediate stuff." Peter, the new co-ordinator for IT in Europe, said that from his previous experience the group lacked focus and was simply trying to tackle too much at once. Bill agreed: "We try to please. We should be more honest." Sven said: "It is a speed issue. We need to move faster." He also cautioned against being excessively gloomy: "We shouldn't only see the holes in the cheese."

Lars appeared on the afternoon of the first day and soon took centre stage. He reinforced the message about Sales and Marketing's dissatisfaction. He told the group frankly that it was under pressure to get its act together and produce results.

Lars went on to shift the priorities for IT. Like a magician, he produced out of his bag one overhead slide that he said set out the direction he wanted the group to consider (the slide became "Lars's picture"). Lars explained the picture by saying that he had been talking to Sven and that they had decided to change the priorities. It was no longer practical to work towards common IT systems for all group companies. The focus of effort should instead be to build a common interface for handling customer data and relating to other systems.

Lars's impact was dramatic. There was an almost audible sigh around the room, as if a great weight had been taken off people's shoulders. No-one had felt able openly to challenge the previous direction even though privately everyone said it was unrealistic. Now Lars had punctured the balloon and there was a rush of energy around the group as people began to engage with the new direction and think through how it might work.

▶

After the day's session closed, Lars held a private review with Sven. He was very direct. He said the situation of IT was difficult. Customers were unhappy. It was time for Sven to be less facilitative and more directive. Sven had been in post for more than a year. He knew the subject now. The reorganisation was complete. Sven should provide clear authoritative leadership (in fact be more like Lars) so that the IT group could sort out its act and begin to perform. Then Lars left.

It was interesting to see the reaction, both the group's and Sven's, to Lars's intervention. In the moment, they were captivated by his personality and persuaded by his arguments. Here was the sort of leader who fitted the company role model: fiercely intelligent, driven, demanding and direct, speaking truths that needed to be said. Afterwards, however, there was a bad taste. Team members expressed a sense of being "seduced" by Lars who had seemed so powerful in the moment. In the cold light of day, were his arguments really so persuasive? What did his proposed direction really mean? How could even his slimmed-down vision be achieved? What impact would his humiliation of Sven have on him and the group?

In private discussions after the meeting, Sven took an important step to distance himself from Lars. He said that he had become aware of Lars's negative impact on him. He said that he needed to find his own way of leading the group. He could not simply follow Lars's advice but had to find the approach that would work for him, Sven, in this situation.

Lars's position in the company was also weakening and it was possible that he might leave the company. Lars had promised Sven that if he left the company he would take Sven with him, but Sven now questioned if this would make sense for him.

Meanwhile the group was showing that it had developed. It had enthusiastically embraced the reorganisation that Sven had made and was impatient to press ahead with the remaining aspects of implementation. Bill, the leadership challenger seven months before, had been given the role of strategist in the team and appeared to enjoy the role and be valued in it by others. Bill was at pains during the meeting to be supportive of Sven and to be a co-operative member of the group. He said at one point: "I feel for Sven – he expected to get things done on IT globally but he has to work across the strong reporting lines which are still to business units." Bill was included in the new four-man leadership group along with Sven, Don and Peter, the co-ordinators for North America, Europe and Asia.

A sense of identity was emerging. People acknowledged their need for help and support from each other and their dependence on each other. The national and company splits that were visible a year before were no longer in the front of people's minds. There was much more reference than before to the corporate picture and less to local priorities. People seemed to identify with the new structure and were keen to make a success of it. There was a tangible sense of common endeavour. There was tolerance of distinctive voices and contributions. Three members of the group acted from time to time as mavericks but they were heard by other members (with some occasional jokes or mockery) and their contributions valued.

From this base Sven and the team could – and did – go on to improve performance and tackle the most pressing needs of the business divisions. It took 18 months but Sven and the team had emerged with a realistic set of objectives and a strong understanding about how to work together. Sven had changed and the group had changed.

The process of Sven gradually separating from Lars, his charismatic boss, and finding his own way to lead the team struck us as very powerful. Sven and the team had a very difficult task – how to arrive at do-able objectives and contribute to group performance when business was bad, budgets were being cut and divisional "barons" had a lot of power. When Sven started he came across to us as in love with the vision Lars had painted of using IT to change the culture of the company. He had to discover his own objectives and his own way of leading – that was neither the consultative style he often adopted at first nor the visionary leader Lars wanted him to be. He had to find the role he could play, aware of his own needs and the real priorities of the situation.

What a leader wants others to do, he has to do first

Moritz and Max were two brothers leading a family owned and managed software business in Germany. Until the mid-1990s they rode the boom in Germany associated with reunification, and the elder brother, Moritz, became a well-known and heroic figure in the software world in Germany.

When the reunification boom ended, the business hit problems. Customers no longer had lots of money to spend, there was overcapacity in the industry and the tax environment became less friendly. As the company went from success to struggling, the younger brother, Max, was appointed Chief Operating Officer and an implicit division of labour was institutionalised. The big brother inhabited only the future and spent his time being strategic and troubleshooting problems. He refused to hear negative messages from customers – and senior managers in client organisations actually covered up the problems so as not to "rock the boat". Senior executives of client organisations met him in luxurious hotels and resorts and assured him that everything was OK. Moritz gained a reputation inside the company of wanting to hear only good news. "Bring me solutions, not problems," he would say.

As a result, staff in the company began to detach from Moritz and look to Max for leadership. Max heard many of the customer and staff complaints. The spilt between the brothers grew. It got deeper and more forceful and their relationship was dominated by fear of getting real with each other. They feared that they would split apart. They feared they would have to look at how bad the company's situation had got and how long it would take to repair. They even worried that they might have to start the business all over again.

With outside help, the brothers reflected individually and both came to see that the position of the other was reasonable.

Max said about Moritz: "He has become a God. He has disconnected from his people. He does not recognise when people lie to him. He does not realise that people tell him what they think he wants to hear – in order to keep him off their backs. He thinks only he is still effective.

All the rest of us are not. The truth is that neither he nor us are effective and that it's awful. All we can do is try and try again."

Moritz said: "I am as negative now as the people I sacked for being negative two years ago. I think I have been too harsh on my younger brother. I have talked to some partners outside that he has recently worked with. It has become clear that he simply relayed to me how negative they feel about us as a company. I have been unfair and not seen that he has really tried more than his best – just like me. Neither of us seem able to cut the Gordian knot. I suppose there is no simple answer. We have to try and try again. At the end of the day we are brothers and he is the only one I really trust. He is the only one I believe is loyal when it gets tough."

The critical realisation was that the difficulties were a product of the business context, not of the other's weaknesses. The younger brother let go of his paranoia and realised that Moritz needed to be positive for investors and customers. This shift enabled them to talk issues through together and be constructive. Each became capable of seeing the other as having tried his best and not acting with malignant intent to the other. They were then able to tolerate each other's pictures of how things really were.

Following the meeting between the brothers, it was possible to bring key players in the company together and for them to get real with each other about what needed to be done, what could be done, what must be done. It did not change the whole company but it reinvigorated key players to take responsibility. This gave hope to most of the people in the company. They began to believe that they could survive and thrive – and this strengthened their attachment to the company.

As consultants, we learnt that living through the cycle did not mean the patient had recovered completely. This was not because the leaders were incompetent but because the context kept changing. The brothers faced one shock after another as government policy changed, key individuals were head-hunted away from the company, sales faltered and then personal tragedy intervened – the brothers' mother died. The brothers had to get their heads around all these changes and they had to shift their pictures of the world. Once they had done this together, they could invite others to work with them. By getting real themselves they could help others to get real.

what the leader wants others to do, she has to do first

What the leader wants others to do, she has to do first. If she wants them to "grow up and take responsibility", she has to try first. If she wants others to stop blaming and see what it is in them that may be contributing to the problems, she has to go first. The only person you can really change is you. When the others you are dependent on experience your change they become more willing to change for you. Don't deny this interdependence. What the brothers did was to say: "I am inviting you to notice that I have changed and I am linking up with you to see whether you can change too – and then we can look to others as well."

The leader allows people to express how awful it really is for them and thereby, paradoxically, enables people to move back into a positive and hopeful framework. If other people experience being accepted as they are, then they will have a go at changing. They know you will not persecute them if they get it wrong. They feel safe enough to try and change.

MARY'S STORY

Allowing yourself to say "I don't know"

In her early days Mary, the new head of nursing in a leading hospital, was naturally anxious. She was concerned about how she was going to make her mark in this demanding environment and whether she would be able to cope with all the pressures of driving through the government's change agenda with many powerful colleagues, not least the senior doctors who had traditionally held the reins. In her early days, rather than hear the issues and concerns of her new reports, she appeared to dump her anxiety on them.

An example was when she tried to use a consultative process that had worked for her in a previous job. She was so keen to make her mark that she imported a process from her previous job without thinking enough about whether it would work in her new environment. She assumed that her team were more capable at that moment than they were, and she ignored the impact of a previous tyrannical leader who had not allowed expression of views and had imposed her own ideas. The response that she got from her team to her request for comments and ideas was poor and she made the mistake of allowing colleagues on the hospital's executive board to see it. She complained, "I come from a provincial hospital. This is supposed to be a world-class organisation, yet they can't even produce decent input for a strategy paper."

When Mary took the work to Executive Management Board, she was criticised by her peers for its poor quality. However, the Chief Executive came in strongly to support Mary. He praised her effort to involve her colleagues and said that an involving style of leadership was what he wanted. He made clear his belief that if the management team was going to carry through the changes expected of them, they would have to take their teams with them. He recognised the problems with the nursing paper but said he was confident that Mary's team would do better with more experience.

She was able to transfer that experience of being supported into her own executive group and change her own approach. Where previously she had given them the problem to solve and waited for results, and then found them wanting, she now decided to spend some time thinking with them, asking for their input while also producing some herself. She gave herself and the two assistant directors the job of editing the final paper. The changed process legitimised her authority; the team recovered their sense of competence and the attacks on the "new kid" in the Executive Management Board stopped.

change and continuity must be balanced

Our view was that the episode was an important one for Mary. She got connected, she got real and she recognised what she could offer to her team and what she could not. She could not transfer previous experience in a straightforward way but had to learn to adjust and make what she knew work in the new context.

Leaders need to change, to enable others to change

We found that it is damaging to take an "all change" approach as a leader. Far better to recognise that change and continuity must be balanced and that the leader needs, in connection with others, to take responsibility for weighing up how much continuity and how little change is needed at any one time.

A little bit less belief, therefore, that you can reinvent this world on your own – and a little bit more belief that you can reinvent yourself would be good. Change does not come about to order. It starts to happen when leaders get involved in the muck and bullets of change processes and demonstrate that they are willing to invest themselves in the process. If you want others to change, you have to change yourself. Going through that process is both frightening and exciting. Experiencing it first hand will make you open to your people's difficulties on their challenging change journey. When they can feel your empathy and when they experience you as accepting of their ambivalence, they will lose their fear of letting go more easily.

What you can do

Think about the choices

Our suggestion is to make time and space to think about the three fundamental choices we have outlined. Where do you stand on these questions:

▍ Do you really see yourself as part of the change process – or are you *doing change to* others?

▍ What's the mix of change and continuity needed in your organisation?

▍ How do you handle the "negative" feelings?

Then there are a number of supplementary questions:

Be part of change

We encourage you to keep part of your mind open to the possibility that something in you may need to change:

▌ What is it I could learn from this role?

▌ What is it I should be prepared to *not know*?

Lead continuity

Think about:

▌ What needs to be continued or built on from the past or present and what really must change?

Tap into the negative

Consider:

▌ How can I give space for people to express their negative feelings?

▌ How and where do I take my negative thoughts?

▌ How can I use my awareness of the resistance to change in myself when I ask others to change familiar ways of doing things?

Development
Get real

One manager in the research told us of his disappointment with the personal development his company had sent him on:

> "Most of the management programmes I have been on have been a waste of time. They analyse you, identify your weaknesses and tell you what you should do to address them. Then you go back to work. For about two weeks you try to follow their advice – before deciding that you can't really change who you are and you give up, feeling inadequate and humiliated."

Leadership development has become increasingly popular in recent years. The suppliers make up a big, and growing, industry. One major company after another has decided that the lack of leadership at many levels is a constraint on its development. In some cases, it is seen as a "make or break" issue. If the corporation cannot develop more leaders, it will not survive. The challenge – from the point of view both of the individual leader and of managers organising development for others – is how to do it? What really works? How can you evaluate the outcome of programmes? Is any of all this leadership development activity delivering results? Can you really develop leaders? What is most effective? Is there an adequate return on the investment?

We believe you can learn about leading. Leading happens *between* people and is not an innate ability you or others possess. It is a process that can be learnt about and improved. If leadership development is to be effective, however, it needs to be firmly connected to the organisational context. Leading is shaped by the context – by the business situation, the organisational culture and the social and political environment. Learning how to be a more

Making sure you're pushing people up – not dragging them down

effective leader must also be anchored in the context. Reg Revans, the British pioneer of "action learning", was clear, as long ago as the 1960s, about the need to link leadership development to the context in which leaders work. At the time, many management development experts saw him as rather strange, but his assumptions have been proved largely correct.

> if leadership development is to be effective, it needs to be firmly connected to the organisational context

Off-site leadership programmes *can* serve an important purpose. They can help people to improve their self-awareness and develop new skills such as coaching, giving feedback, delegating or speaking clearly and confidently in public and give leaders a "safe environment" to experiment with new approaches and behaviours. Off-site events can provide an opportunity for managers to step back from day-to-day pressures and work out what's important for them and what they want to give priority to.

However, learning about leadership is not something that happens solely (or even mainly) on courses or programmes. It happens as people try different ways of doing and being and then step back and make sense of their experience. It happens all the time as leaders work, as they have new experiences, as they exchange ideas with colleagues and friends. We encourage you to learn more consciously about leadership, what works for you and others and what the context needs.

Just as people learn best how to operate a computer when they have a combination of some support and a real task to perform, so people learn most about leading when they do it and stop long enough to see what they are learning. It is bizarre that some consultants or business schools seem to suggest that people learn about leadership, separated from the work they have to do. No one would think much of a swimming lesson that was all theory and didn't involve going near a pool. So why do we take seriously efforts to develop leadership that are all in the classroom and don't touch the real leading that people do?

Business schools and consultants can bring their expertise and experience in a given leadership context. Managers can bring their own experience. When there is a real exchange of the two, learning occurs.

We believe that "thinking spaces" are required, where managers can step back and reflect on what they take from their experience. Most of what individuals learn about leading is like the proverbial iceberg: it is hidden beneath the surface. It is tacit or implicit knowledge and understanding. If you are to have choices about how you lead, you need to be aware of how you are leading at the moment and of the assumptions that inform what you do. If you are to improve, you need to try out different ways of being and doing – and then reflect on what works for you.

A lesson from the research is that leadership development is best done *with* the people that the leader is called upon to lead. The big potential for development is not working with individual leaders on their own but addressing the real life issues, with the real working group, in real time.

If learning about leading is out of context, then leadership development may result in a series of New Year resolutions – well meant but fantasy statements of "What I ought to do". Resolutions like: "I ought to listen more"; "I ought to consult more"; "I ought to coach more"; "I ought to think of the other person's perspective more". It may be that the resolutions are valid. However, what is really required is to question what is needed for a specific leader, with specific others, in a specific context.

Some of the focus needs to shift away from developing the skills and qualities of individuals in isolation. Certain skills and qualities are likely to be valuable to leaders in any situation but they are not enough. Individual development meets only one part of the need. More significant changes happen when individual, group and organisational work is linked.

The challenge in the development of professionals is to find ways of linking individual, group and organisational development for maximum effect. If fewer organisations are buying the "silver bullet", "seven steps to leadership" solutions, it is because they are becoming more aware of the limitations of leadership development out of context.

Part of being sensitive to the context involves thinking through the nature of leadership in your situation. This does not mean espousing some textbook ideal but getting some sense of what leadership means to you, in your business, your organisational culture and the dynamics of your group. Some key questions are: "What is really admired and respected in this organisation?" "What works and what doesn't?" "How does leadership relate to management – that vital business of getting things done and achieving results, day-to-day?" "What is the real business challenge and what type of leadership is required to address it?" "How can I contribute to that leadership, given the person I am?"

Integrating this thinking about the nature of leadership with some reflection on what is happening "in the moment" with your reports makes development a direct and powerful, if sometimes uncomfortable, process.

Finding "thinking spaces"

A leader needs space and time to reflect. He needs to escape (a little) from the addiction to extreme "busyness" and step back to look at the context, the group and himself. This is a process for "recovering your wits". The essence of this process is the opportunity for the leaders to get in touch with their own feelings, fears and hopes, sense of inadequacy and power, and enthusiasms and sense of energy. Once the feelings are expressed, they can begin to think more clearly, begin to see what their real intentions are and how to realise them. They can begin to let go of fantasies about what might be and engage more with the reality around them, however difficult.

An example of a "thinking space" is the research process we used. Typically we visited the case study companies once a month, for a day. We followed a step-by-step review process, usually organised around times when the leader and his immediate team came together for management team meetings. We held a preparatory session of about 45 minutes with the leader. We focused on understanding and clarifying the leader's intention with regard to the management meeting by asking three questions:

▌ What are your objectives for the meeting?
▌ What reaction do you expect from your colleagues?
▌ How will you respond to their likely reactions?

Often, these preparatory sessions gave the leaders an opportunity to step back and reflect on their intentions and possible courses of action in a way, they said, that otherwise they would not have done.

The leader and his team then held the management meeting and worked through their normal business, with the research team observing. Immediately following the business meeting, we initiated a review of the meeting, a "joint sense making" of what had happened, what the leader and others had intended and how far they had achieved it. We focused particularly on the moves and stance of the leader and how others had interpreted and reacted to these. After the meetings we usually talked one-on-one with individual managers and explored their sense of the context, the group and the leader. Later on

▶

the same day, we held a review session, privately, with the leader, to help him to consider what he had achieved and what he had learnt.

The outcome of the reviews was often dramatic. Strongly-felt issues about the leader and the team, and about their interactions, tumbled out. We were repeatedly surprised by how quickly people were able to voice their views and feelings, often ones they had not expressed before. We were taken aback by the ability of the group to put pretence aside and "tell it like it is". We were impressed particularly by the maturity of the conversations. Where, a moment before, people blamed others for all the problems, had scapegoats and simplified complex issues, here, quickly, groups seemed to address problems head on, as they were, without flinching. And yet, the strain on the leaders in holding open the space for this dialogue was intense. In one of the review sessions, the leader was almost physically holding himself together to endure the open discussion of his relationship to the group. He was shaking, and holding tightly to the table in front of him. The open review in the group seemed to be near the limit of what he could endure.

So, we were left with a paradox. Here was a review process that got to the heart of issues that disturbed management teams and that seemed to be critical to their effectiveness. Here was a method that, in a few hours, exposed issues that months of work in "Awaydays", team building or management consultancy exercises had failed to tackle. The groups seemed eager to tackle the issues and had the maturity to do so. And yet the leaders found it too hard. This form of "thinking space" was, for them, too threatening.

We concluded that a much longer building of relationships with leaders was essential if they were to tolerate the open review of leadership in the group. The leaders need to feel "held", supported by outsiders or others, over weeks and months, before they can relax enough to bring themselves to an open review. The leaders also sometimes need protection from the group who may want to make them scapegoats for any problems.

We also concluded that the feedback process invited leaders to attend to a whole new domain of knowledge and information – the perceptions, assumptions and meanings that others gave to shared events. Uncovering these, in an appreciative manner, created a new and creative context. The review process created new information for the leaders and the other members of the groups. By conducting a slow but attentive enquiry into the minute goings-on in the meeting that had just been completed, two important things happened. First, people understood each other better. By taking off the mask, and stating openly, "The reason I said what I said to so and so in that way was this: . . .", people gave each other precious information about each other. Secondly, because people were displaying trust that others would not abuse the new vulnerability they were revealing, a new quality of closeness and informality developed and spread.

We further found that "thinking space" should be integrated into day-to-day processes of running an organisation, not separated out in an "Awayday", or similar activity. Our experience shows that the issues are there and can be identified quickly – even in a 45-minute review – as part of a normal team meeting. They are all the more powerful because they are current, and directly linked to the work the group has been doing. They are not the theoretical or "nice to have" issues that often emerge in "Awaydays". They are the "here and now", pressing issues that shape how the group works together. What we offer could, and should, be integrated into day-to-day activities. It would be revolutionary if the "Awayday" could be rethought as a salami that can be worked with, slice-by-slice, meeting-by-meeting.

> "thinking space" should be integrated into day-to-day processes of running an organisation

RANESH'S STORY

Streets ahead

It started with quality. We had helped Ranesh, the director of Environmental Services in a large local authority, to find a realistic and effective way to implement quality assurance. When the quality work was finished, he called us back. He said, "I would like your help in developing Environmental Services. If we are going to improve the

▶

service, we have got to break down the barriers between different teams – and we have got to encourage staff to take more responsibility."

Ranesh was in his late fifties. His family belonged to a minority group that had had a privileged role in British India. His father had been an officer in the Indian Army. Following Independence, Ranesh's extended family emigrated to different parts of the world. Ranesh and his parents came to London. He seemed marked by the experience. He worked hard to keep in touch with his extended family around the globe. He was part of British society and yet also on the edge of it. He came across as a "boundary person", able to get close to people and teams but also sometimes looking at the organisation with the eyes of an outsider. He could identify with the needs of voters but also see the priorities of local politicians and chief officers.

An engineer by training, Ranesh was used to working in a measured, careful way. Important projects took time and required several stages. Colleagues described him as "a gentleman". He was flexible in his approach to leading. He was prepared to wait for some issues to mature but he could also be decisive. He was sympathetic and a good listener but also knew the limits of dialogue.

Ranesh had worked for the local authority for 15 years and was now responsible for 600 staff providing core services – everything from mending the roads to enforcing parking controls and collecting rubbish. He had multiple bosses – politicians, central government, chief officers, local voters – and was facing the aftermath of the "Thatcher Revolution" – under constant pressure to privatise services, to cut costs and measure outputs.

With Ranesh, we developed a process for working with individuals, groups and the whole organisation:

Every fourth week, the weekly management group was designated as an open space. There was no fixed agenda. The objective was to break the pattern of endless good news in the top team and become more open about the issues and challenges ahead. Managers brought problems in their own team and sought the help of other managers in making sense of their issues and in tackling them. We facilitated these meetings for the first six months.

Each member of the senior team took on a major improvement project that cut across the Council departments. Once or twice a year each manager brought his project for review by the top team. The focus was on connections across the whole Council – how to handle group dynamics, organisational politics, the public relations of the team. Ranesh saw the process as an insurance policy for himself and his team – to prevent attack by others in the Council.

When managers felt comfortable to bring real issues to the senior team, another process was added. This was a quarterly review day, not just for the leaders of projects, but for middle and senior managers together. Between 80 and 120 people were present at these sessions. The quarterly reviews were designed and run by the managers, not by the consultants (though we were around to encourage and to challenge). The senior team decided which project would be the subject of the next review day and which manager would take responsibility for it. Every project was reviewed once a year; plus there was a spot for urgent issues. The designated manager got two or three people who were going to present their projects to design the day with him. The idea was to model trust – to live with the fact that some would be very good designers of the day, others less so. The chief executive of the Council was a very controlling person from a financial background so it was important to set a different pattern in Environmental Services.

Every two months Ranesh had a half-day session with us. We aimed for monthly meetings but this proved impossible because of diary constraints. Each time he spent an afternoon with us reflecting on what had happened and what was needed now. It provided a proper thinking space for him.

Members of the senior team also had the option of one-to-one coaching with us – to help them with their projects. Forty percent of the team took up regular coaching, 20 percent had coaching now and then and 40 percent didn't take up the offer.

The process proved successful in different ways. Managers developed and were recognised as being more effective. All the managers in the senior team were subsequently promoted. Four of the eight managers were soon promoted twice.

After three years Ranesh retired. At his retirement party Ranesh made a powerful speech. Addressing one of us, he said: "You have restored my

▶

faith in the existence of one humanity and reminded me that that is just as important as difference. You retaught me that all cultures have authority built in to them and that it is important to use authority in a considerate way. I have tried to do that all my life. Working with you has made me realise it is worth using authority much more consciously. Our people rely on us doing that."

Ranesh also thanked the politicians who had protected him when there had been problems and some people had looked for a scapegoat: "You disbelieved what you heard about me and continued to believe what you knew about me."

What seemed to us important about the method of supporting Ranesh and his group was that the intervention was at a number of levels – individual, group and organisational – and dealt with the work the organisation had to do at the same time as relationships and feelings, structures and strategies. Managers "learned while doing". The outside support helped to provide enough sense of safety for managers to express their true thoughts and feelings and enough "thinking space" to be conscious of what they were learning.

What you can do

Avoid development work that mimics the problems

In our research we saw some development efforts that, despite the best efforts of the managers involved, became disconnected from the realities of the workplace and mimicked the problems they needed to address:

▌ Awaydays with packed agendas and a requirement to think positively, at which managers avoided the topics that mattered most to them;

▌ team-building weekends in North Wales which, far from tackling chronic divisions in a management team, reinforced an "us and them" split;

▌ sending managers on courses that were a useful opportunity for them to draw breath and reflect but where any learning was held by the individual alone and not shared with colleagues;

▌ management consultants who had a management team work through a series of exercises that confirmed an issue but did not seem to lead to any change in thinking or behaviour.

We were struck by the fact that leadership development processes often repeat the "chop, chop, busy, busy" activity that stops managers stepping back to think and learn together. Carefully controlled agendas were often a barrier to progress. The agenda may stipulate that the task be dealt with but sometimes, in order to move on, the group needs to address its own dynamics or some change in the wider world. Performance, tasks, the group dynamics, the external world, the politics and the culture of the organisation in the here and now may need to be dealt with at different times.

Think about:

▌ Do we make space and time to work on leadership development?

▌ How can we do so in a way that encourages people to step back and think and does not repeat the pattern of manic activity?

Find protected "thinking spaces"

We talk in Chapter 9 about the importance of "thinking spaces", where you have an opportunity to step back, to make sense of what is happening and decide how or what to focus on or do next. When you do this with others in a group, it can have an important developmental effect. It can become real-time leadership and team development.

We saw the effective team building that happened in some of the cases when the group took time out at its regular meetings and stepped back to review with us their underlying dynamics. It was clear that building relationships in context, dealing with the actual issues that created friction, was more meaningful and much faster than development outside the workplace. It also enabled the groups to work together more directly.

The prerequisite for effective "thinking spaces" is enough sense of safety for you and your colleagues. People need to feel able to say what they think and voice their feelings about the work issues facing them.

Think about:

▌ How could you make space and time in the course of your normal meetings to step back and learn?

▌ What support and what environment do you need for you and your colleagues to learn?

Work with the whole of people – good and bad

As we explain in Chapter 5, we are concerned about the use of leadership or management competencies – the lists of what management and leaders should be and do. Introduced to help to make development and assessment processes more objective, they can encourage people to focus on their weaknesses and to try to remedy those weaknesses in ways that are unrealistic and damaging.

strengths and weaknesses go together

In fact, with all managers and leaders, you never quite get the ideal competencies you want. Instead you get a package, good and bad, great qualities, experience and skills – and characteristics that are less desirable. The strengths and weaknesses go together – they are two sides of the same coin. Indeed the strengths become weaknesses when overplayed or used in the wrong situations and the defects become strengths in certain contexts. All these are age-old truths from history and literature. Our suggestion is that the business and organisational world should act on them more often.

The starting point is a never-ending task of increasing self-awareness. Questions like, "What's most important to me?" "How do I live out what matters to me most?" "What can I learn from what I do – as opposed to what I espouse?" "What impact do I have on others?" "How can I have more of the impact on others that I want to have?"

Think about:

▌ What processes do you have for stepping back and thinking about your own needs and wishes, who you are and what you want?

▌ How do you get help from others to do this?

▌ How do you get feedback?

▌ How do you make best use of your unique talents?

▌ How do you manage your weaknesses?

▌ How could you use competency frameworks as a prompt to talking about unique contributions – not a vehicle for focusing on weaknesses?

Connect coaching to the organisation

Executive coaching has become popular as a way of relieving the pressures on leaders. (By executive coach we mean the use of an outside consultant, not as an expert, but a sounding board, support and challenge, to help leaders to find their own ways forward on the issues that most concern them.) In many cases it is an essential safety valve, a way of processing all that has been happening and working out what it means. But there is a problem. Coaching can mirror the isolation of a leader. It can provide a secret compartment in which a leader talks about his issues but does so in a way that is not connected to the realities of his organisation. Without feedback from the organisation to a leader and vice versa, coaching can be work in vacuum. It can reinforce the picture of the leader, heroic and apart, having to work through all the issues on his own. Individual coaching can reinforce the transformational model. It is often important therefore to connect up coaching with the organisation. This requires careful attention to boundaries and confidentiality but it can be done very successfully.

If you have coaches in your organisation, consider:

▌ How could you link up the coaching to the organisational issues – without infringing individual confidentiality?

Connect other development activities to the context

As with coaching, so also with other development activities. Leadership programmes need to be rooted in the real-life context of participants if they are to be effective. Examples that we saw include:

▌ the increasing use of projects before and between leadership development activities to make use of ideas and tools and to learn how to apply them in the real-life situation;

▌ action learning groups in which managers of roughly equal seniority and experience, from different organisations, support and challenge each other in tackling their real-life issues;

▌ linking development and coaching for individuals with parallel work with teams and organisations.

Think about:

▌ How could you link individual, group and organisational development?

Look after your network

The reliance on professional external coaches reminds us of the incident in the film *Crocodile Dundee* when the Australian outback hero is in New York and hears someone refer to her analyst. "What is an analyst?" he asks. His friend explains that an analyst is someone who listens to your problems and tries to help you to reflect on ways of dealing with them. "What do you need them for?" the hero asks. "Don't you have any mates?"

In our research we saw leaders maintain informal networks and use them to great effect as a way to step back and think. Some leaders were particularly skilled in developing and maintaining networks of old colleagues and friends. Whenever they faced a big issue, they took it round their network, looking for ideas, different points of view and sometimes feedback on how they were perceived. The networks were critical in relieving the tensions that build up and gaining some perspective on the issues the leader faced.

Support new leaders

One of the shocking findings of our research was the degree to which organisations invest money and effort in finding new leaders and then, once they are appointed, abandon them. Hundreds of thousands of euros or dollars are spent on head-hunters and many hours of top management time are spent seeking out and interviewing possible candidates, yet after the new person starts, he often feels on his own.

The imbalance of effort makes no sense. Organisations know that senior appointments are risky, particularly if they are from outside. Often new leaders do not work out as hoped and the costs of an unsuccessful appointment can be very high.

If you have a role in appointing new leaders, we strongly suggest:[1]

A cold dash of reality in job and person specifications

Sometimes organisations look for the fantasy perfect leader, and individuals think they are getting the fantasy perfect job. It is vital to keep people's feet on the ground and help them to be realistic.

▌ How could you help to bring realism to the job and person specifications?

Giving personal support

We saw that occasional, personal support from a business leader or Human Resources professional could provide guidance or encouragement at critical moments. Examples included:

▌ helping a new leader back on his feet after a setback;

▌ making sense of the culture of an organisation for a recruit from outside;

---

1 For more information on our research findings on support for new leaders, see E. Braiden, and G. Binney, *New Leaders – Improving the Odds of Success*, Ashridge/Richmond Events, 2004.

▌ clarifying the expectations of top management and others.

Consider:

▌ How could you provide the necessary personal support for a
new leader?

Encouraging the new leader to practise "healthy selfishness"

As we discussed in Chapter 9, new leaders are often reluctant to
acknowledge their own needs.

Think about:

▌ How could you help a new leader to see that he should give
priority to keeping in good enough shape to lead?

▌ What ideas or help can you offer to support "healthy
selfishness"?

Offering "thinking spaces"

The need for "thinking spaces" is particularly acute for new
leaders faced with the anxieties of a leadership transition and the
weight of expectations to transform a culture or process.

Consider:

▌ How can you help to provide "thinking spaces" for a new
leader?

Helping new leaders tackle the "here and now"

Given the pressures on new leaders, we saw a risk that they escape
into the future. Today's realities seem too complex and
uncomfortable to tackle. It seems easier to dwell on creating
visions and strategies for the future.

Think about:

▌ How can you help a new leader to find the confidence to tackle
the few key issues that are most urgent and important?

part

What comes next?

In Part 3 we step back and look at the social, economic and political context for leaders and organisations today. We offer our reflections on the transformational hero picture of leadership, the social and political trends associated with it and the signs that new perspectives are emerging.

We conclude with a restatement of the key features of *Living Leadership*.

Living with permanent transition?
The disturbed context for leading

There is much that goes on in the modern organisational world that is a little mad. It's crazy to think that one individual can change the DNA of a large organisation in months. It's mad in workplace after workplace for directors to say they want a transforming hero irrespective of their business situation. It's mad to focus so much attention on the individual leader as hero and then expect others to give of their best. It's absurd to ask people to take responsibility, to seek to "empower" them while imposing endless measurement, auditing and control that signals loss of trust and denies employees the ability to use their own judgement. It's crazy to reorganise again and again and leave people confused about what's expected of them, where they belong, sometimes even who their boss is. It's daft to rush around at speed and rarely have time to stop and reflect about what needs to be learnt from events. It's absurd to talk about partnerships and long-term relationships while moving leaders and others around every 12 to 18 months.

These contradictions do not arise by accident. They are part of a pattern.

In our research we saw many organisations that were in a state of permanent transition. Before one reorganisation was complete, the next one rolled along as leaders sought to bring about transformation. Before one merger or takeover was absorbed, the next one started. Before the impact of one boss had been worked through, a new one was in place. And, often, all these things were happening at the same time. What we experienced was one part of a bigger picture in which endless upheaval and chronic insecurity

Is the transformational hero falling and the living leader emerging?

has become the norm. In many large organisations, there is no
settled structure. The abnormal has become normal.

> the abnormal has become normal, endless
> upheaval and chronic insecurity has become
> the norm

The old pattern of "freeze, unfreeze, refreeze" no longer applies (if
it ever did) in the organisations we observed. Some now say:
"Change is the only continuity." Though there are periods of
relative calm, there are complex transitions going on all the time.
In many companies people have become used to organisational
upheaval. They are resigned to seeing their roles and work being
frequently restructured. They don't ask whether the next
reorganisation will come, but when and how.

We found in our case studies that stability was expected but never
arrived. It was always just around the next corner. Though
transition is a normal part of human life and essential to the
renewal of organisations, the speed and frequency of transitions

seemed unnatural and counter-productive. It was as if an individual or family had to move house, change job or face the death of a close relative every month.

Some have argued that endless transitions are an inherent part of the organisational world. We disagree. We came to feel strongly during our observations that periods of both stability and disturbance are vital for the leader, the executive group and the organisation. They need reliable and continuous structures *and* they need to be able to survive in a river of change.

Transitions, in our view, remain disturbances and can't be reduced to something that is a permanent state. We do not all move house every day; we do it sometimes but not continuously. So it is with disturbances to the organisational culture and structure. What seems important to us is to understand why disturbance is often self-inflicted and not driven by the external world.

Among the case study organisations, relentless upheaval was usually justified by reference to change in the external world. Reorganisation was felt by managers to be necessary to enable companies and workplaces to adapt and thrive in changed landscapes. We found that, on the contrary, much of the turmoil was self-inflicted.

Ironically, in the light of the ostensible objective, the turmoil sometimes had the effect of stopping groups and organisations from responding to change in the external environment.

The need for transforming heroes is part of this picture. Equating leadership with transformation flows from a "hamster wheel" of inflated objectives, inadequate performance and trying ever harder. If this is the model, then the leader has to be the hero, the "saviour", the magical figure who will bring about change.

So what's going on? Why the endless upheaval? And what does the desire for transformational heroes tell us about our times?

In this chapter we share what we notice from our research – and our hunches about what's happening.

We notice:

The crisis of authority

The pattern of building up business heroes, giving them celebrity and money and then later knocking them down is a bit like the *Big Brother* show on TV. Look at the dotcom boom, the irrational, and sometimes corrupt, hype about businesses that never had any sales, let alone any profits; then the crash, the scandals and the investigations with so many wanting to be wise after the event. The cycle of boom and bust in reputations repeats itself. Stock exchange analysts often seem to make their judgements of leaders for reasons of fashion. They are, often, first unrealistically optimistic about leaders; later, unreasonably harsh. *Big Brother* takes the pattern to its extreme conclusion. The best people for the role of messiah and scapegoat are those who have personality or charisma but are relatively empty of substance, of character, like footballers, pop stars, fashion models. Perhaps, however, *Big Brother* provides a clue as to what is happening in the organisational world.

Our hunch is: Maybe the point of the "hero to zero" pattern is to develop heroes who in time will be destroyed. Ours is a sceptical age where the old certainties have gone. Once authority came to those born to it. No longer. The power of religion has weakened, most politicians are not respected any more and the professions no longer enjoy the position they once had. The institutions that provided authority figures are not respected as they once were.

There is a crisis of authority. Richard Sennett argues that we have difficulty acknowledging our need for authority figures. We want and need them but we can't talk openly about it. In public conversation we talk about teamwork and flat organisations. We tend to associate authority with the abuse of power. "What sex was to the Victorians, authority is to us," he says.[1]

The hero to zero phenomenon is linked to the identity crisis caused by what Tony Giddens calls the "disembedding" of societies and institutions, linked to globalisation.[2] People are left

1 R. Sennett, *Authority*, Alfred A. Knopf, 1980.
2 A. Giddens, *Runaway World – How Globalisation is Reshaping our Lives*, Profile Books, 1999.

without a strong sense of belonging, rank and security. Identity is no longer firmly rooted in reliable social structures or national boundaries but is propped up through an association with fashions, sub-cultures and attachments to a brand or company. Status and fame rather than character and authority count towards recognition and self-worth. There is a hunger for more possessions and attention. The act of consumption itself (so-called shopping therapy) becomes the holding activity which keeps at bay the realisation that one is a nobody rather than a somebody. What the stockmarket analysts must keep at bay is the realisation that their speculative gains are out of kilter with the creation of real value in the economy rooted in continuity rather than exponential change.

There is an urgent need to bring the discussion about authority out into the open, to recognise the need for it and to develop it in a way that is legitimate and credible for this age.

We notice:

Fleeing into the future

Only change is valued. Perfectly intelligent people who know change can't be tolerated without stability go along with the religion that change is all that matters. Again and again we saw leaders getting trapped in the future, focused on what they wanted to change but unable to hold in mind the difficulties and uncertainties of the present. Tony Blair was the epitome of this trend – a brilliant and persuasive politician who talked sometimes as if the good things he wanted had already arrived. We see the tendency to pretend to ban risk (through standards, control and audits), as if risk and uncertainty were not an essential part of life. We hear incessantly that only the future counts; the past is no guide. It is at best a half-truth.

We also notice that the belief in "all change" exists even though we do *not* live in an era of unique social, technological, political and economic change. Past eras have had much more rapid change. The upheavals that we are living through would not have impressed the generations who, in the first half of the 20th century, lived through two world wars, the collapse of the

European empires, the emancipation of women, the development of communism and fascism, the emergence of a mass middle class, the spread of industrialisation throughout the western world, modern medicine – and much more. The belief in ever-accelerating technological change is unhistorical. Just pause for a moment and look around you. Yes, your computer and mobile phone are recent developments. But your car is essentially the same technology as emerged in the 1920s – as is your landline phone and aeroplanes. Clothing, furniture, housing and many other familiar items – with the exception of plastics – have not changed fundamentally in 80 years.

Our hunch is: The pressure on leaders to be transforming heroes is unbearable to the point of self-destruction. The transformational leader deals with this pressure by fleeing into an idealised future. She draws a line between herself and the good future, on the one hand, and other people and the bad past and present, on the other.

We notice:

Empowerment is often a veil for tyranny

Targets close down the space for creativity. They have removed or restricted freedom, self-management, creativity, spontaneous commitment, and the space in which to be different and find new niches for survival and adaptation. It is as if we want to fatten the pig by weighing and measuring alone and feeding is no longer necessary.

The empowerment religion is a version of magical thinking that has more to do with wishful thinking than the here and now. We found in the research that empowerment was often talk and not reality. The leaders in our research were highly ambivalent about it because it implied dependency and lack of control. The followers often were either already empowered and waiting for the leader to find their power, or they felt that "empowerment" was abusive – that the leader dumped the hard stuff on them while she played at managing her bosses. Or they were frightened by the freedom offered and did not want to take more responsibility.

we found in the research that empowerment was often talk and not reality

Our hunch is: That the spaces to be free have closed up because leaders can't hold the anxiety connected with not knowing and having things beyond their control. They defend against personally unbearable uncertainty by fleeing into control, manic activity and the delusion that there is no alternative to their way of seeing the world.

We notice:

Disturbing echoes of the totalitarian regimes of the 1930s

Transformational leadership is reminiscent of the dictatorships of the first half of the 20th century when people had put all their power at the disposal of "one and only" charismatic leaders to use as they saw fit. Do we really want this as a model for business leaders – and for politicians and public sector managers? Isn't it time to step back and take stock of this flight into yet another age of heroes?

In Stalin's Russia and Mussolini's Italy, as in modern organisations, there was an obsession with the increasing speed of change. Under Stalin, the image was that of the speeding train; under Mussolini, the fast car. For those on the train or in the car, life outside became a blur. Other people became less human and their lives and fates were stripped of specificity and depth.

There are other echoes:

- more than one generation was taught that the present did not matter; what was important was progress to a better future;
- an endless focus on measurement and production that attempted to show that the glorious future was coming nearer and nearer;
- a focus on planning and control from above;

▌ abrupt and unpredictable changes of policy and senior personnel;

▌ the development of a new language: people had to learn how to recite the politically correct language if they were to deal with the authorities;

▌ the use of an idealised future to justify cruelty and tyranny in the present.

Our hunch is: Transformational leaders are not so much the cause of the permanent change and transition culture but a symptom of it. They symbolise our need for safety and protect us from being at the mercy of our fear of falling apart or being swallowed up when faced with overwhelming changes beyond our control and full comprehension. Once the heroic leader is in place, the dependent mass is also in place. The one cannot exist without the other: the mass is held together by love and fear connected with the leader and by colluding with each other and then in pursuing an enemy within or without. The world is divided into what is pure and what is dirty, what is in and what is out, what is friendly and what is hostile, what needs to be protected and what needs to be eradicated. All forms of modernisation have these mechanisms attached to them and so does the present version called "Transformational Leadership".

We notice:

The personification of complex issues

Complex business, social and political issues are discussed in terms of individual leaders – Blair and Bush, Chirac and Schroeder. It seems that we can't bear the complexity of the issues so we talk about them as if the heroes or scapegoats were uniquely responsible. We often seem to need to find fault, to blame events on individuals, when our rational selves know the reality is much more complex.

Our hunch is: That the tension between individual responsibility and collective interaction is experienced as intolerable at present.

People need to feel that their own actions make a difference; yet they know also, at some level, how difficult it can be to trace the cause and effect and how they are shaped by the context. In order to make sense of the world, we personify issues and exaggerate the importance of individuals.

We notice:

The need for security

The anxiety produced by the push towards faster and faster change as the only way to be has produced, in most people we observed, a pull towards security and safety. In the absence of structures within organisations that are safe from permanent re-engineering, people have ended up personifying the problem of insecurity by placing their hope for security and survival on to the heroic, the strong and the transformational leader. They feel perhaps that an unbearably uncertain context can be made more bearable and safe by knowing that one leader takes on the burden and promises a way out. In fact, the leader is cast in the role of the messiah, the rescuer. At the same time he is, when taking on this role and accepting the projection, ideally placed to be the scapegoat when things go wrong again.

Our hunch is: Transformational leadership is a symptom of a lost awareness of our connection with others, the reality that we are social animals and that we depend on others to fail or succeed. When we lose the awareness of our connection with a wider community for which we are equally responsible, we feel we can do what we like – the trap for self-centred leaders – or we feel fearful and want to be rescued by charismatic leaders – the trap for followers. Our fear creates the heroic leaders, then we submit to them, then we test them in action, then they turn out to have feet of clay – and then we resent them; and then it is often too late.

> transformational leadership is a symptom of a lost awareness of our connection with others

We notice:

Manic activity is a symptom of transition

That manic activity, the drug of being forever in the fast lane and the sense of hysteria in organisations, is typical of what happens to people during transitions – times when an old order dies and a new one is being born. People often can't think straight. They are too unsettled, too anxious during the transition. They only have a clear sense of who they are and who they are working with once the old order dies and the new one becomes established.

People get stressed out by not knowing when this organisational turmoil will end. Perfectly intelligent and sensible people have come to believe that organisational spaghetti and destabilised organisations attached to a permanent change ideology driven by supermen and superwomen are the only routes to progress and security.

Our hunch is: By thinking that we have arrived in the golden age of chaos, we define change as the only state of being which is legitimate and – without spelling it out – make continuity a taboo and therefore a sin. By denying continuity we lose our sense of time and imagine that we are in space without limits and boundaries – everything is possible, everything is thinkable, and everything is do-able, everything is able to be coped with. This makes two things very difficult:

1. Working in the moment with a sense of good timing and a feeling for what the people you depend on can handle at present.

2. Thinking ahead, planning change and continuity together, and accepting that change and development are a process of recovery and recreation rather than revolution and alteration beyond recognition.

The belief in an age of constant change is characteristic of the magical thinking used to defend against the fear caused by the disembedding process which promises permanent self-recreation but is, in reality, experienced as an attack on a sense of self, identity and personal security. The burden is greater because heroic leadership requires organisational members to speak only in positive terms, to smile and hide their inner anxiety and worry.

Leaders and members of an organisation collude in speaking in false tongues. Over time, the ability to speak frankly with each other, to get real about what is going on, is restricted to the remaining uncontrolled spaces like coffee breaks and the toilet.

It is time to start to return to *Living Leadership* and the art of the possible and to acknowledge that change happens between people and is inseparable from continuity.

We would like you, as a living leader, to make a start in reconnecting continuity and change and thereby complete the move from permanent transition to something more recognisably settled. Everyone needs a sense of time and space to remember what they know, who they are, what history they have and how they relate and separate on the basis of their inheritance.

We want to encourage a return to authority rooted in the human life cycle.

We notice:

The end of transformational leadership?

We should acknowledge that we need authorities to develop. Leaders should earn their right to be in that role by recognising that their power has been lent to them and they have a responsibility to use it with judgement and hand it on. We need leaders who see themselves as interdependent and as located in a generational hierarchy, not godlike figures who can use power arbitrarily. We need leaders who recognise their obligation with and to other members of the organisation – not members of a tyrannical system or a feudal court where safety and security is exclusively placed in proximity with the boss.

Our hunch is: That the transformational leadership age is coming to an end and that we are moving towards something new. *Living Leadership* is saying that it is time to ring the death knell for the heroic leader and the age of permanent and ever-faster change. Both imploded when the e-commerce bubble burst and Enron was exposed for what it was – an empty shell inhabited by cannibalistic leaders who ate up the company before they could be eaten by it.

what we are living through is transition mistaken for a new age

Constant change and upheaval, the sense of dislocation, the insecurity and the manic activity are not there for ever but signals of a wider transition. What we are living through is transition mistaken for a new age.

A summary of living leadership

What you have said is, in a way, obvious – but we have forgotten it.
A German manager responding to our presenting the concept of Living Leadership.

Being prepared to look foolish enough to become an authority

Leading is a social, in-between activity. Leaders, groups, organisations and the environment around them are interdependent. **Leaders are not just at the top but in the middle of a complex network of relationships. Living leaders recognise this interdependence and relish discovering what is possible.** Respect the context and the culture of your organisation. Engage with people around you and look for exchanges and a sense of mutual obligation. Come down the mountain and work in the moment.

Living leaders have the courage to use their life experiences as a guide. They do not look to the ideal or competency frameworks but are comfortable with their experience and instincts. As leading and change mirror the life cycle of human development, it is your own experience that is your inner compass for working in the moment, for finding the right mix of continuity and change and tolerating uncertainty in a thoughtful and not panicky or hyperactive way.

To lead in the moment requires that you understand yourself as you are. The bad news is that at some moments you feel as if you are sinking or just getting through the water. The good news is that you know from your life experience how to get through it. Each time the cycle is repeated it is not really the same. It is more like a familiar journey into something that is, as yet, unknown. Don't be too hard on yourself. Many leaders are very self-critical. Allow yourself the luxury sometimes of noticing when you do things well and when your needs must be put first.

Accept yourself and respect people as they are; learn to see that you are not alone and not responsible in isolation. You can work out the key issues with others.

Don't get trapped into dividing everyone and everything into for and against, good and bad. We encourage you not to give in to this pressure to divide people into sheep and goats. To be human is to value people in the round and suspect the ideal. Recognise that most people are both good and bad. If you impose alignment, misalignment is bound to be the result.

There is always a third group with whom you can work – the don't knows. You can invite the bystanders to step in and work with you to think through a way forward. For this approach to succeed, you must **let go of the ideal, the perfect plan and vision and open up a space in which to think and trade,** where people can explore what they think is going on – a good mix of continuity, change and risk-taking.

We encourage you to resist the idea that you can change the world at will and not be subject to the limits of time and space. Treat this as a relief, not a problem. If your people experience you as realistic, they will be freer to give you more. Inspiration does not come from the vision statements that seem unreal. People feel inspired when they feel accepted, heard and can give of their best without fear.

Learn to recover a sense of working with the grain and with the organisational culture as it really exists and give up chasing a change wish-list for a transformation of everything and everyone in one go. Issues can't and shouldn't be tackled all at once. Timing and pacing are critical skills. **Trust in small steps to move forward. Don't burden yourself with efforts to map the whole picture and see everything that is needed.** No-one can in reality – why burden yourself with an impossible task?

Organisations need *many authorities*, not one leader, and they need people who are both managers and leaders, both organising delivery and working to release the collective potential of people.

The "transforming heroes" idea makes leaders think they have to live up to an ideal that they cannot reach. Rather than inspire them to greater things, this ideal ends up making them underperform. We advocate *living leaders* – as opposed to transformational ones – so that ordinary managers and leaders, in times that are not extraordinary times, can succeed again.

We suggest that organisations need ordinary heroes. They are essential if workplaces and their magic are to be maintained. Ordinary heroes have character, integrity and can serve as role models; they resist the temptation to gather unquestioning followers; and they extend conversations, enlarging the ways in which things are done here.

We encourage you to help your organisation to do more of what it has shown it can do well; to release more of its collective capacity for developing work of value. What is important is to help people to get better at what they do and to use the resources they have. **If you're uncertain about the future, consider what's special about your organisation from the past.** Don't set up others for approval, but let them fly.

A child thrives on "good enough" parenting. A group will, we believe, thrive on "good enough" leadership. Dependants need help to get better at what they do and who they are – until they themselves become helpers. Until that point, they depend on parental figures who fill their role by being an authority.

We suggest that leaders need to find a basis for their authority that is human, liberal and based on contribution – not on prescription, alignment and control; leaders who give permission to people to find their own voice.

We have seen many of you do what we are suggesting. We know you can do it. Good luck!

The research

The work we did[1] differed from most management research in that we lived alongside leaders and their organisations for periods of 12 to 24 months. We were with them in the moment, as their stories unfolded. The view of leading that we had was very different from that reported when you ask people after the event what they did. We all have a tendency to tidy up our memories of past events and feelings, to rationalise them. When you are there, as it happens, you see what is really involved in leading and following.

Our research took four years and was in three phases:

1. **The first phase involved over 40 interviews with company chairmen, chief executives, human resources directors and senior head-hunters across Europe. The purpose was to hear the issues as perceived by these key players in leadership transitions and thereby map out the ground we needed to cover in the main part of the research. Already in this phase we were told by some senior people that the current expectations of leaders were unsustainable and that it was increasingly difficult to find capable candidates for chief executive roles.**
2. **The centrepiece of the work was a set of eight "case study" stories that we researched in depth. We accompanied new chief executives, general managers and heads of function – and the people around them – for between 12 and 24 months in their new jobs. We talked to a range of people – such as non-executive directors, senior and middle managers, human resources specialists, as well as chief executives – in each organisation. We observed and**

▶

1 G. Binney, E. Wilke and C. Williams, *Leadership Transitions: The Dramas of Ordinary Heroes*, Ashridge, 2003.

exchanged views on important meetings and discussions, key decisions, strategies, actions and behaviours. Most valuable, we held review sessions with each leader and their team and made sense together of the leading and following in the group.

3 **We checked out what we found in the case studies with many hundreds of managers and leaders in meetings, workshops and conferences across Europe. We were struck by how the themes resonated with very diverse groups.**

The research team of 12 was drawn from Ashridge, the international business school based in the UK; Groupe HEC in France; and a number of independent consultants and researchers. The research team was deliberately drawn from people with diverse backgrounds and disciplines to encourage the sharing of alternative views and the effective challenging of pre-existing ideas. The group contained those with backgrounds in strategic consulting and organisation and management development and others whose expertise is in group and psychoanalysis. We ended up with a truly diverse and international team including British, French, German and Belgian nationals who regularly work across Europe and beyond.

Acknowledgements

The research was made possible by generous and patient support provided by the business school at Ashridge. Alex Knight, the former Managing Director of the consulting arm of Ashridge, gave us practical and financial support, allowed us to follow the enquiry in the way we believed was most valuable and was tolerant of a two-year study becoming a four-year one. Bill Critchley provided important encouragement and challenge and Ina Smith, the current Managing Director, was instrumental in bringing the research to completion.

Groupe HEC in France gave us valuable support and contacts and helped us to work on a truly pan-European basis.

The core team who undertook the research, in addition to ourselves, was:

Richard Elsner

and from

Groupe HEC	**Ashridge Consulting**
Gilles Amado	Howard Atkins
Rachel Amato	Elizabeth Braiden
	Kathleen King.

Bill Critchley, Robert Dickson, Michel Roger and Ina Smith helped to shape the research and provided important contacts.

We are grateful to the many companies and individuals who participated in the interview phase of the research and the later validation work. They enabled us to frame the issues and check the validity of our conclusions.

Elizabeth Braiden, Phillipe Coullomb, John Higgens, Mary Kennedy, Michaela Rebbeck, Janet Smallwood and Stefan Wills have read drafts of the book and given us valuable feedback.

Kate Campbell has supported the development of the book with style, enthusiasm and humour.

Above all we are indebted to the organisations and leaders who worked with us on the case studies. It was not always easy for them to have outsiders observing and commenting on what they did and how they behaved in real, sometimes difficult, situations. As our case studies are anonymous, they did not participate for the greater glory of themselves or their organisations. They worked with us in order to learn more about their situations and about themselves; such an inquiry is an act of leadership in itself. They made it possible for us to have a fascinating and intimate view of leadership transitions. We learnt a huge amount from being with them.

George Binney, Gerhard Wilke and Colin Williams

Publisher's acknowledgements

We are grateful to the following for permission to reproduce copyright material:

Cartoons
Cartoon on page 95, 'What a divinely damaged person' by Bud Handelsman © Methuen London Ltd from *Families and How to Survive Them* by Robin Skynner and John Cleese. Reprinted by permission of The Random House Group Ltd.

Text
Quote on page 23 adapted from "What leaders really do", *Harvard Business Review* (Kotter, J. P. 2001). Reprinted by permission of *Harvard Business Review*. From "What Leaders Really Do" by John P. Kotter, December 2001. © 2001 by Harvard Business School Publishing Corporation; all rights reserved.; Quote on page 30 from "Holes at the Top: Why CEO Firings Backfire", *Harvard Business Review* (Wiersema, M. 2002). Reprinted by permission of *Harvard Business Review*. From "Holes at the Top: Why CEO Firings Backfire" by Margarethe Wiersema, December 2002. © 2002 by Harvard Business School Publishing Corporation; all rights reserved.; Quote on page 33 adapted from "The curse of the

Index

acceptance, need for 88
action learning 240
adaptability 16
Alcatel 61
alignment 24, 74, 225, 226
answers, not knowing 11, 53–5
appreciating others 180–1
attitude of leader 223–4
attractors 94–6
  demons as 96
authority 113, 117–18, 267
  based on contribution 272
  crisis of 260–1
  importance of 12
  need for 260, 261
    many 271
Awaydays 166, 245, 248

Barnevik, Percy 22, 28
BCG Honda report 69
benchmarking 74
Bennis, Warren 23, 24
Blair, Tony 261
body language 7, 197
bosses 133–52
  expectations from 141–2, 149,
    150
  as Greek gods 133–4
  overidentification with 136
  unrealistic expectations
    133–4
  see also organisations
boundaries 117
  defining 167
  personal 155
Boydell, M. 155
bringing oneself to lead 6–8,
  19

Brooks, J. 36
Buffett, Warren 61
Burgoyne, J. 155
Burston-Marsteller CEO study
  37

Casey, David 178–9
change 5, 221–37
  and attitude of leader 223–4
  case study 226–31
  and change in leader 226–31,
    236–7
  compliance as resentment
    225, 226
  constant 62–5, 257–68
    belief in 266
  and continuity 214, 224–5,
    236, 267, 270
  different voices 231
  and heroic leadership 22–3,
    25
  leader as part of 236, 237
  negative feelings about 114,
    225
  participation in 223
  of personnel 175–6
  phasing of 141
  pressures for 25, 26
  as religion 261
  resistors 55–6, 225
  role of leader 222–6
    and choice 236
  trapped in 224
  see also transition
character 17–18
charisma 3, 17–18, 137
choice 111–21, 132
  areas of 111, 112–21

choice (*continued*)
made by leader, and change
226
questionnaire 119, 120–1
of staff 171
Churchill, Winston 8
Cleese, John 94
Clinton, Bill 87
coaching
and context 251–2
and development 252
reinforcing isolation 251
Collins, Jim 18
coming alive 103, 105–6
and healthy disillusionment
107–8
commitment 116–17
of staff 218
communication 27, 56–7
competencies approach 92–3,
250, 251
and deficit thinking 16, 92
competitive advantage 71, 214
compliance 266
culture of 225, 226
conflict 14, 45
connection with people 4, 19,
41–60
admitting vulnerability 53–5
case study 46–8
coming alive 105–6
components of 13–14
destroyed 37–8, 60
examples 43–4
good enough 52, 57–8
group as whole 58
importance of 41–2
lack of 135–6
and managing upwards 49–50
obstacles to 14
and self-care 158–9
signs of good enough 45
signs of inadequate 45
in tackling problems 53–4
and transition 266
unplanned moments 53

working together 58–9, 60
context 61–2, 142
adapting to 77–8
case studies 65–7
disturbed 257–68
importance of 62, 80
and leadership 4–5, 19, 235
and nature of team 178–9
power of 65–7
respecting 269
shaping leadership 239–40
shaping results 62
and strategy 68–71
understanding of 16
continuity
and change 236, 267, 270
change as 258
leading 80, 224–5, 237
as sin 266
coping mode 103–4, 105, 108
value of 106
creativity and targets 262
Critchley, Bill 178–9
culture of organisation 5, 6, 14,
62
and new leader 253
respecting 269
Sven's story 66

de Pree, Max 76
debriefing the moment 106–7
decision making 18
deficit thinking 16, 92
delegation 118, 183–4
tasks not roles 193
demons 87–92, 99, 156, 165
as attractors 95–6
enjoying 98
examples of 88–9, 91–2
and inner security 97–8
making use of 91, 169–70
results of denial 97
understanding 86, 87, 90–2,
97
and unrealistic expectations
150

value of 90
development 239–54
    avoiding mimicking problems
        248–9
    connected to context 240,
        241, 242, 252
    inclusion of reports 241, 242
    projects and 252
    see also learning
Diane's story 43, 137–42
dictators, heroes as 263
dimensions of leadership 113,
    128
direction 113, 114–15
    setting 24, 122
discomfort, signs of 197
disembedding process 260, 266
disempowerment of leaders 22,
    38, 39
disillusionment, healthy 107–8,
    135, 217
dreams 107–8
    unrealised 33–4

elephant in the room 68, 128,
    187–90
    cost of not confronting 189
    developing skills for 198–9
    getting real about 190
    when to confront 199
    see also unspoken issues
Eliot, T.S. 153
emotions 16
    awareness of 123–4
empathy 236
empowerment 22, 23, 117, 257
    of leaders 19
    as religion 262
    as tyranny 262–3
Encyclopaedia Britannia
    214–15
Enron 28, 33, 146, 176, 267
environment: business and
    social 14
Essner, Bob 31–3
ethics of leadership 18–19

execution power 72–4
executive group 136, 171
    focusing on 181–2
    fostering common ground 182
    selection of 178–80
    see also groups
expectations
    clarifying for new leader 254
    of leaders 25
    management 137
    negotiating realistic 141–2,
        149, 150–2
    reducing 213
    unrealistic 8–9, 36–7, 102,
        133–4, 150
experience
    lessons from past 113–14
    life 7, 57, 84–5, 106, 132, 270
expertise, valuing 180–1

fear, voicing 191
feedback 83, 251
    need for 36
    obtaining quality 169
    in thinking space 244
feelings 16, 17
    and thinking spaces 243
    using 168
followers *see* groups; staff
fragmentation 218–19
frustration 191, 221
future
    escaping into 254, 261–2
    trapped in 261–2

General Electric 28–9
    meetings 210
Gerstner, Lou 185
Giddens, Anthony 260
gifts, giving and receiving 178
Gilmore, Tom 52, 158
globalisation 260
Goethe, J.W. von 77
good enough
    group 43, 57–8
    leadership 9, 271–2

good enough (*continued*)
  relationships 60
Gorbachev, Mikhail 67
Gordon's story 205–8
Grasso, Dick 22
great man theory 3, 24
Greenspan, Alan 26
group think 182, 218–19
groups 185–99
  and context 178–80
  not confronting issues 188–9
  off the table issues 185–99
  patterns of disconnections
    49–51
  see also executive group

Hamel, Gary 68
healthy disillusionment 107–8,
  135, 217
healthy selfishness 153–6,
  165
  components of 155
  new leader 254
Heifetz, Ron 54
help 83–99
  accepting 105
  asking for 16–17, 97, 104,
    158, 159
  offering to others 16
  see also support
here and now 83, 254
hero/es
  created in fear 265
  leaders as 21–39, 264
  looking for 22–3
  not trying to be 196
  to zero 28–33, 260
heroic leadership *see*
  transformational hero
Hitler, A. 25
Hock, Dee W. 21
Hodgson, Phil 58
Hoeneker, Erich 67
Honda 69–70
HR professionals, support from
  168

hub and spokes working 43,
  192–5
humanity of leader 17

Iacocca, Lee 52
IBM 186
identity crisis 260–1
imperfections of leader 9–10,
  54–5, 85, 98
inner review 150
insecurity
  of leader 88–9
  and transition 258, 268
inspiring others 15, 24, 27, 59
  Living Leaders 271
interdependence 60, 234, 267,
  269
  of groups 172
  organisational context 61
intuition 16, 17
  suppressing 123
  for unspoken issues 196–7
issues
  personification of 264–5
  unspoken 187–90, 191

James' story 44
John's story 43, 65–6, 125–7,
  142–8, 192–5
judgement 199
  avoiding 197–8

Kanter, R.M. 23
Kennedy, John F. 8, 52
Khurana, Rakesh 33
King, Martin Luther 8
Kohl, Helmut 67
Kotter, John P. 23

language, politically correct 264
Lay, Kenneth 22, 28
leaders
  adapting to context 77–8
  admitting vulnerability 53–5,
    97, 98, 118, 121
  appreciating past 224–5

being on top 52–3, 60
character not charisma
    17–18
as example of change 233,
    234
expectations of 25
and formal power 11–12
getting real 61–81
as heroes or scapegoats 264
imperfections 9–10, 54–5, 85,
    98
inner deficit 87
inner drive 87–92, 96, 156
internal 'agenda' 86
letting go 183–4
and life experience 57
in the middle 4, 52, 60, 136,
    157, 269
need for many 11–12
and organisations 4, 94–6
overidentification with bosses
    136
personal needs of 153
qualities of 7–8, 11
role in strategy 203–5, 212
self-awareness 85
self-disclosure 191–2
as storyteller 75–6
unexpected impact of 35–6
unlearning ideas 219–20
using senses 190–2
working with 'what is' 14
see also connection with
    people; transformational
    hero
leadership
and context 4–5, 235
dimensions of 113, 128
ethics of 18–19
good enough 9, 271–2
idealised 19
in the moment 111–29
purpose of 10–11
shaped by context 239–40
shortfall 22
three themes of 4–8

and uncomfortable moments
    190
unexpected results 65
versatility 111
leadership development see
    development
learning
action 240
strategic 71
to lead 239–42, 253–4
unlearning 219–20
see also development
Lenin, V. 25
Leonhard, Wolfgang 36
lessons from research 19
change process 223
context 80
getting connected 60
getting real 98–9
heroic ideal 39
leading in the moment 128
unspoken issues 187–90
letting go 183–4
life experience 57, 84, 106, 132
examples 84–5
use of 7, 270
limits, personal 120, 122, 155
listening 45
first 100 days 78
to non-verbal signs 197
Living Leadership
change and continuity 267
characteristics 15, 59, 83,
    270–1
implications of 13–19
many people as leaders 11–12
summary 269–72
three themes 48
see also connection; context;
    leaders; leadership
loneliness of leader 157–8
loyalties 113, 116–17, 126

magic of organisation 213
magical thinking and change
    266

management 133–52
    expectations 137
managing upwards 49–50, 135
mandate, clarifying 134–5,
    143–4
Manfred's story 160
Mao Tse-tung 25
Marks and Spencer 30–1
Mary's story 44, 234–5
Max's story 44, 66–7
meetings 210–11
    avoiding judgement 197–8
    confronting elephants 198,
        199
    signs of discomfort 197
    time for reflection 198
middle, in the 4, 52, 60, 136,
    157, 269
Miller, Herman 76
Mintzberg, Henry 69, 204
moment, in the
    leadership development 242
    leading 111–29, 185, 190,
        269, 270
Moritz and Max's story 232–3
motivation: leader's role 24
Mussolini, B. 263

Nasser, Jacques 33
needs
    personal 153
        acknowledgment of 156
    prioritising 159–60, 169
negative feelings 114, 236,
    237
    working with 225
Netco 125–7, 142–3, 192–5
networks 167
    maintaining informal 252–3
NHS case study 62–5
Nietzsche F. 25
Nokia 73, 215
    culture of 79
non-verbal signs 7
    of discomfort 197
Novartis 75

objectives 117, 141–2
    changing 68, 70
    management by 134–5
obligation, mutual 172–3, 178,
    180, 269
obstacles to connecting 14
offending others 169
openness 13, 14
opportunity, zones of 112
organisations
    choices made by 217
    constant change 257–68
    culture of 5, 6, 14
    disembedding 260
    hidden agenda 96
    and leaders 15
        unconscious attractors 94–6
    magic of 78–9, 213
    reorganisations 62–5, 257–8
    serving 120
    unfinished business 93–4, 99
    see also transitions

panic, avoiding 101
Pascale, Richard 69–70
Pedler, M. 155
people 171–84
    aligning 24
    focusing on 8
    relating to 13
    selection of team 171
    work for people 4
    see also connection with
        people
perfectionism 182
Peter and Sven's story 43–4, 48,
    229
Pfizer 71
Pierre's story 44, 51, 161–5
politically correct language 264
Poussot, Bernard 31
PowerPoint
    festivals 45, 46, 128, 166, 186
    preoccupation with 72, 185
projects
    and development 252

as experiments 180
Pullman, Philip 17, 90

qualities of leaders 7–8, 11
questionnaire on choice 119,
    120–1

Ranesh's story 148–9, 245–8
rationalisation 70
real, getting 61–81, 233, 239–42
    fear of 232–3
reality
    accepting 170
    articulating 217
    current 213
    implications for leaders 75–6
    of leadership 3
    working with 21, 77
reflection 106–7, 108, 109
    allowing time for 198
    on choices 112
    as healthy selfishness 155
    inner review 150
    leadership dimensions 129
    process 99
relationships 14, 113, 116
    as basic 41
    good 40–1
    good enough 60
    maintaining distance 116,
        120
reorganisations 62–5
    constant 257–8
research, description of 273–4
    see also lessons from research
resistance to change 55–6, 225
respect 13, 14, 37, 42, 60
Revans, Reg 240
risk 261
role
    models 8
    playing a 7
role of leader
    in change 222–6
    in strategy 203–5, 212
Rose, Stuart 30–1

Rosenberg, Merrick 26
Ryan, Barbara 33

scapegoat, leader as 4
self 153–70, 266
self-awareness 85, 169, 182–3,
    221, 250
self-belief 113, 118
self-care 140, 158–9
    accepting reality 170
    and offending others 169
    pleasing others 161, 165
    prioritising 159–60, 165
self-confidence 111, 119
self-disclosure 191–2
self-esteem of leader 104, 156
Sennett, Richard 260
Shaw, George Bernard 28
Shaw, Patricia 71
Simpson, George 22, 29
sinking 101–9
Skilling, Jeff 28
Skynner, Robin 94
Srdjan's story 208–12
stability
    lack of 258
    need for 259
staff
    changes 174–6
    commitment of 218
    good enough 43
    healthy disillusionment 107
    passivity 33, 37, 49, 51, 107
    see also connection with
        people; executive; groups
Stalin, J. 263
storytelling 75–6
    strategy 204–5, 218, 219, 220
strategic conversations 217, 218
strategic learning 71
strategy 201–20
    bringing different voices
        214–15
    connecting thinkers and
        doers 215–16
    and context 68–71

strategy (*continued*)
development of 70–1
engaging with people 212–13
exercises 206–7, 210–11, 212
and learning 71
marketing 71
and middle managers 201–2,
203
power of small steps 219
prioritising issues 216
questions 213–14
reviews 206–7, 210, 214
role of leaders 203–5, 212
storytelling 204–5, 218, 219,
220
timing 216
strengths and weaknesses
250–1
Superman, end of 21–39
see also transformational
leadership
support 150, 152
emotional 165
from HR professionals 168
mutual 158
for new leaders 253–4
over-dependence on 168–9
personal 155
prioritising 165–6
surfing 101–9
Suroweicki, James 10
survival mode 102–4
cost of 104–5
value of 106
Sven's story 12–13, 43–4, 46–9,
66
change 226–31
mutual appreciation 177
and vulnerability 54–5
swimming 101–9

targets
adapting 136
paralysis of 73
realistic 135
stifling creativity 262

Tchuruk, Serge 61
teamwork
effective team building 249
hub and spokes 192–5
nature of 178–9
template management 12, 46–7
Thatcher, Margaret 8
thinking spaces 155, 166–7,
241, 243–5, 248, 270
integrated into day-to-day
245
for new leader 254
protected 249–50
research example 243–5
review days 246–7
timescale for impact 35
timing 113, 115–16, 266
as critical skill 271
strategy 216
tough guy image 27
trading 172–4, 177, 270
projects as experiments 180
valuing expertise 180–1
transformational hero
characteristics of 23
as damaging ideal 19, 21,
33–4, 36–9, 49–51, 121–2
destroyed connections 37–8,
60
as dictatorship 263–4
as dominant ideal 26–8, 39
and expectations 38–9
first 100 days 213
and future visions 72
heroism/passivity cycle 26
hype 32
limitations of 18
loneliness of 157–8
as myth 28, 39
passive followers 33, 37, 107
pressures on 37, 123–4, 262
preventing versatility 122,
128
as saviour 259
as symptom of change 264
trapped in future 36

as unattainable ideal 28,
38–9, 92, 271
unreasonable expectations
102
transition 257–68
and chronic insecurity 258,
268
constant 257–9
crisis of authority 260–1
heroes as symptom 266
manic activity as symptom
266, 268
mistaken for new age 267–8
personification of complex
issues 264–5
timescale 35
see also change
trust 13, 14, 37, 42, 43
in group 54
and self-care 158–9
and working together 60

uncertainty 5–6, 10–11, 179,
215
escape from 263
tolerating 74–5, 270
understanding 113–14
unexpected, responding to 71

unspoken issues 187–90
making time and space for 191
see also elephant in the room

values 13, 14
Vandevelde, Luc 30, 31, 154–5
Vasella, Daniel 75
Veronique's story 56–7
Viagra 71
visions 23, 72
trapped in future 36
Voltaire 3
vulnerability 53–5, 97, 98, 118,
121

Washington, George 26
weaknesses and strengths 88,
250–1
Webster, Jean 83
Weinstock, Arnold 28–9
Welch, Jack 22, 26, 28, 33, 52
Wiersema, Margarethe 30
work-life balance 117, 140
working relationships 87
good enough 14, 60
Wyeth 31–3

zero to hero 176